SQUADRON

SUPREME

FINDING NAMOR

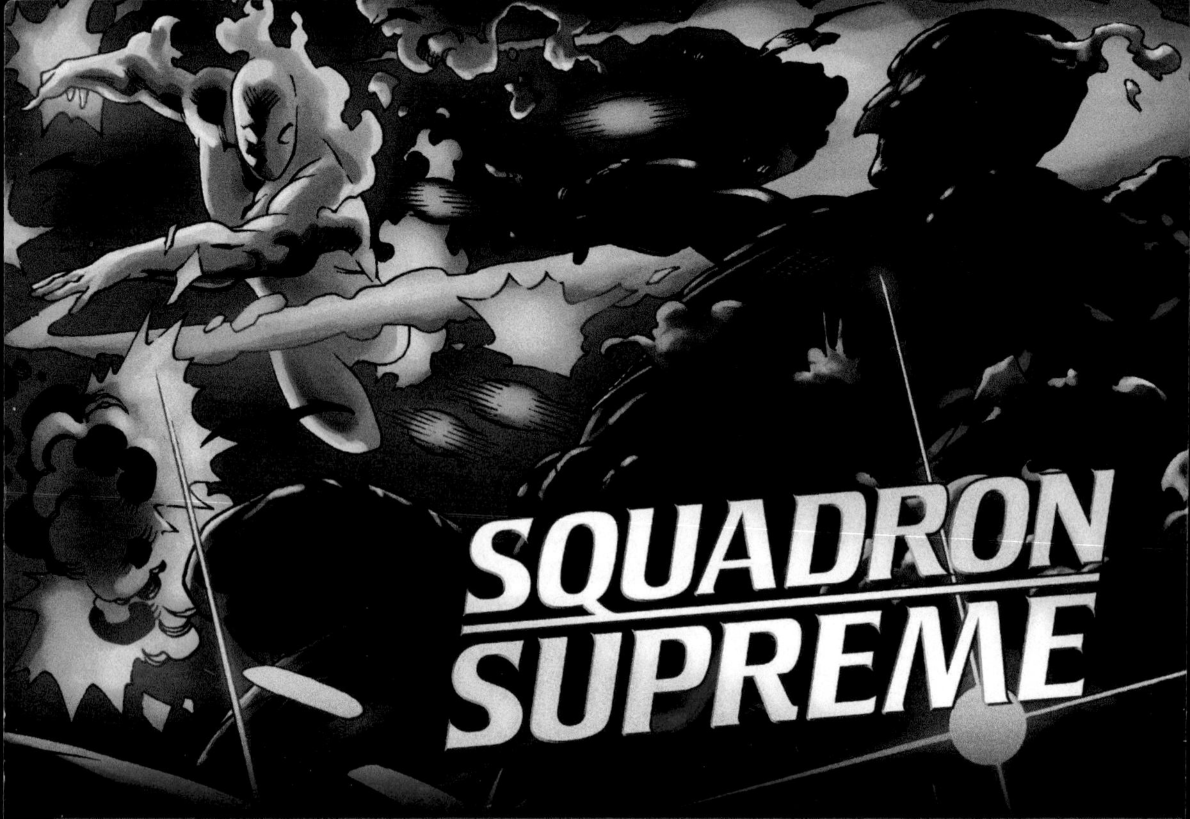

SQUADRON SUPREME

JAMES ROBINSON
WRITER

#10-14

LEONARD KIRK WITH **PAOLO VILLANELLI** (#14)
PENCILERS

PAUL NEARY WITH **MARC DEERING** (#11-12)
INKERS

CHRIS SOTOMAYOR
COLORIST

#15

EMILIO LAISO
ARTIST

CHRIS SOTOMAYOR
COLOR ARTIST

VC's TRAVIS LANHAM
LETTERER

ALEX GARNER
COVER ART

CHRISTINA HARRINGTON
ASSISTANT EDITOR

KATIE KUBERT
EDITOR

MARK PANICCIA
SENIOR EDITOR

COLLECTION EDITOR: **JENNIFER GRÜNWALD**
ASSISTANT EDITOR: **CAITLIN O'CONNELL**
ASSOCIATE MANAGING EDITOR: **KATERI WOODY**
EDITOR, SPECIAL PROJECTS: **MARK D. BEAZLEY**

VP PRODUCTION & SPECIAL PROJECTS: **JEFF YOUNGQUIST**
SVP PRINT, SALES & MARKETING: **DAVID GABRIEL**
BOOK DESIGNER: **ADAM DEL RE** WITH **JAY BOWEN**

EDITOR IN CHIEF: **AXEL ALONSO**
CHIEF CREATIVE OFFICER: **JOE QUESADA**
PRESIDENT: **DAN BUCKLEY**
EXECUTIVE PRODUCER: **ALAN FINE**

SQUADRON SUPREME VOL. 3: FINDING NAMOR. Contains material originally published in magazine form as SQUADRON SUPREME #10-15. First printing 2017. ISBN# 978-1-302-90285-8. Published by MARVEL WORLDWIDE, INC., a subsidiary of MARVEL ENTERTAINMENT, LLC. OFFICE OF PUBLICATION: 135 West 50th Street, New York, NY 10020. Copyright © 2017 MARVEL. No similarity between any of the names, characters, persons, and/or institutions in this magazine with those of any living or dead person or institution is intended, and any such similarity which may exist is purely coincidental. **Printed in the U.S.A.** DAN BUCKLEY, President, Marvel Entertainment; JOE QUESADA, Chief Creative Officer; TOM BREVOORT, SVP of Publishing; DAVID BOGART, SVP of Business Affairs & Operations, Publishing & Partnership; C.B. CEBULSKI, VP of Brand Management & Development, Asia; DAVID GABRIEL, SVP of Sales & Marketing, Publishing; JEFF YOUNGQUIST, VP of Production & Special Projects; DAN CARR, Executive Director of Publishing Technology; ALEX MORALES, Director of Publishing Operations; SUSAN CRESPI, Production Manager; STAN LEE, Chairman Emeritus. For information regarding advertising in Marvel Comics or on Marvel.com, please contact Vit DeBellis, Integrated Sales Manager, at vdebellis@marvel.com. For Marvel subscription inquiries, please call 888-511-5480. **Manufactured between 4/7/2017 and 5/9/2017 by QUAD/GRAPHICS WASECA, WASECA, MN, USA.**

10 9 8 7 6 5 4 3 2 1

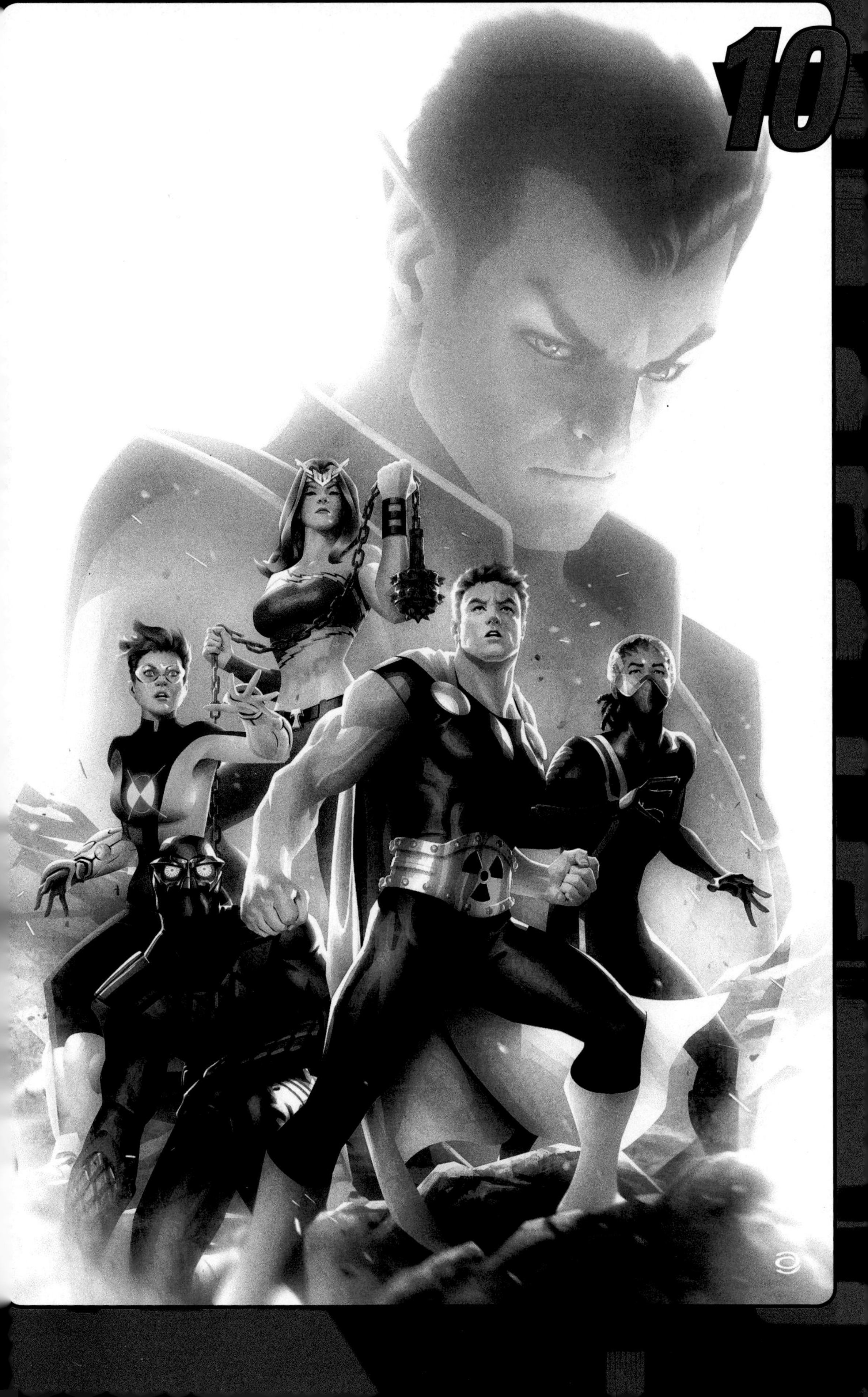
10

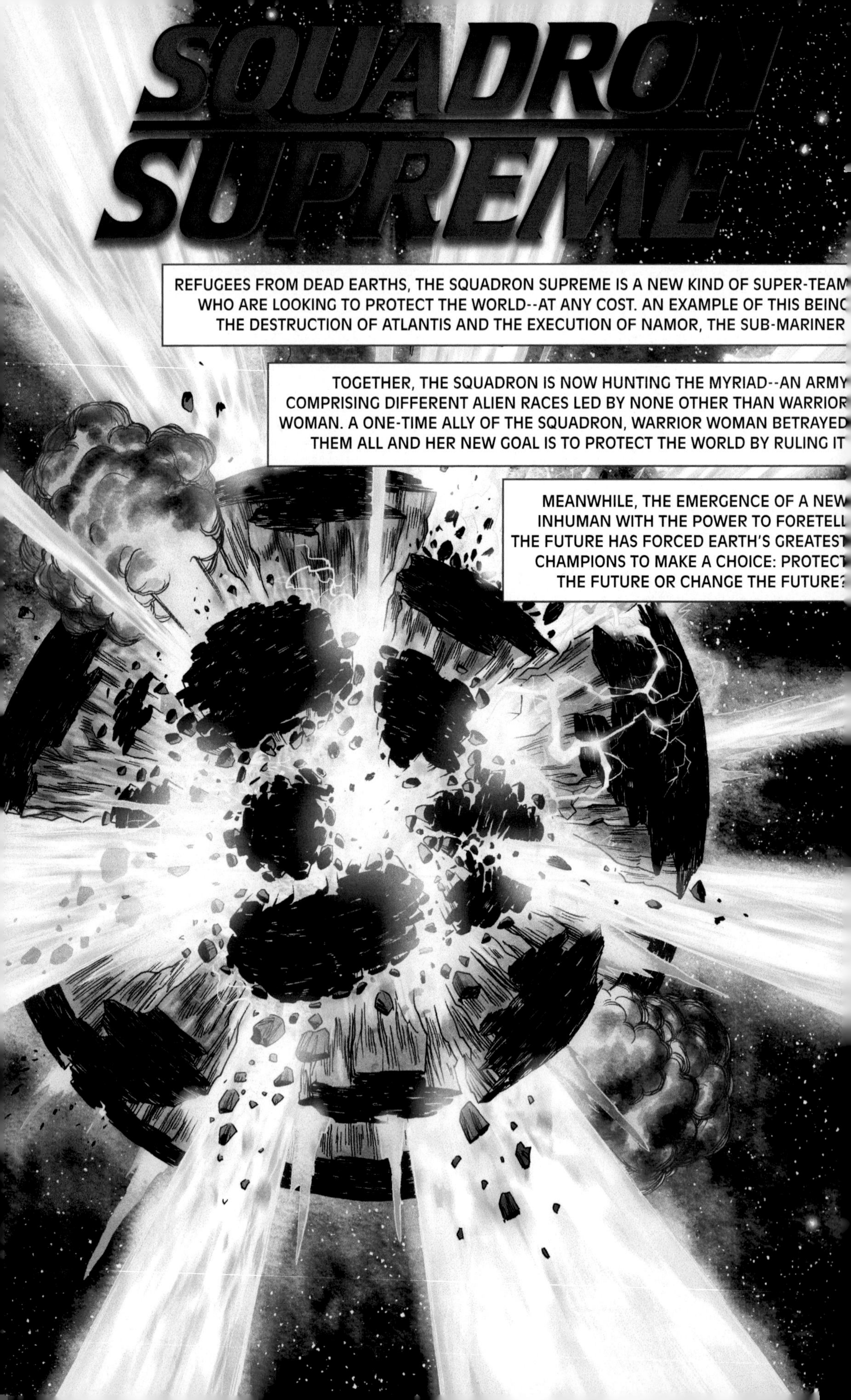
SQUADRON SUPREME
REFUGEES FROM DEAD EARTHS, THE SQUADRON SUPREME IS A NEW KIND OF SUPER-TEAM WHO ARE LOOKING TO PROTECT THE WORLD--AT ANY COST. AN EXAMPLE OF THIS BEING THE DESTRUCTION OF ATLANTIS AND THE EXECUTION OF NAMOR, THE SUB-MARINER
TOGETHER, THE SQUADRON IS NOW HUNTING THE MYRIAD--AN ARMY COMPRISING DIFFERENT ALIEN RACES LED BY NONE OTHER THAN WARRIOR WOMAN. A ONE-TIME ALLY OF THE SQUADRON, WARRIOR WOMAN BETRAYED THEM ALL AND HER NEW GOAL IS TO PROTECT THE WORLD BY RULING IT
MEANWHILE, THE EMERGENCE OF A NEW INHUMAN WITH THE POWER TO FORETELL THE FUTURE HAS FORCED EARTH'S GREATEST CHAMPIONS TO MAKE A CHOICE: PROTECT THE FUTURE OR CHANGE THE FUTURE?

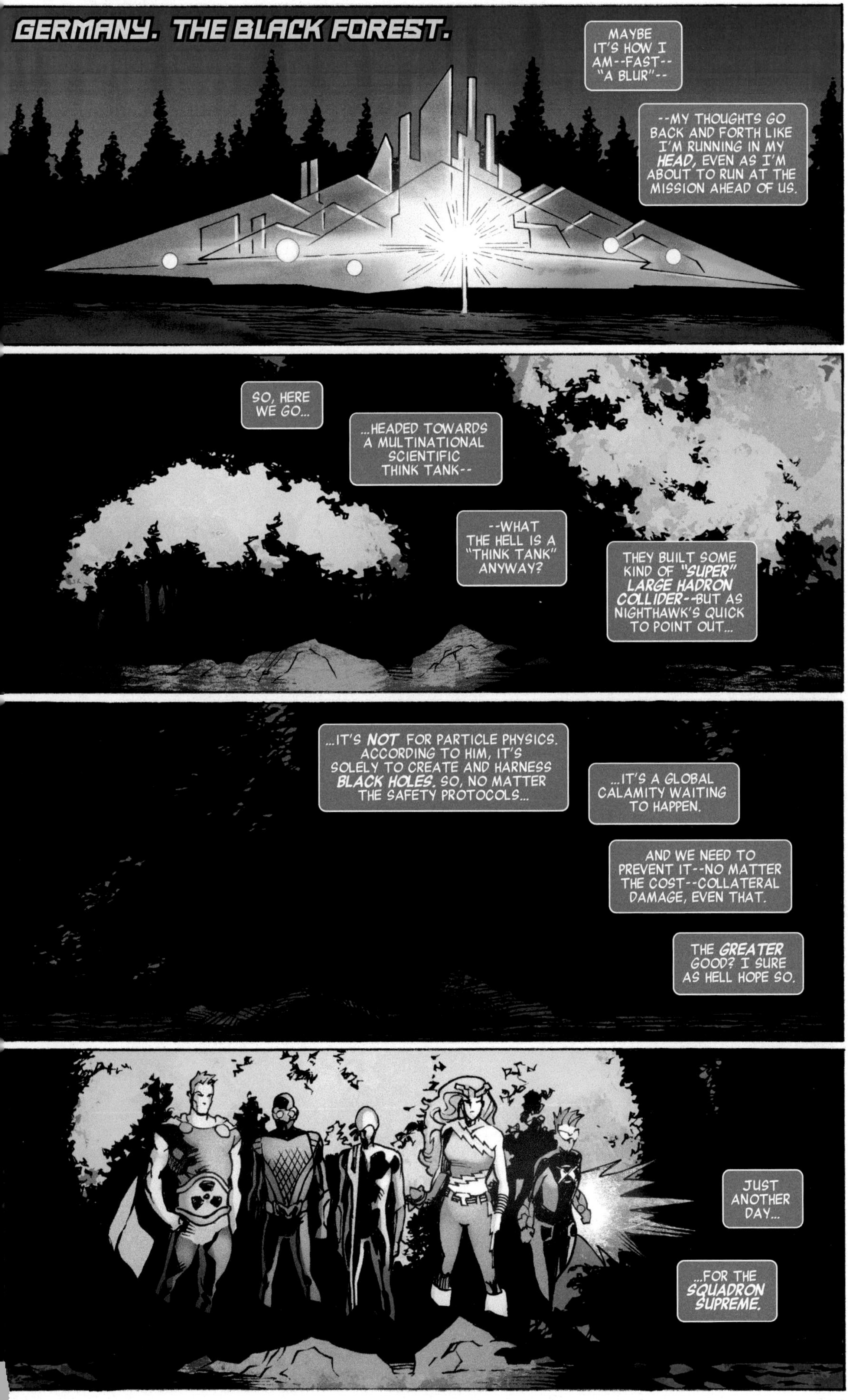
GERMANY. THE BLACK FOREST.
MAYBE IT'S HOW I AM--FAST--"A BLUR"--
--MY THOUGHTS GO BACK AND FORTH LIKE I'M RUNNING IN MY HEAD, EVEN AS I'M ABOUT TO RUN AT THE MISSION AHEAD OF US.
SO, HERE WE GO...
...HEADED TOWARDS A MULTINATIONAL SCIENTIFIC THINK TANK--
--WHAT THE HELL IS A "THINK TANK" ANYWAY?
THEY BUILT SOME KIND OF "SUPER" LARGE HADRON COLLIDER--BUT AS NIGHTHAWK'S QUICK TO POINT OUT...
...IT'S NOT FOR PARTICLE PHYSICS. ACCORDING TO HIM, IT'S SOLELY TO CREATE AND HARNESS BLACK HOLES. SO, NO MATTER THE SAFETY PROTOCOLS...
...IT'S A GLOBAL CALAMITY WAITING TO HAPPEN.
AND WE NEED TO PREVENT IT--NO MATTER THE COST--COLLATERAL DAMAGE, EVEN THAT.
THE GREATER GOOD? I SURE AS HELL HOPE SO.
JUST ANOTHER DAY...
...FOR THE SQUADRON SUPREME.

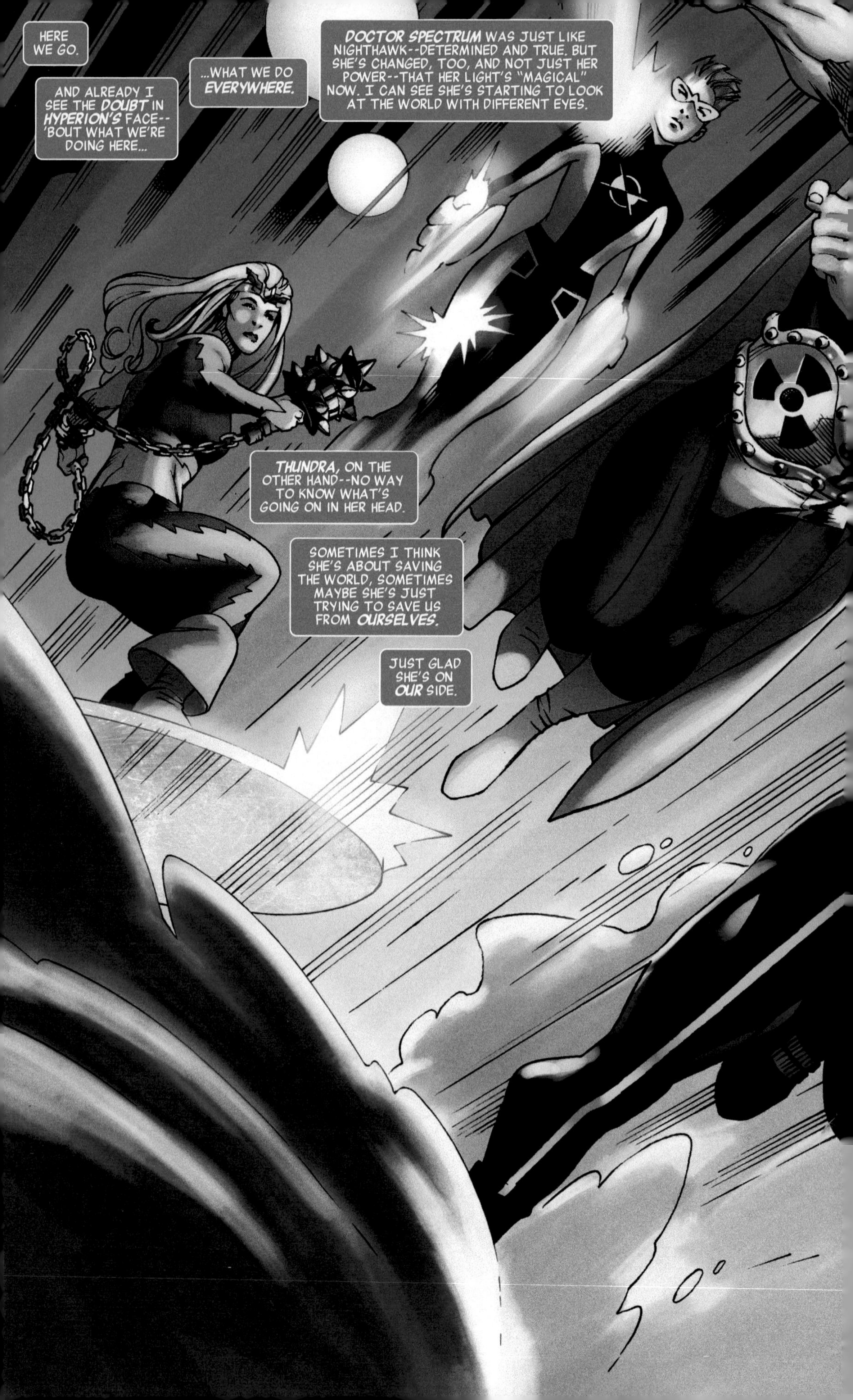
HERE WE GO.
AND ALREADY I SEE THE DOUBT IN HYPERION'S FACE--'BOUT WHAT WE'RE DOING HERE...
...WHAT WE DO EVERYWHERE.
DOCTOR SPECTRUM WAS JUST LIKE NIGHTHAWK--DETERMINED AND TRUE. BUT SHE'S CHANGED, TOO, AND NOT JUST HER POWER--THAT HER LIGHT'S "MAGICAL" NOW. I CAN SEE SHE'S STARTING TO LOOK AT THE WORLD WITH DIFFERENT EYES.
THUNDRA, ON THE OTHER HAND--NO WAY TO KNOW WHAT'S GOING ON IN HER HEAD.
SOMETIMES I THINK SHE'S ABOUT SAVING THE WORLD, SOMETIMES MAYBE SHE'S JUST TRYING TO SAVE US FROM OURSELVES.
JUST GLAD SHE'S ON OUR SIDE.

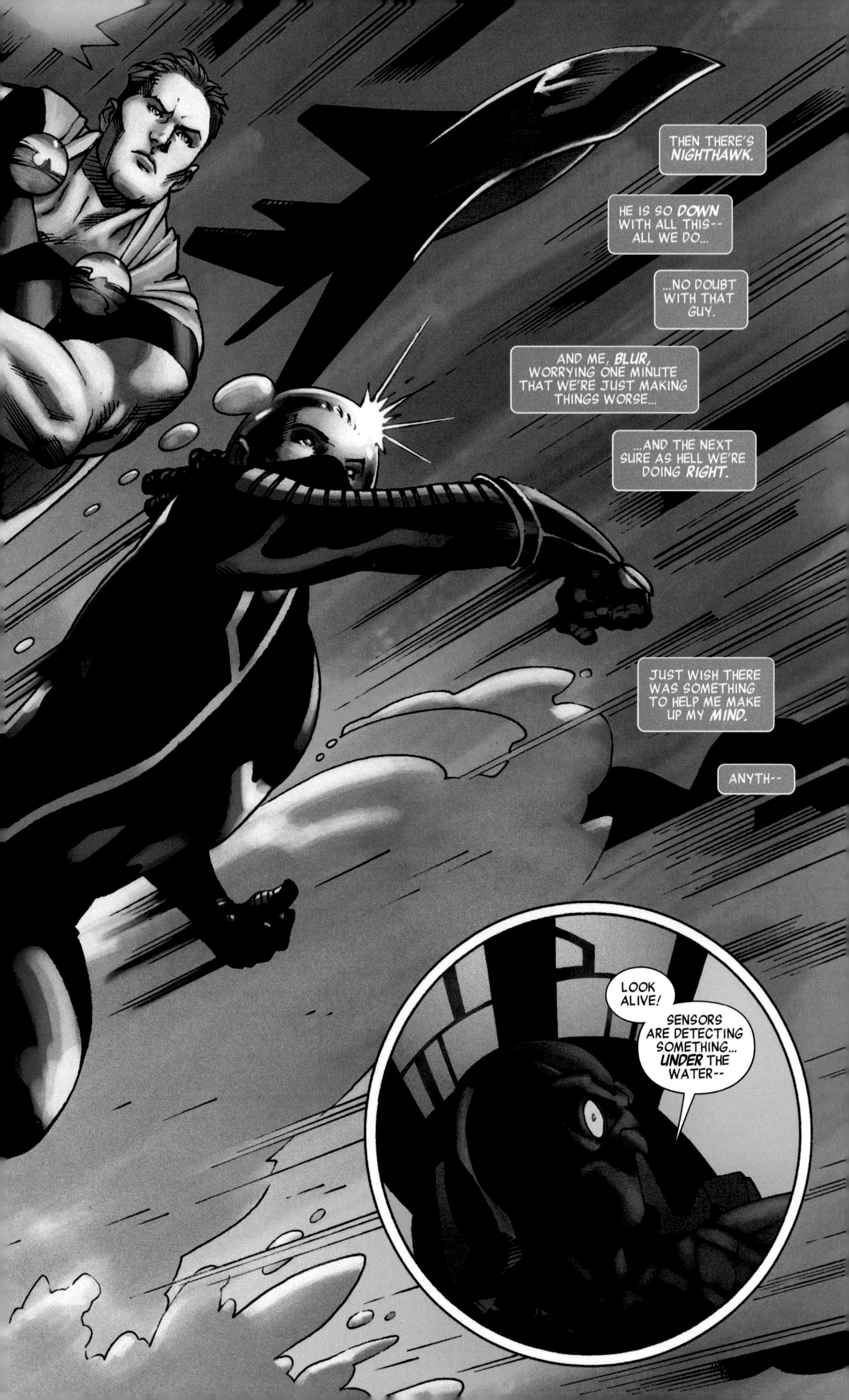
THEN THERE'S NIGHTHAWK.
HE IS SO DOWN WITH ALL THIS--ALL WE DO...
...NO DOUBT WITH THAT GUY.
AND ME, BLUR, WORRYING ONE MINUTE THAT WE'RE JUST MAKING THINGS WORSE...
...AND THE NEXT SURE AS HELL WE'RE DOING RIGHT.
JUST WISH THERE WAS SOMETHING TO HELP ME MAKE UP MY MIND.
ANYTH--
LOOK ALIVE!
SENSORS ARE DETECTING SOMETHING... UNDER THE WATER--

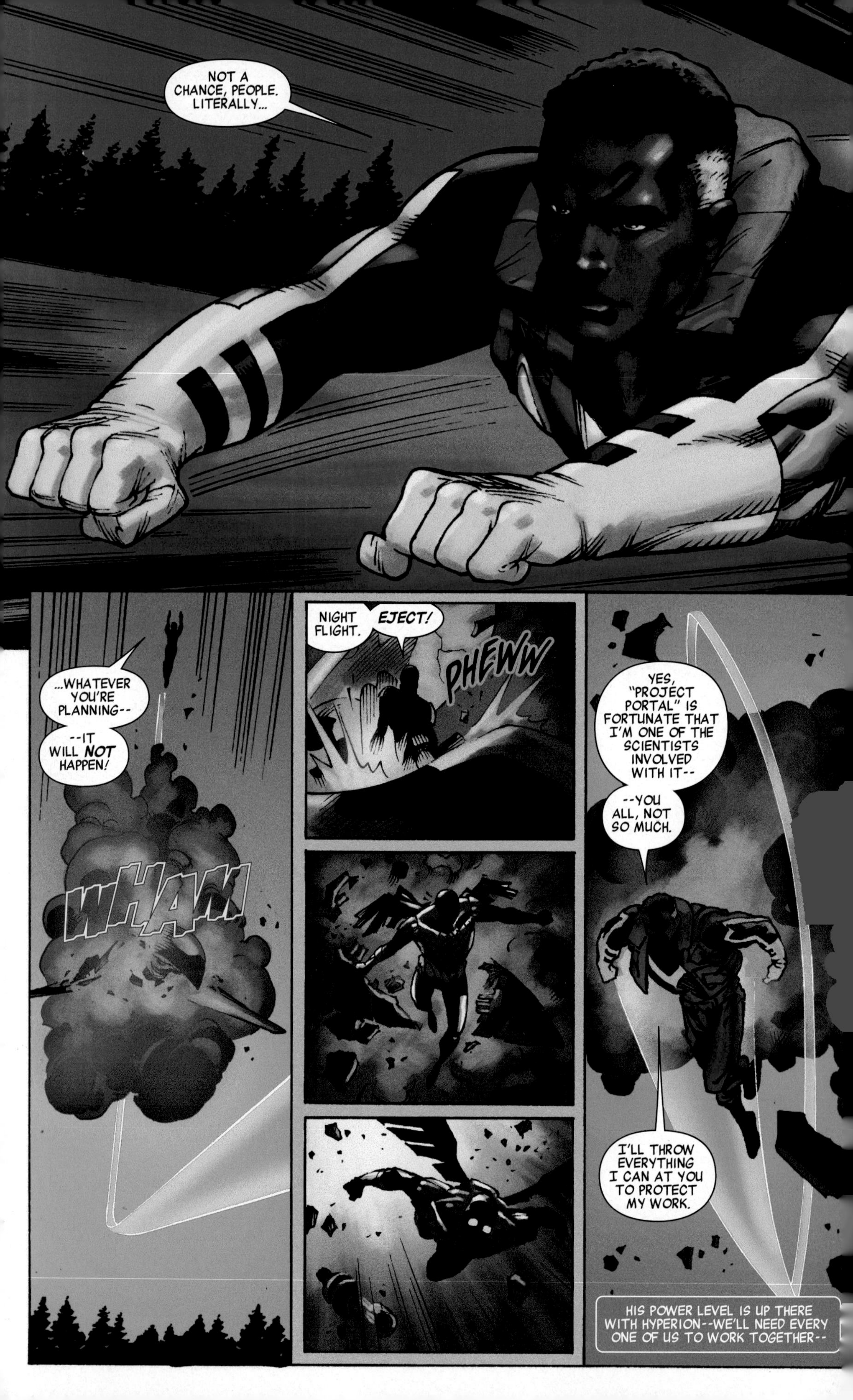
NOT A CHANCE, PEOPLE. LITERALLY...
...WHATEVER YOU'RE PLANNING--
--IT WILL NOT HAPPEN!
WHAM
NIGHT FLIGHT.
EJECT!
PHEWW
YES, "PROJECT PORTAL" IS FORTUNATE THAT I'M ONE OF THE SCIENTISTS INVOLVED WITH IT--
--YOU ALL, NOT SO MUCH.
I'LL THROW EVERYTHING I CAN AT YOU TO PROTECT MY WORK.
HIS POWER LEVEL IS UP THERE WITH HYPERION--WE'LL NEED EVERY ONE OF US TO WORK TOGETHER--

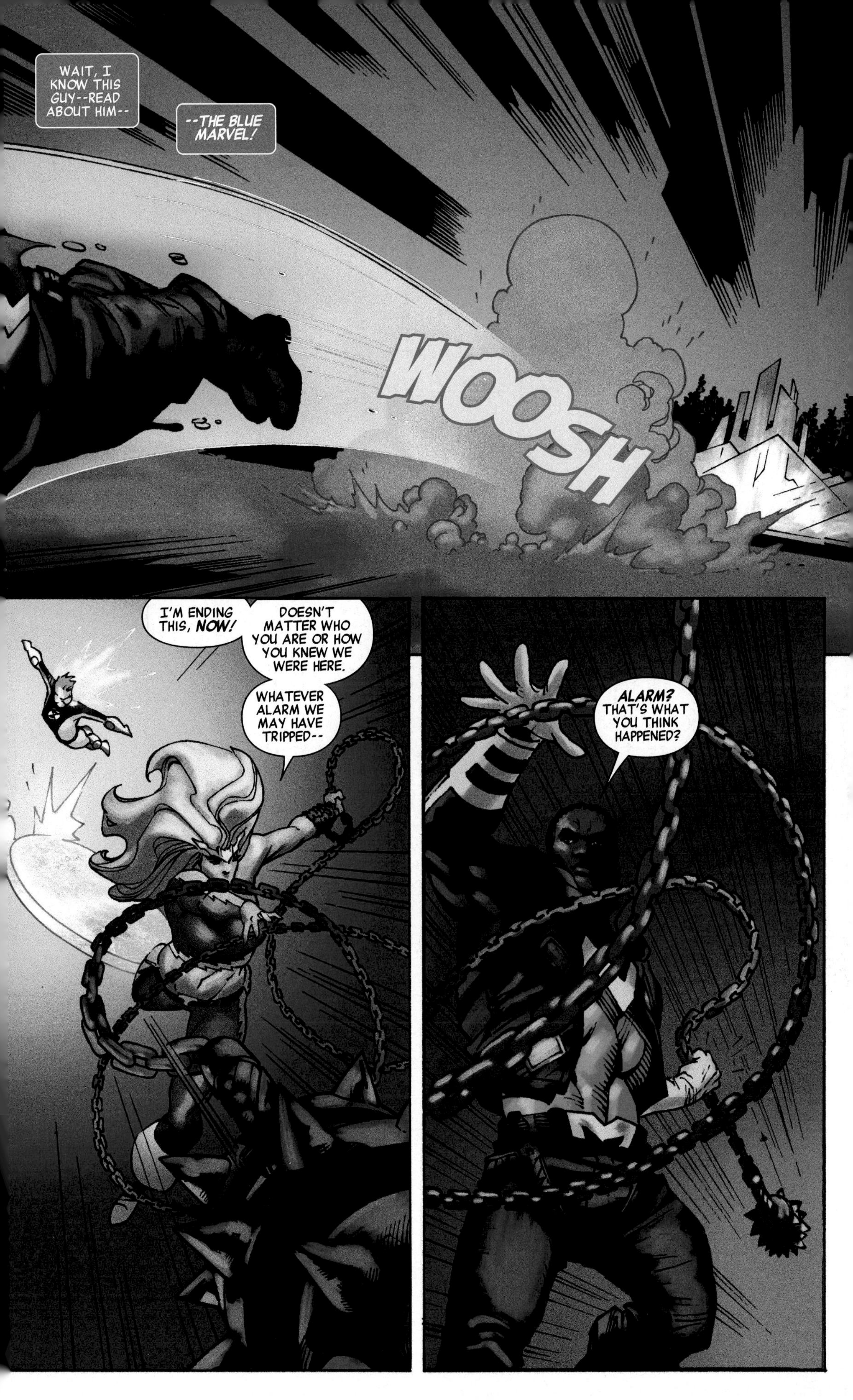
WAIT, I KNOW THIS GUY--READ ABOUT HIM--
--THE BLUE MARVEL!
WOOSH
I'M ENDING THIS, NOW!
DOESN'T MATTER WHO YOU ARE OR HOW YOU KNEW WE WERE HERE.
WHATEVER ALARM WE MAY HAVE TRIPPED--
ALARM? THAT'S WHAT YOU THINK HAPPENED?

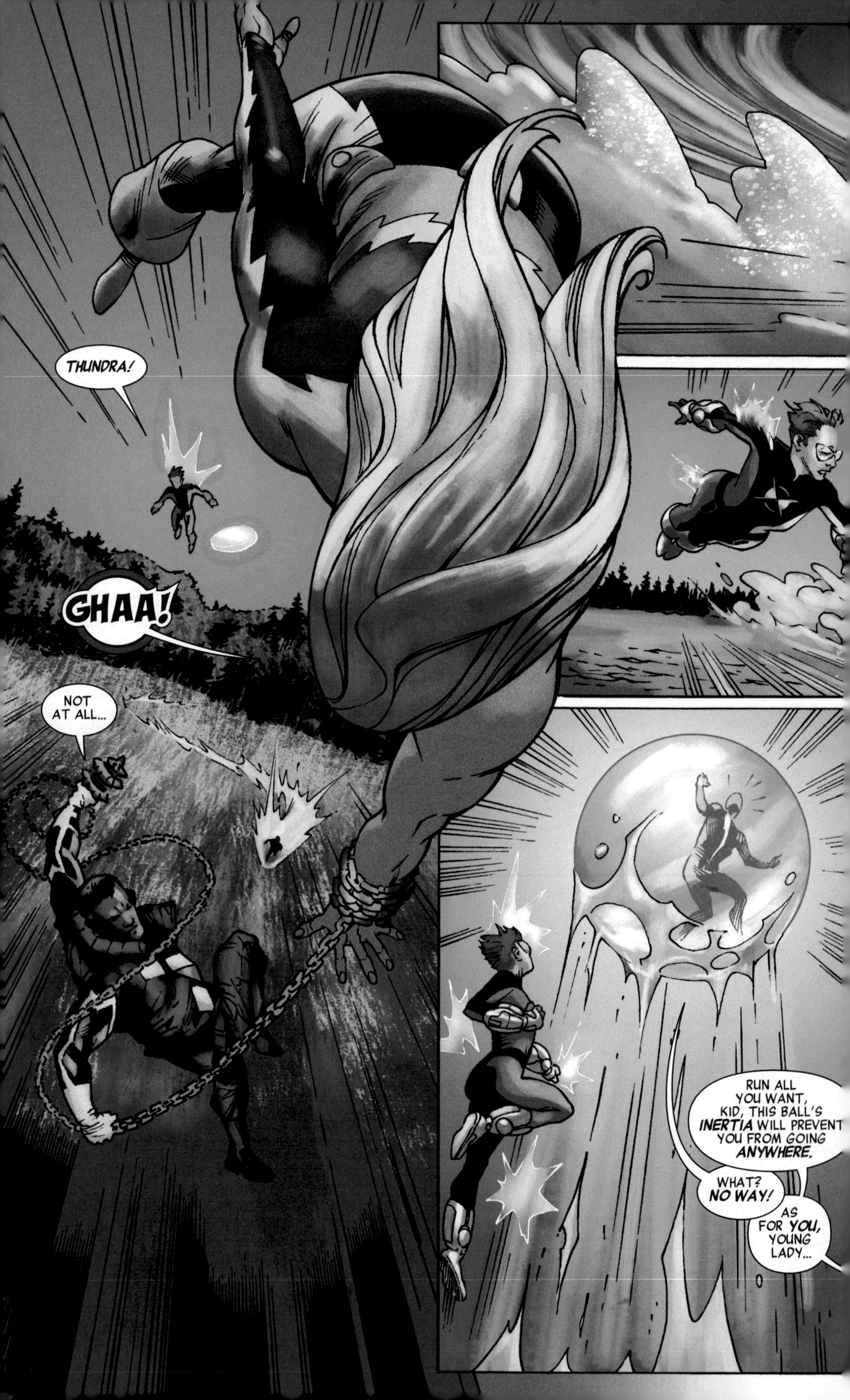
THUNDRA!
GHAA!
NOT AT ALL...
RUN ALL YOU WANT, KID, THIS BALL'S **INERTIA** WILL PREVENT YOU FROM GOING **ANYWHERE.**
WHAT? **NO WAY!**
AS FOR **YOU,** YOUNG LADY...

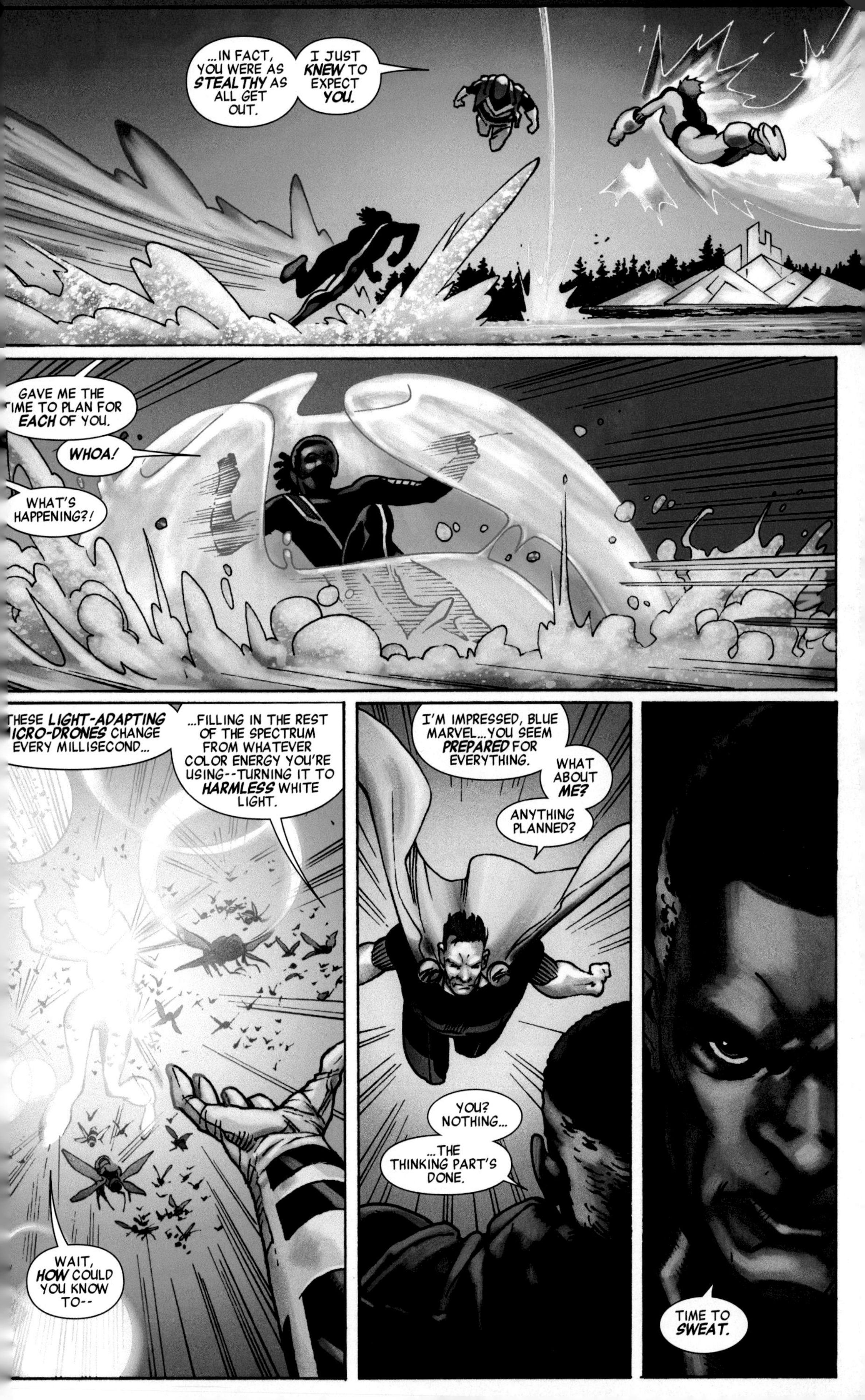
...IN FACT, YOU WERE AS STEALTHY AS ALL GET OUT.
I JUST KNEW TO EXPECT YOU.
GAVE ME THE TIME TO PLAN FOR EACH OF YOU.
WHOA!
WHAT'S HAPPENING?!
THESE LIGHT-ADAPTING MICRO-DRONES CHANGE EVERY MILLISECOND...
...FILLING IN THE REST OF THE SPECTRUM FROM WHATEVER COLOR ENERGY YOU'RE USING--TURNING IT TO HARMLESS WHITE LIGHT.
WAIT, HOW COULD YOU KNOW TO--
I'M IMPRESSED, BLUE MARVEL...YOU SEEM PREPARED FOR EVERYTHING.
WHAT ABOUT ME?
ANYTHING PLANNED?
YOU? NOTHING...
...THE THINKING PART'S DONE.
TIME TO SWEAT.

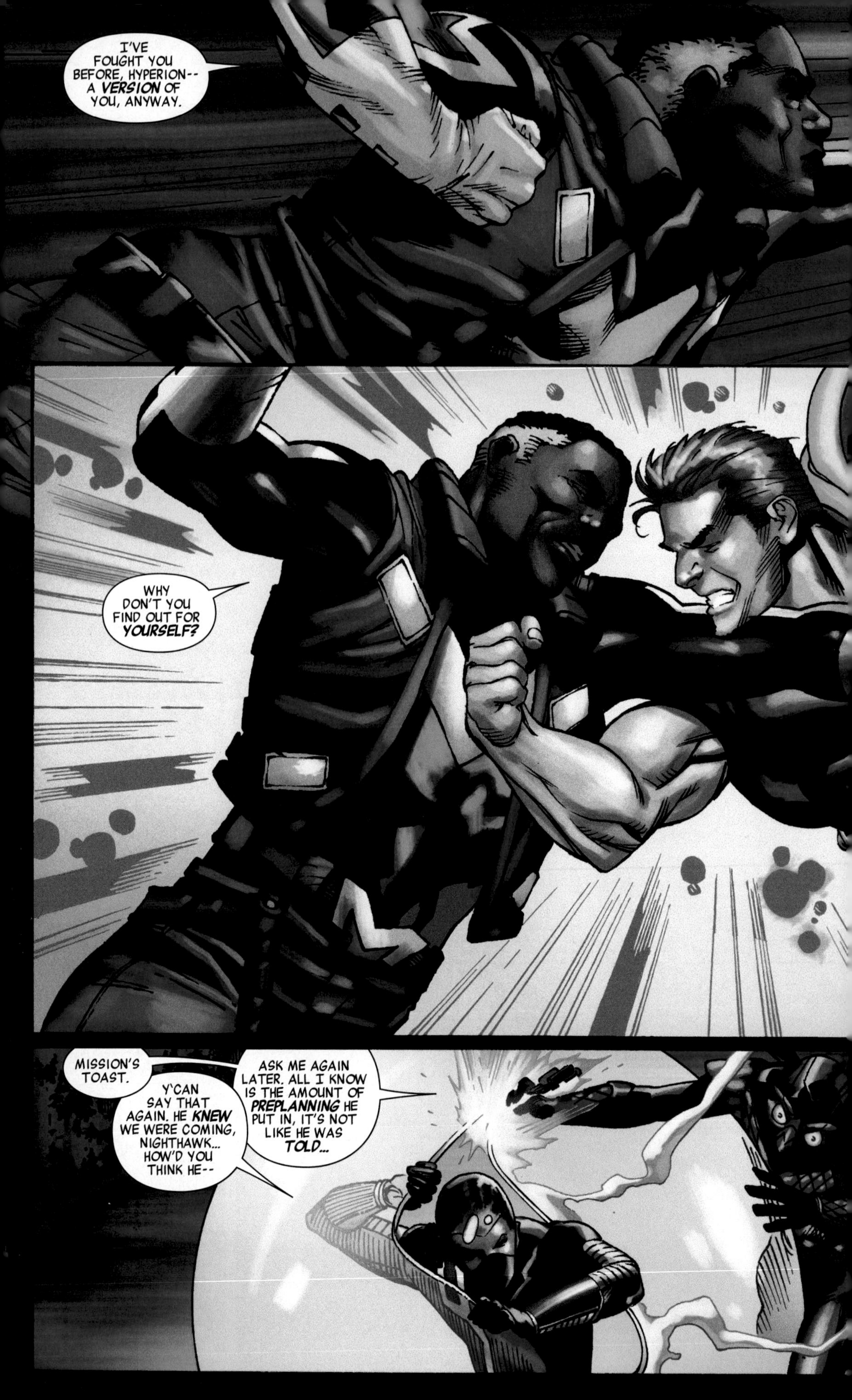
I'VE FOUGHT YOU BEFORE, HYPERION-- A VERSION OF YOU, ANYWAY.
WHY DON'T YOU FIND OUT FOR YOURSELF?
MISSION'S TOAST.
Y'CAN SAY THAT AGAIN. HE KNEW WE WERE COMING, NIGHTHAWK... HOW'D YOU THINK HE--
ASK ME AGAIN LATER. ALL I KNOW IS THE AMOUNT OF PREPLANNING HE PUT IN, IT'S NOT LIKE HE WAS TOLD...

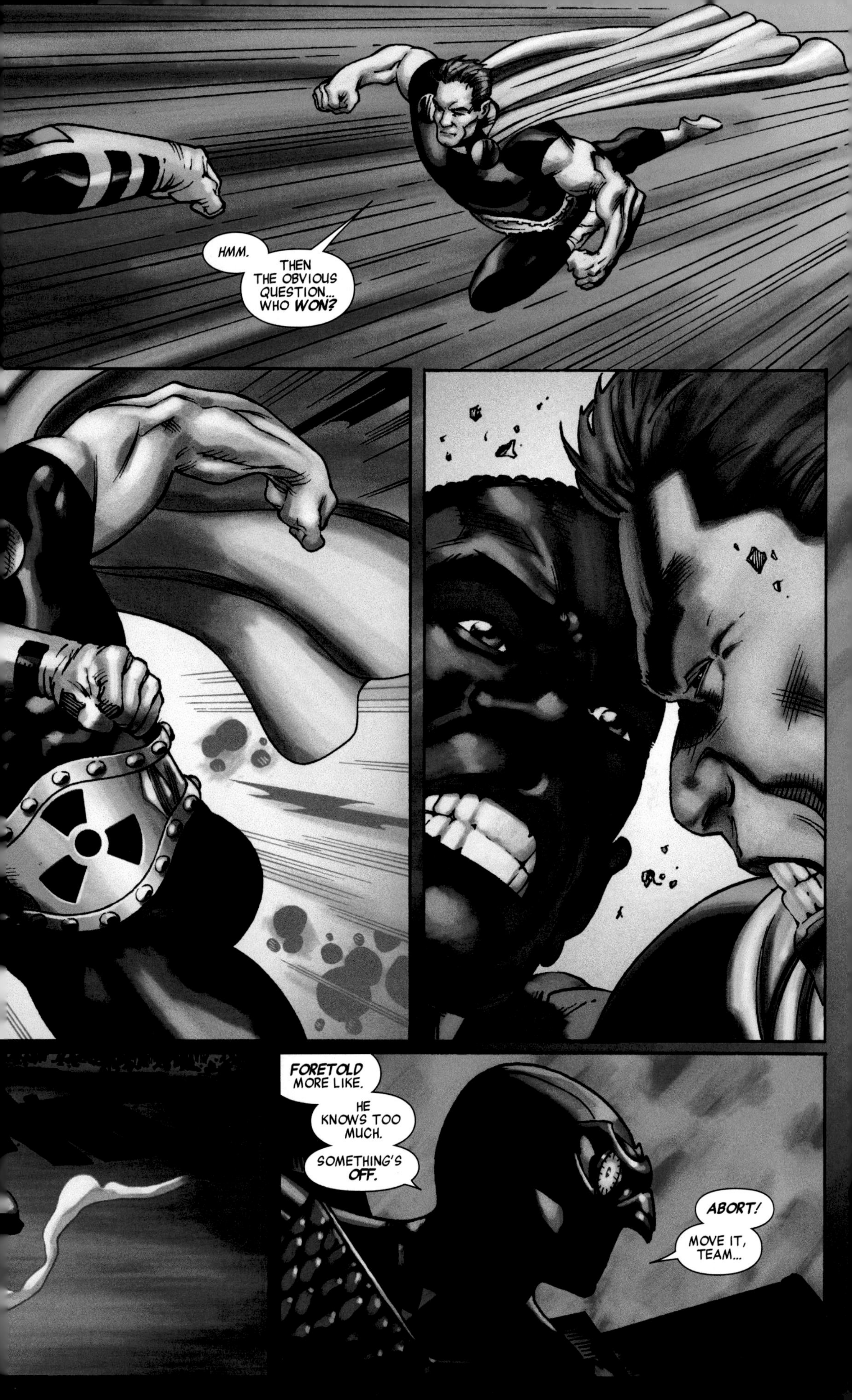
HMM.
THEN THE OBVIOUS QUESTION... WHO WON?
FORETOLD MORE LIKE.
HE KNOWS TOO MUCH.
SOMETHING'S OFF.
ABORT!
MOVE IT, TEAM...

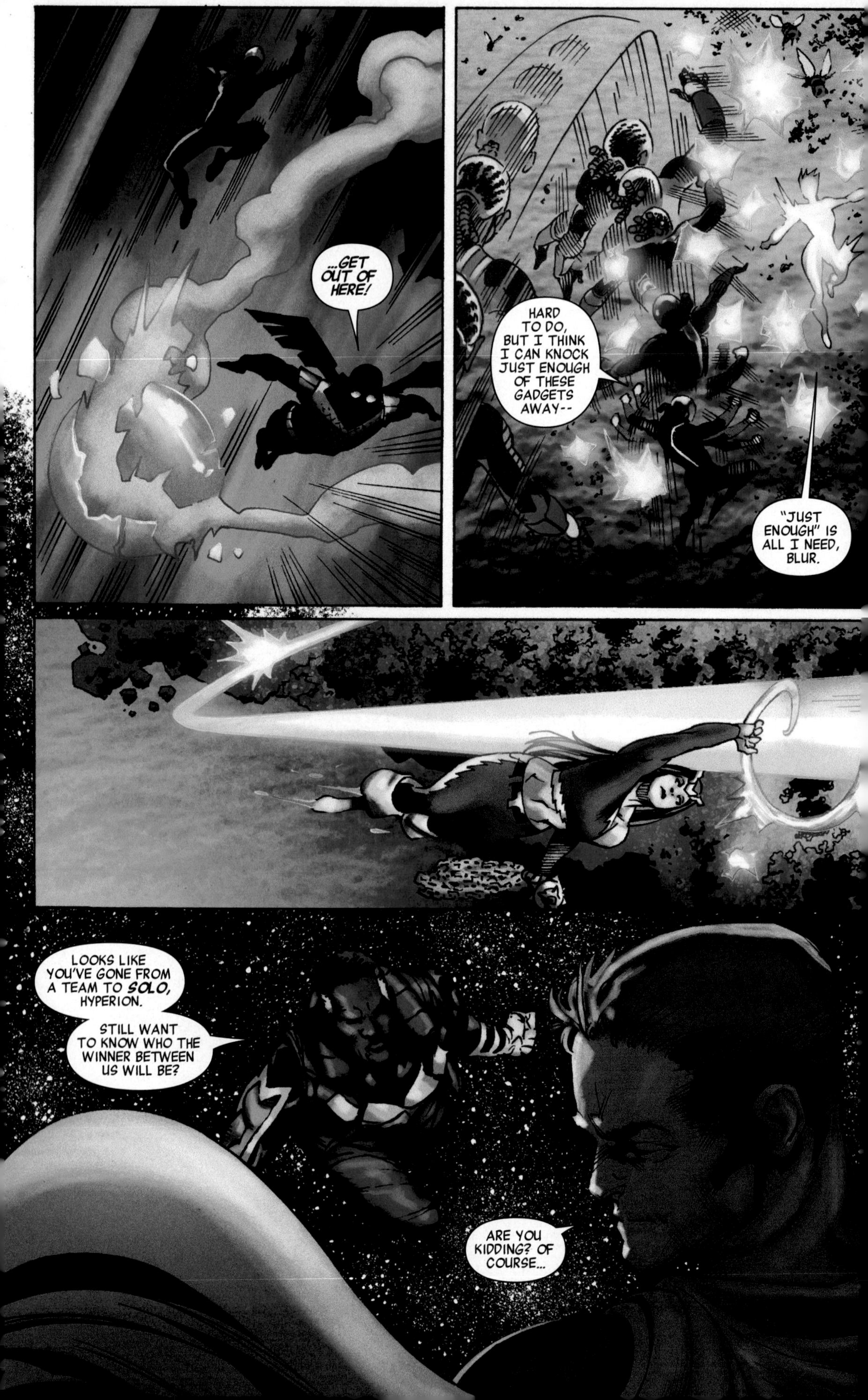
...GET OUT OF HERE!
HARD TO DO, BUT I THINK I CAN KNOCK JUST ENOUGH OF THESE GADGETS AWAY--
"JUST ENOUGH" IS ALL I NEED, BLUR.
LOOKS LIKE YOU'VE GONE FROM A TEAM TO SOLO, HYPERION.
STILL WANT TO KNOW WHO THE WINNER BETWEEN US WILL BE?
ARE YOU KIDDING? OF COURSE...

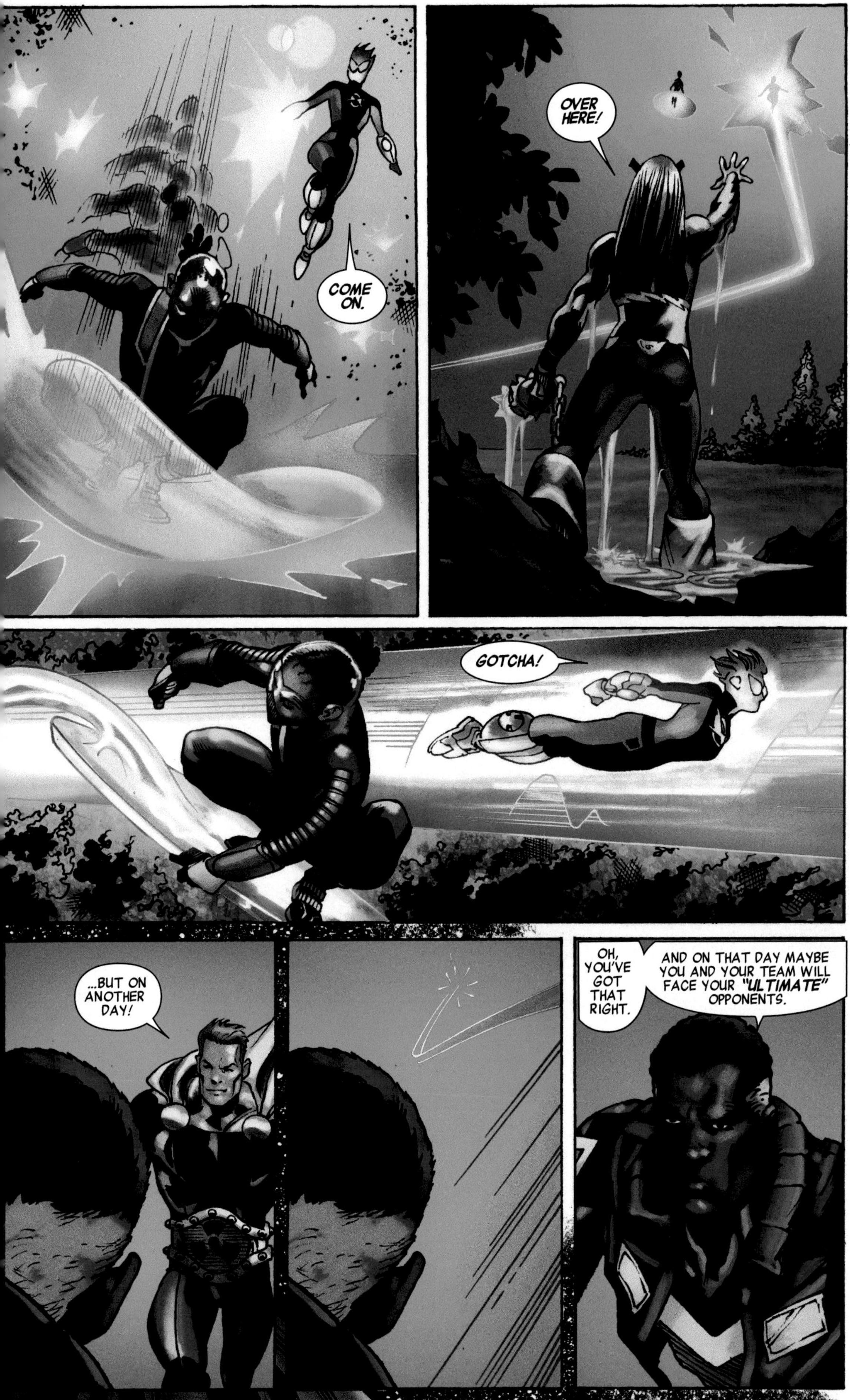
COME ON.
OVER HERE!
GOTCHA!
...BUT ON ANOTHER DAY!
OH, YOU'VE GOT THAT RIGHT.
AND ON THAT DAY MAYBE YOU AND YOUR TEAM WILL FACE YOUR "ULTIMATE" OPPONENTS.

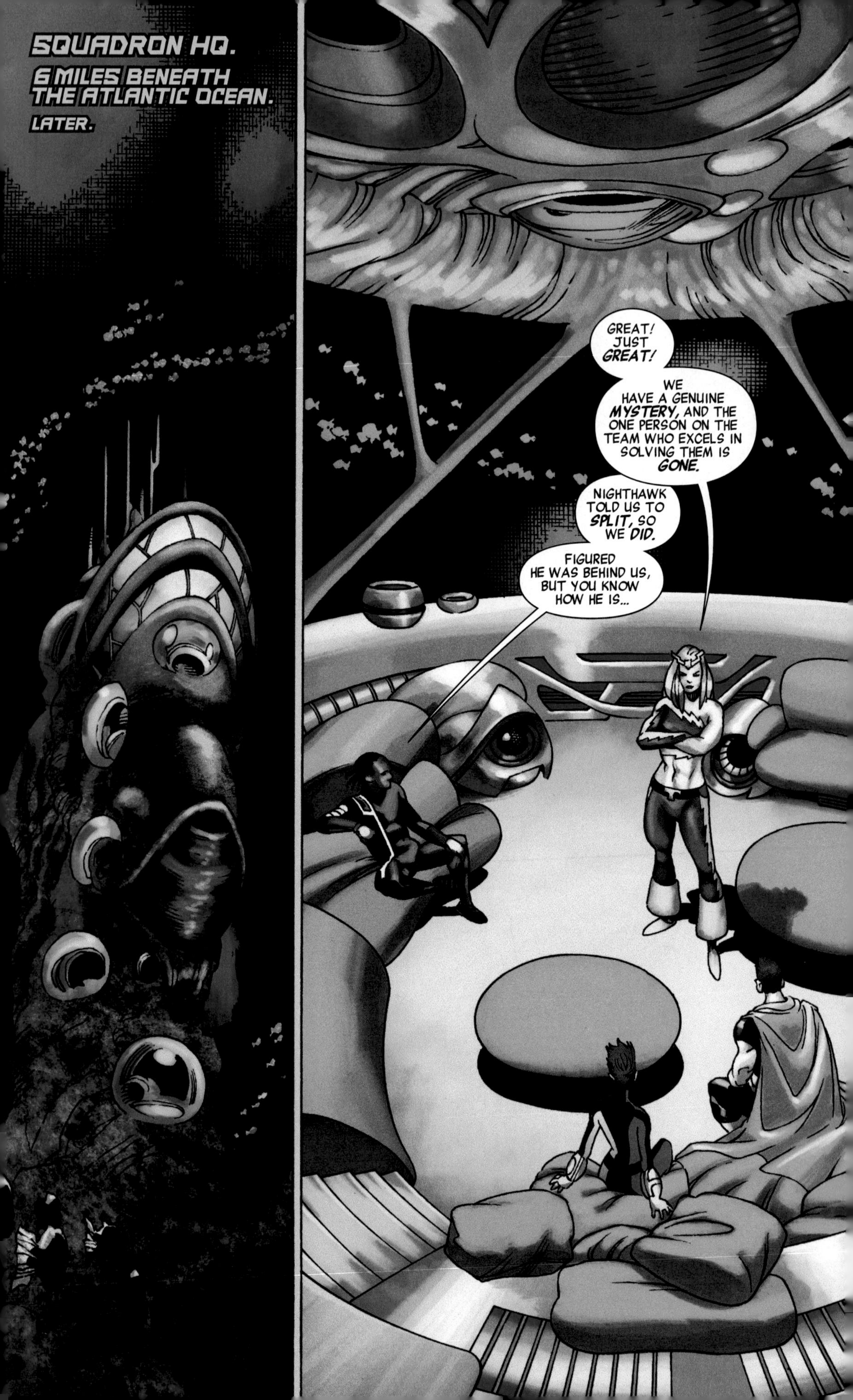
SQUADRON HQ.
6 MILES BENEATH THE ATLANTIC OCEAN.
LATER.
GREAT! JUST GREAT!
WE HAVE A GENUINE MYSTERY, AND THE ONE PERSON ON THE TEAM WHO EXCELS IN SOLVING THEM IS GONE.
NIGHTHAWK TOLD US TO SPLIT, SO WE DID.
FIGURED HE WAS BEHIND US, BUT YOU KNOW HOW HE IS...

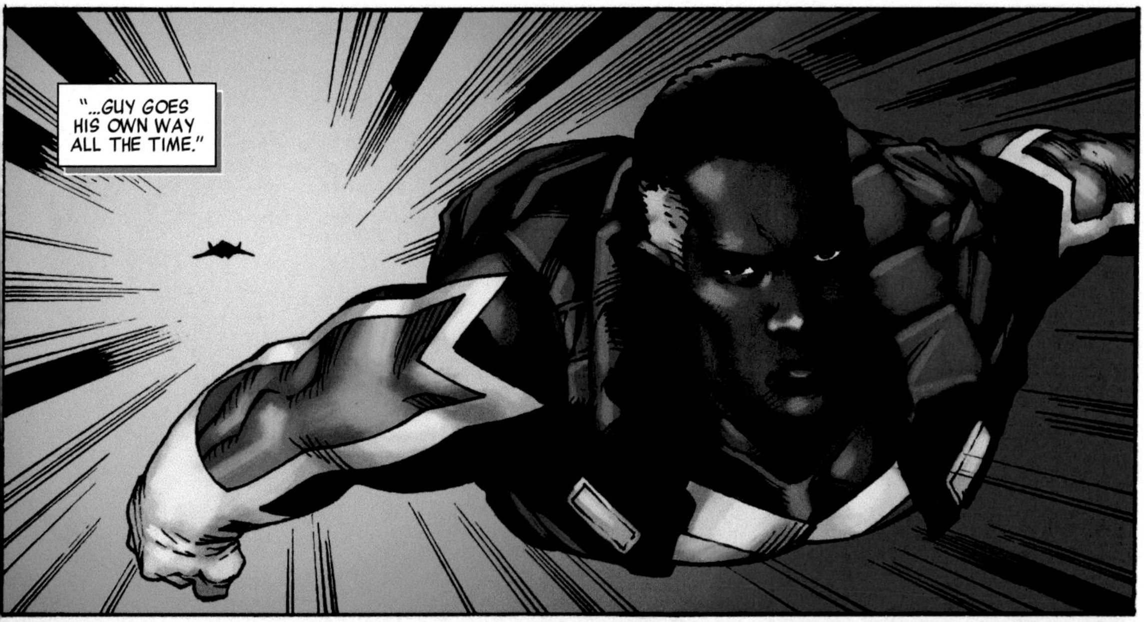
"...GUY GOES HIS OWN WAY ALL THE TIME."

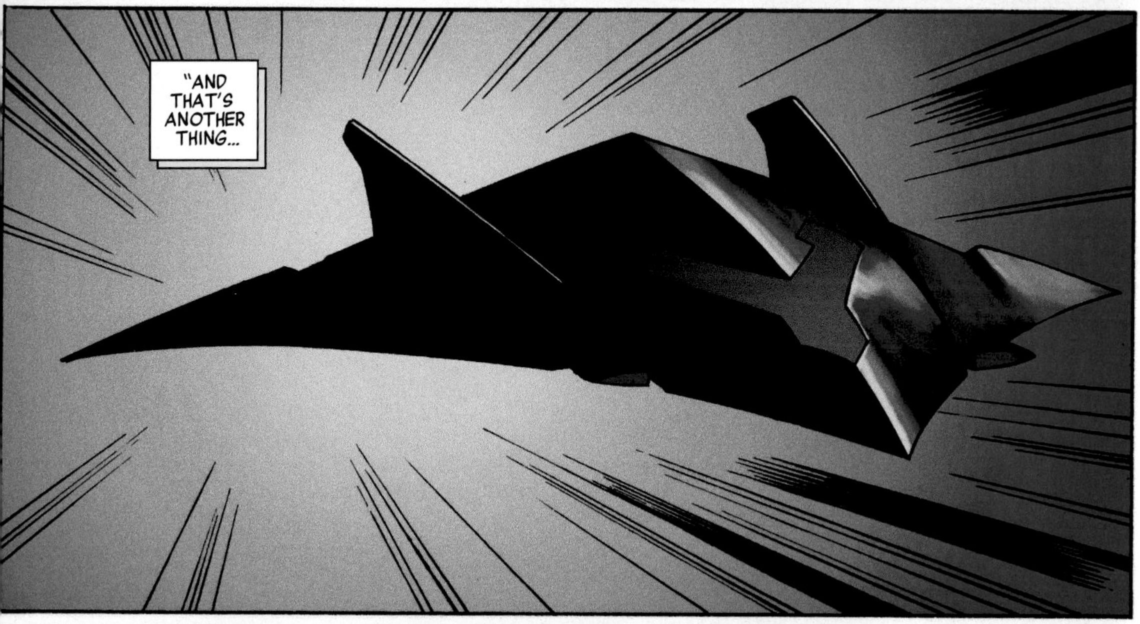
"AND THAT'S ANOTHER THING...

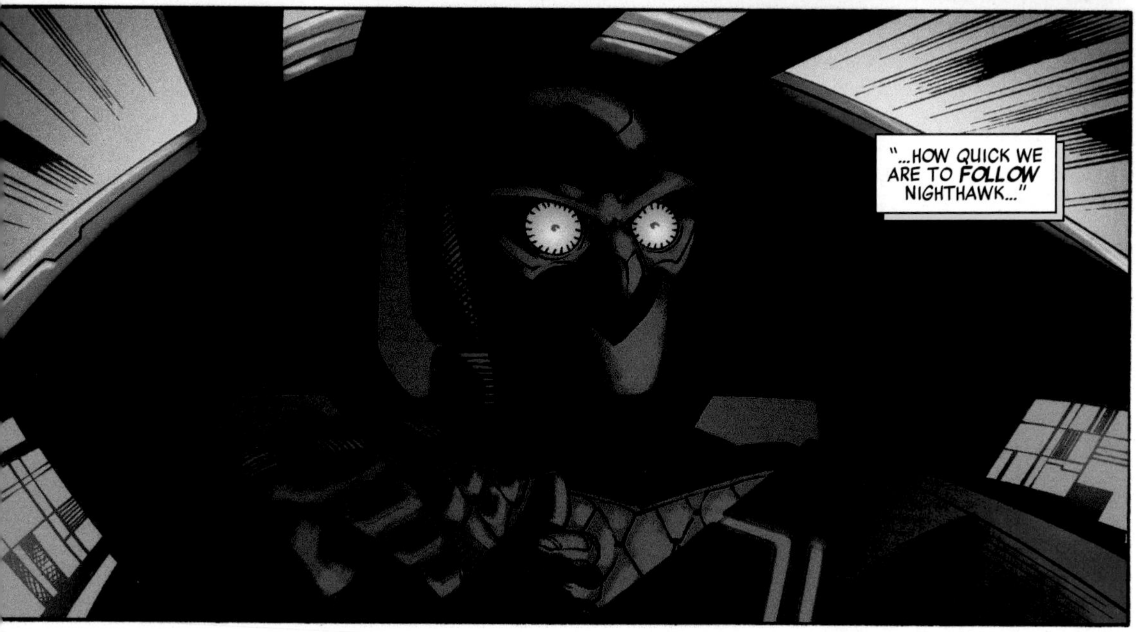
"...HOW QUICK WE ARE TO FOLLOW NIGHTHAWK..."

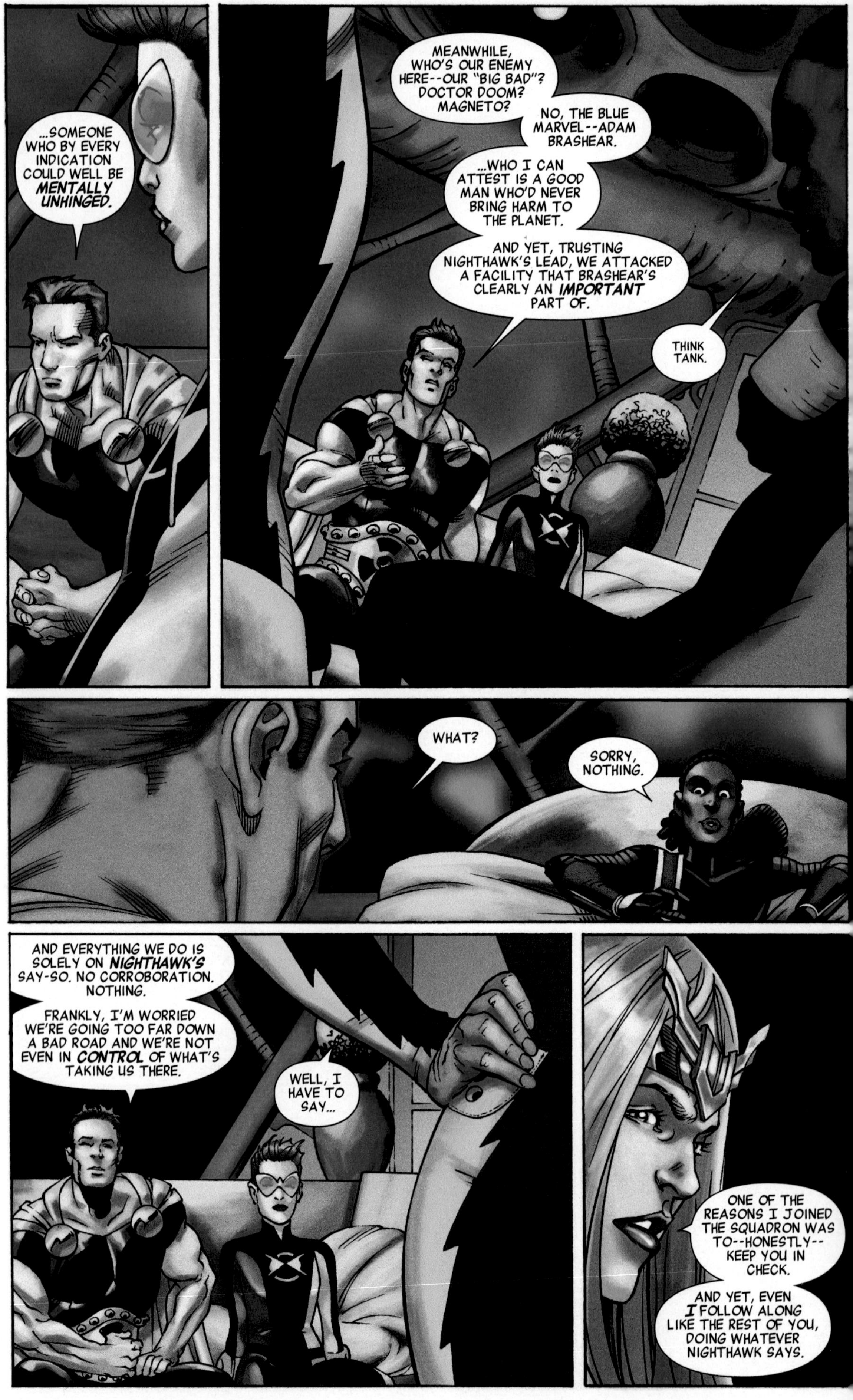
...SOMEONE WHO BY EVERY INDICATION COULD WELL BE MENTALLY UNHINGED.
MEANWHILE, WHO'S OUR ENEMY HERE--OUR "BIG BAD"? DOCTOR DOOM? MAGNETO?
NO, THE BLUE MARVEL--ADAM BRASHEAR.
...WHO I CAN ATTEST IS A GOOD MAN WHO'D NEVER BRING HARM TO THE PLANET.
AND YET, TRUSTING NIGHTHAWK'S LEAD, WE ATTACKED A FACILITY THAT BRASHEAR'S CLEARLY AN IMPORTANT PART OF.
THINK TANK.
WHAT?
SORRY, NOTHING.
AND EVERYTHING WE DO IS SOLELY ON NIGHTHAWK'S SAY-SO. NO CORROBORATION. NOTHING.
FRANKLY, I'M WORRIED WE'RE GOING TOO FAR DOWN A BAD ROAD AND WE'RE NOT EVEN IN CONTROL OF WHAT'S TAKING US THERE.
WELL, I HAVE TO SAY...
ONE OF THE REASONS I JOINED THE SQUADRON WAS TO--HONESTLY--KEEP YOU IN CHECK.
AND YET, EVEN I FOLLOW ALONG LIKE THE REST OF YOU, DOING WHATEVER NIGHTHAWK SAYS.

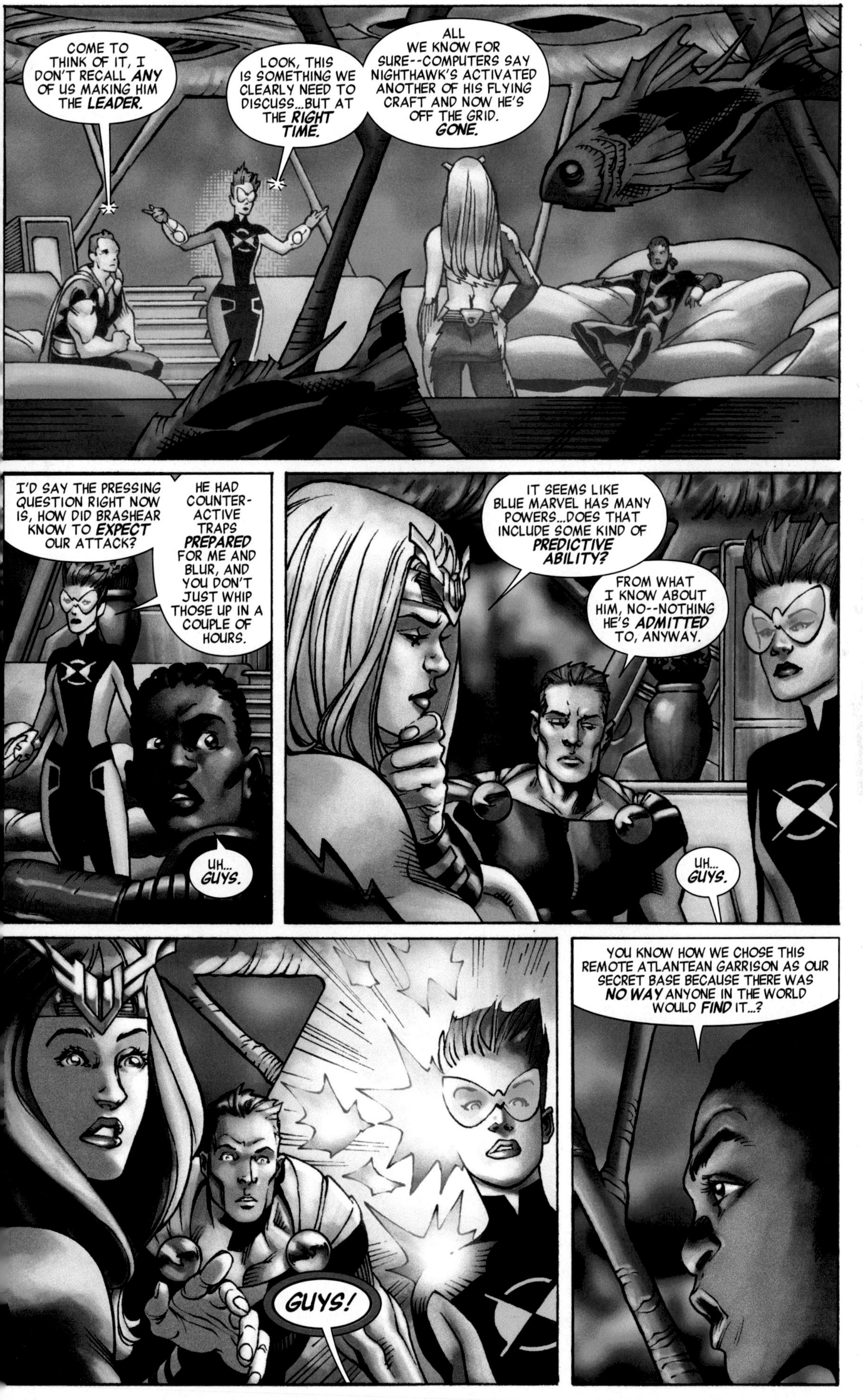
COME TO THINK OF IT, I DON'T RECALL ANY OF US MAKING HIM THE LEADER.
LOOK, THIS IS SOMETHING WE CLEARLY NEED TO DISCUSS...BUT AT THE RIGHT TIME.
ALL WE KNOW FOR SURE--COMPUTERS SAY NIGHTHAWK'S ACTIVATED ANOTHER OF HIS FLYING CRAFT AND NOW HE'S OFF THE GRID. GONE.
I'D SAY THE PRESSING QUESTION RIGHT NOW IS, HOW DID BRASHEAR KNOW TO EXPECT OUR ATTACK?
HE HAD COUNTER-ACTIVE TRAPS PREPARED FOR ME AND BLUR, AND YOU DON'T JUST WHIP THOSE UP IN A COUPLE OF HOURS.
UH... GUYS.
IT SEEMS LIKE BLUE MARVEL HAS MANY POWERS...DOES THAT INCLUDE SOME KIND OF PREDICTIVE ABILITY?
FROM WHAT I KNOW ABOUT HIM, NO--NOTHING HE'S ADMITTED TO, ANYWAY.
UH... GUYS.
GUYS!
YOU KNOW HOW WE CHOSE THIS REMOTE ATLANTEAN GARRISON AS OUR SECRET BASE BECAUSE THERE WAS NO WAY ANYONE IN THE WORLD WOULD FIND IT...?

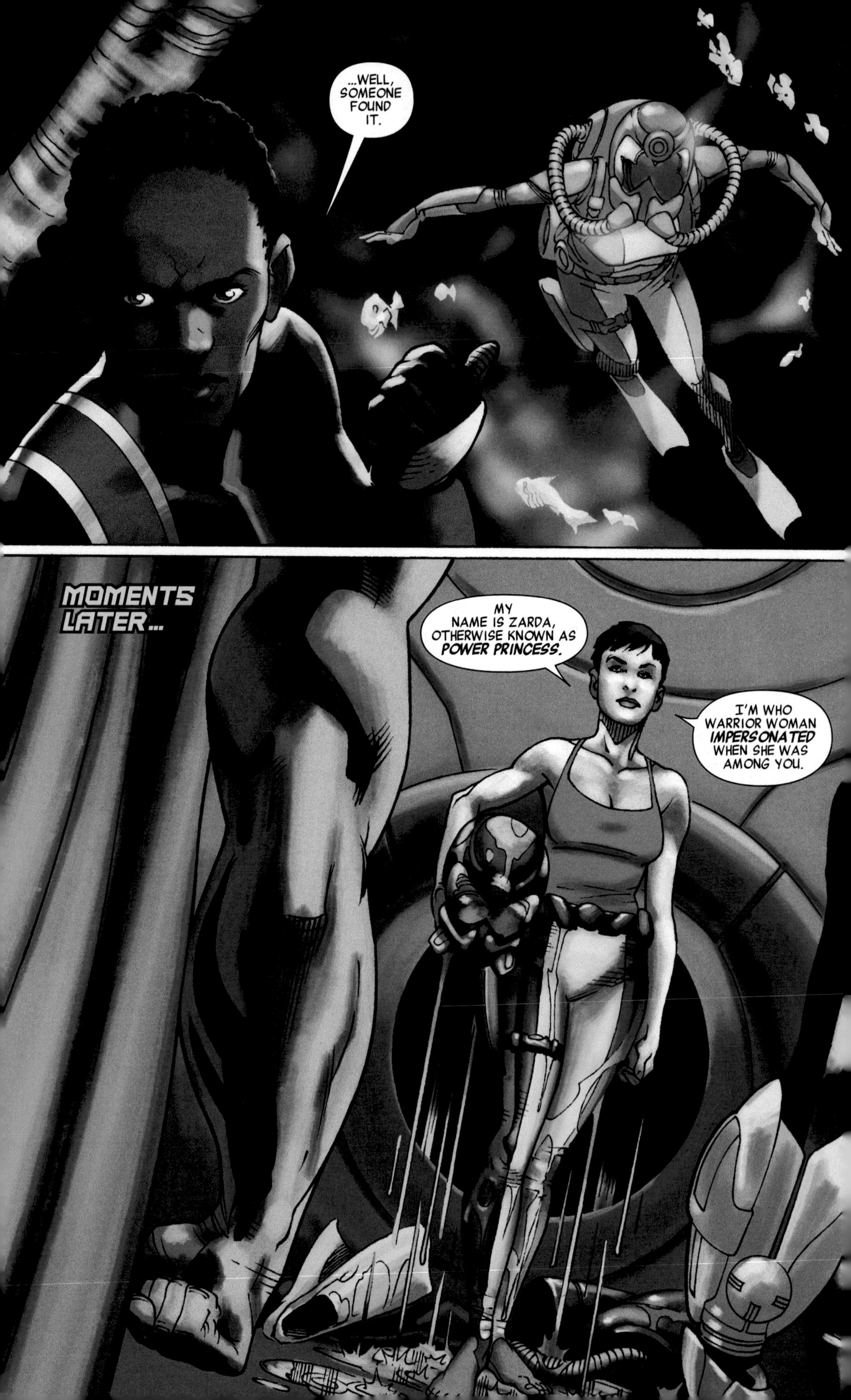

...WELL, SOMEONE FOUND IT.
MOMENTS LATER...
MY NAME IS ZARDA, OTHERWISE KNOWN AS POWER PRINCESS.
I'M WHO WARRIOR WOMAN IMPERSONATED WHEN SHE WAS AMONG YOU.

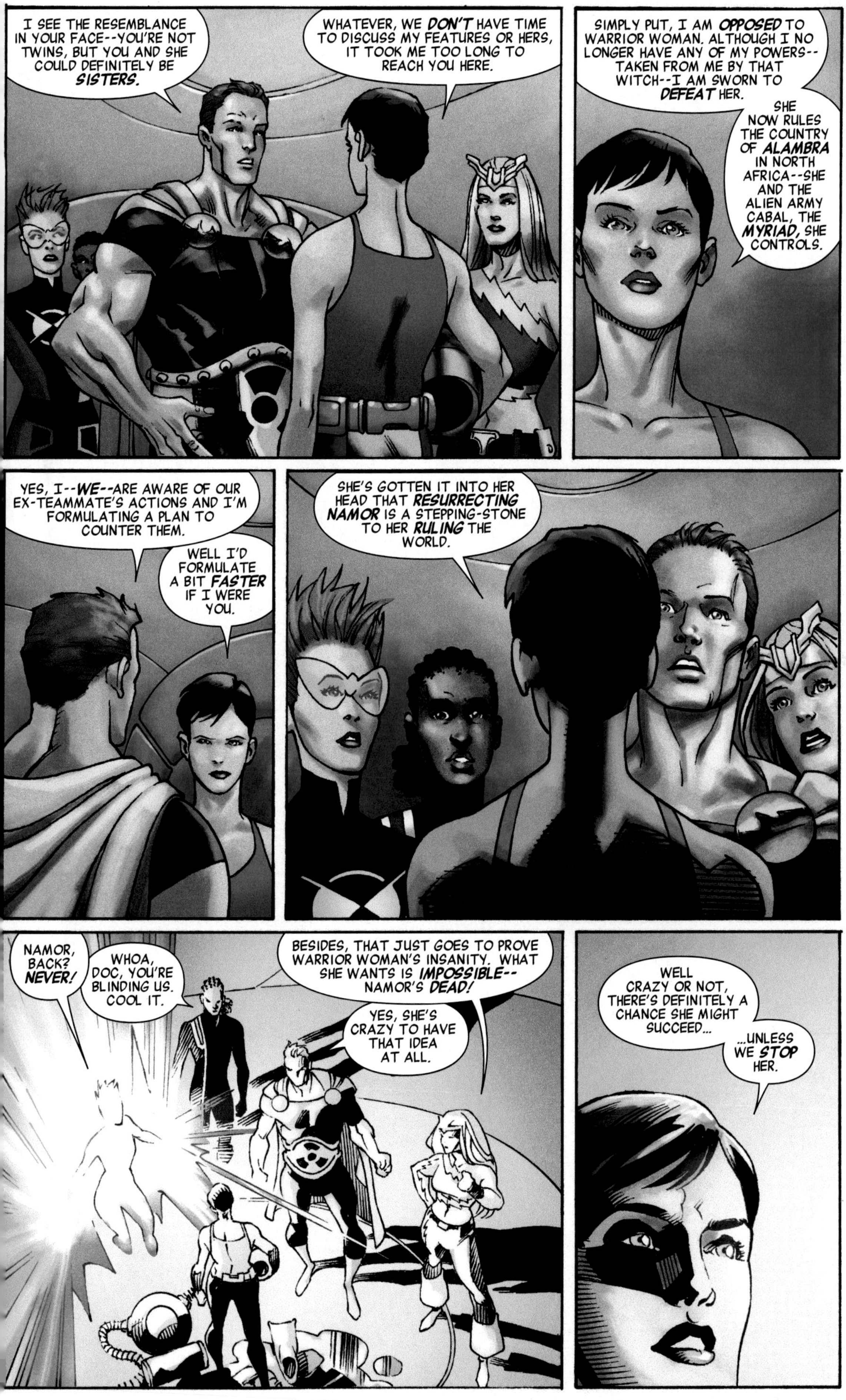
I SEE THE RESEMBLANCE IN YOUR FACE--YOU'RE NOT TWINS, BUT YOU AND SHE COULD DEFINITELY BE SISTERS.
WHATEVER, WE DON'T HAVE TIME TO DISCUSS MY FEATURES OR HERS, IT TOOK ME TOO LONG TO REACH YOU HERE.
SIMPLY PUT, I AM OPPOSED TO WARRIOR WOMAN. ALTHOUGH I NO LONGER HAVE ANY OF MY POWERS--TAKEN FROM ME BY THAT WITCH--I AM SWORN TO DEFEAT HER.
SHE NOW RULES THE COUNTRY OF ALAMBRA IN NORTH AFRICA--SHE AND THE ALIEN ARMY CABAL, THE MYRIAD, SHE CONTROLS.
YES, I--WE--ARE AWARE OF OUR EX-TEAMMATE'S ACTIONS AND I'M FORMULATING A PLAN TO COUNTER THEM.
WELL I'D FORMULATE A BIT FASTER IF I WERE YOU.
SHE'S GOTTEN IT INTO HER HEAD THAT RESURRECTING NAMOR IS A STEPPING-STONE TO HER RULING THE WORLD.
NAMOR, BACK? NEVER!
WHOA, DOC, YOU'RE BLINDING US. COOL IT.
BESIDES, THAT JUST GOES TO PROVE WARRIOR WOMAN'S INSANITY. WHAT SHE WANTS IS IMPOSSIBLE--NAMOR'S DEAD!
YES, SHE'S CRAZY TO HAVE THAT IDEA AT ALL.
WELL CRAZY OR NOT, THERE'S DEFINITELY A CHANCE SHE MIGHT SUCCEED...
...UNLESS WE STOP HER.

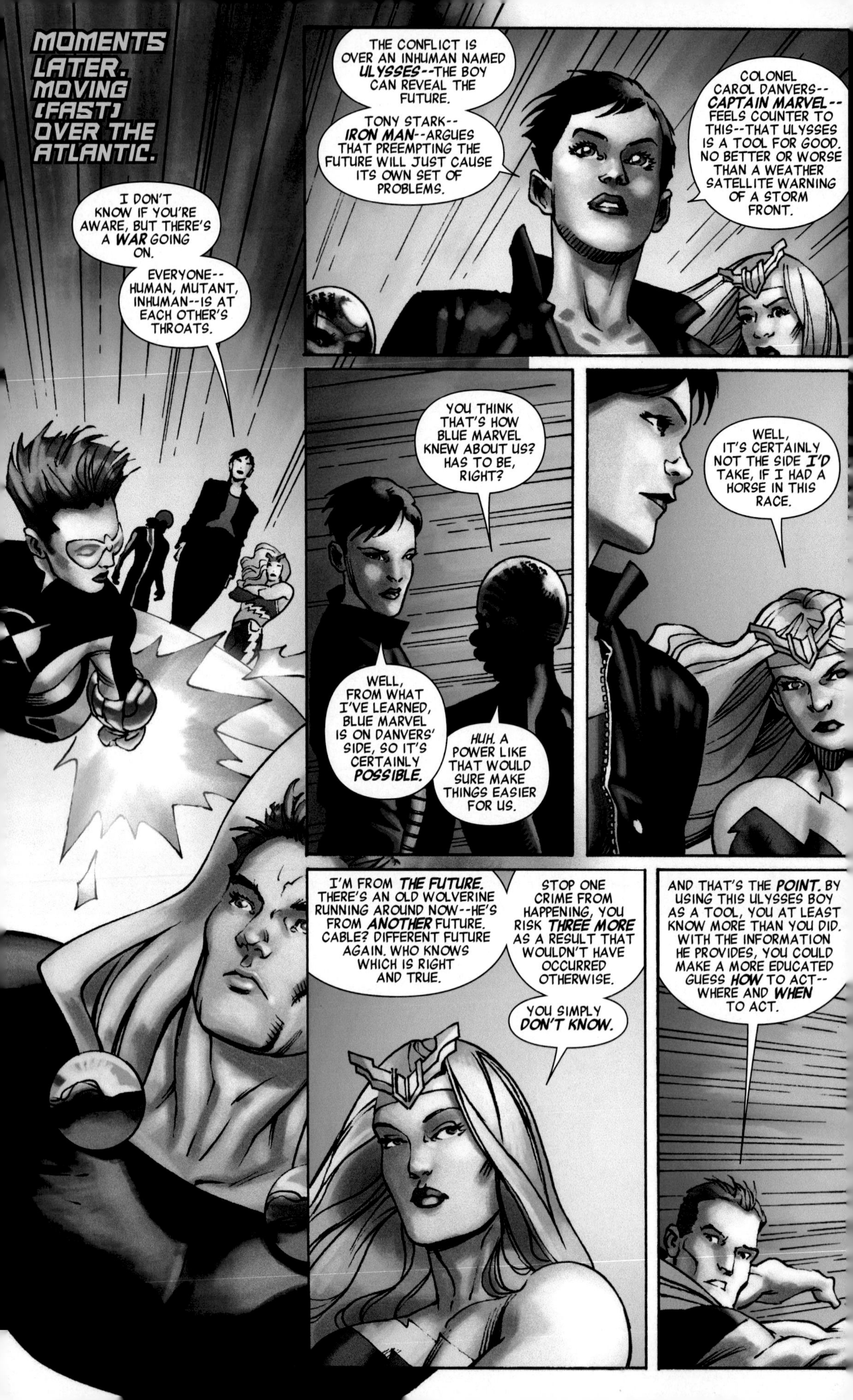
MOMENTS LATER. MOVING (FAST) OVER THE ATLANTIC.
I DON'T KNOW IF YOU'RE AWARE, BUT THERE'S A WAR GOING ON.
EVERYONE--HUMAN, MUTANT, INHUMAN--IS AT EACH OTHER'S THROATS.
THE CONFLICT IS OVER AN INHUMAN NAMED ULYSSES--THE BOY CAN REVEAL THE FUTURE.
TONY STARK--IRON MAN--ARGUES THAT PREEMPTING THE FUTURE WILL JUST CAUSE ITS OWN SET OF PROBLEMS.
COLONEL CAROL DANVERS--CAPTAIN MARVEL--FEELS COUNTER TO THIS--THAT ULYSSES IS A TOOL FOR GOOD. NO BETTER OR WORSE THAN A WEATHER SATELLITE WARNING OF A STORM FRONT.
YOU THINK THAT'S HOW BLUE MARVEL KNEW ABOUT US? HAS TO BE, RIGHT?
WELL, FROM WHAT I'VE LEARNED, BLUE MARVEL IS ON DANVERS' SIDE, SO IT'S CERTAINLY POSSIBLE.
HUH. A POWER LIKE THAT WOULD SURE MAKE THINGS EASIER FOR US.
WELL, IT'S CERTAINLY NOT THE SIDE I'D TAKE, IF I HAD A HORSE IN THIS RACE.
I'M FROM THE FUTURE. THERE'S AN OLD WOLVERINE RUNNING AROUND NOW--HE'S FROM ANOTHER FUTURE. CABLE? DIFFERENT FUTURE AGAIN. WHO KNOWS WHICH IS RIGHT AND TRUE.
STOP ONE CRIME FROM HAPPENING, YOU RISK THREE MORE AS A RESULT THAT WOULDN'T HAVE OCCURRED OTHERWISE.
YOU SIMPLY DON'T KNOW.
AND THAT'S THE POINT. BY USING THIS ULYSSES BOY AS A TOOL, YOU AT LEAST KNOW MORE THAN YOU DID. WITH THE INFORMATION HE PROVIDES, YOU COULD MAKE A MORE EDUCATED GUESS HOW TO ACT--WHERE AND WHEN TO ACT.

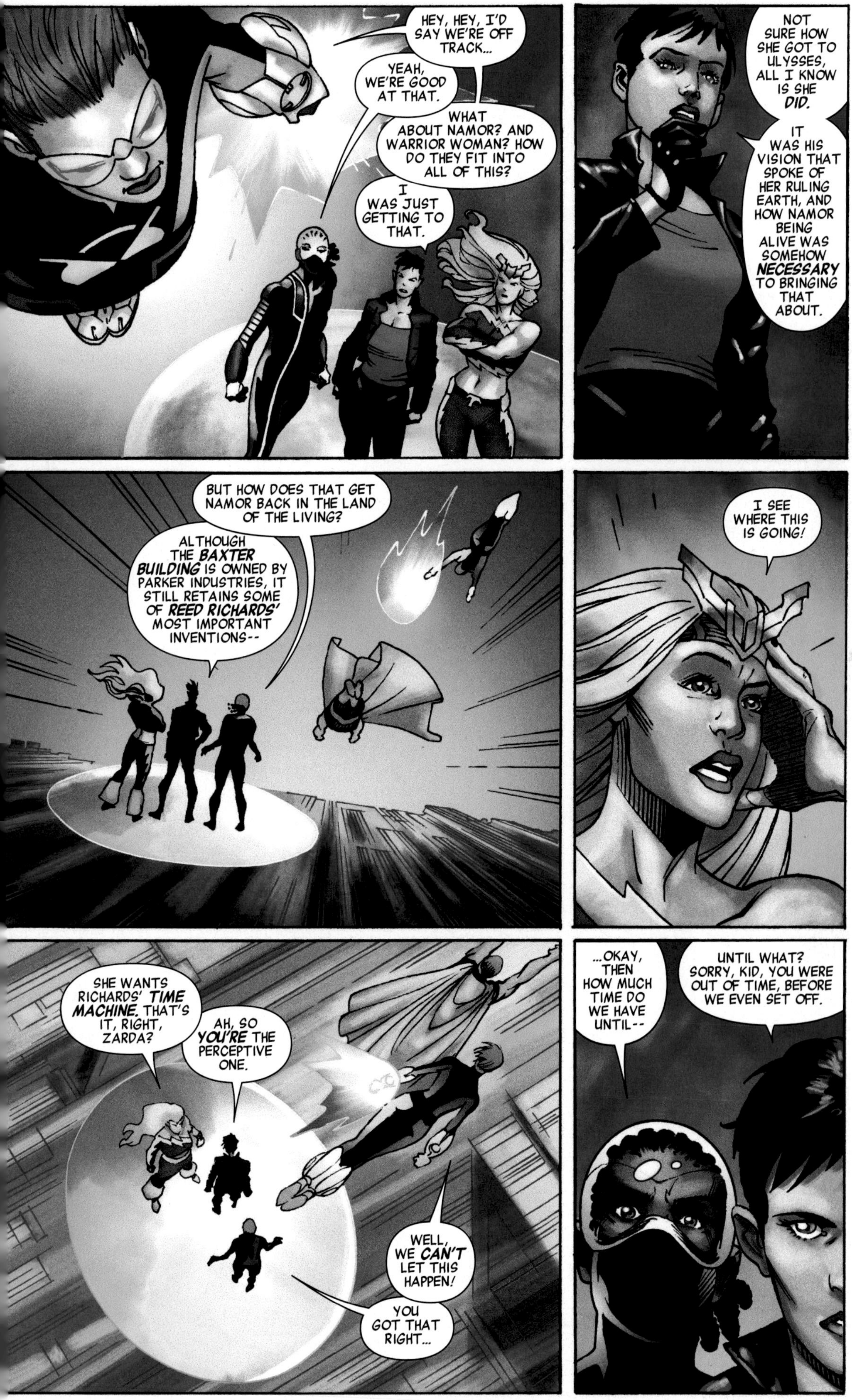

HEY, HEY, I'D SAY WE'RE OFF TRACK...
YEAH, WE'RE GOOD AT THAT.
WHAT ABOUT NAMOR? AND WARRIOR WOMAN? HOW DO THEY FIT INTO ALL OF THIS?
I WAS JUST GETTING TO THAT.
NOT SURE HOW SHE GOT TO ULYSSES, ALL I KNOW IS SHE DID.
IT WAS HIS VISION THAT SPOKE OF HER RULING EARTH, AND HOW NAMOR BEING ALIVE WAS SOMEHOW NECESSARY TO BRINGING THAT ABOUT.
BUT HOW DOES THAT GET NAMOR BACK IN THE LAND OF THE LIVING?
ALTHOUGH THE BAXTER BUILDING IS OWNED BY PARKER INDUSTRIES, IT STILL RETAINS SOME OF REED RICHARDS' MOST IMPORTANT INVENTIONS--
I SEE WHERE THIS IS GOING!
SHE WANTS RICHARDS' TIME MACHINE. THAT'S IT, RIGHT, ZARDA?
AH, SO YOU'RE THE PERCEPTIVE ONE.
WELL, WE CAN'T LET THIS HAPPEN!
YOU GOT THAT RIGHT...
...OKAY, THEN HOW MUCH TIME DO WE HAVE UNTIL--
UNTIL WHAT? SORRY, KID, YOU WERE OUT OF TIME, BEFORE WE EVEN SET OFF.

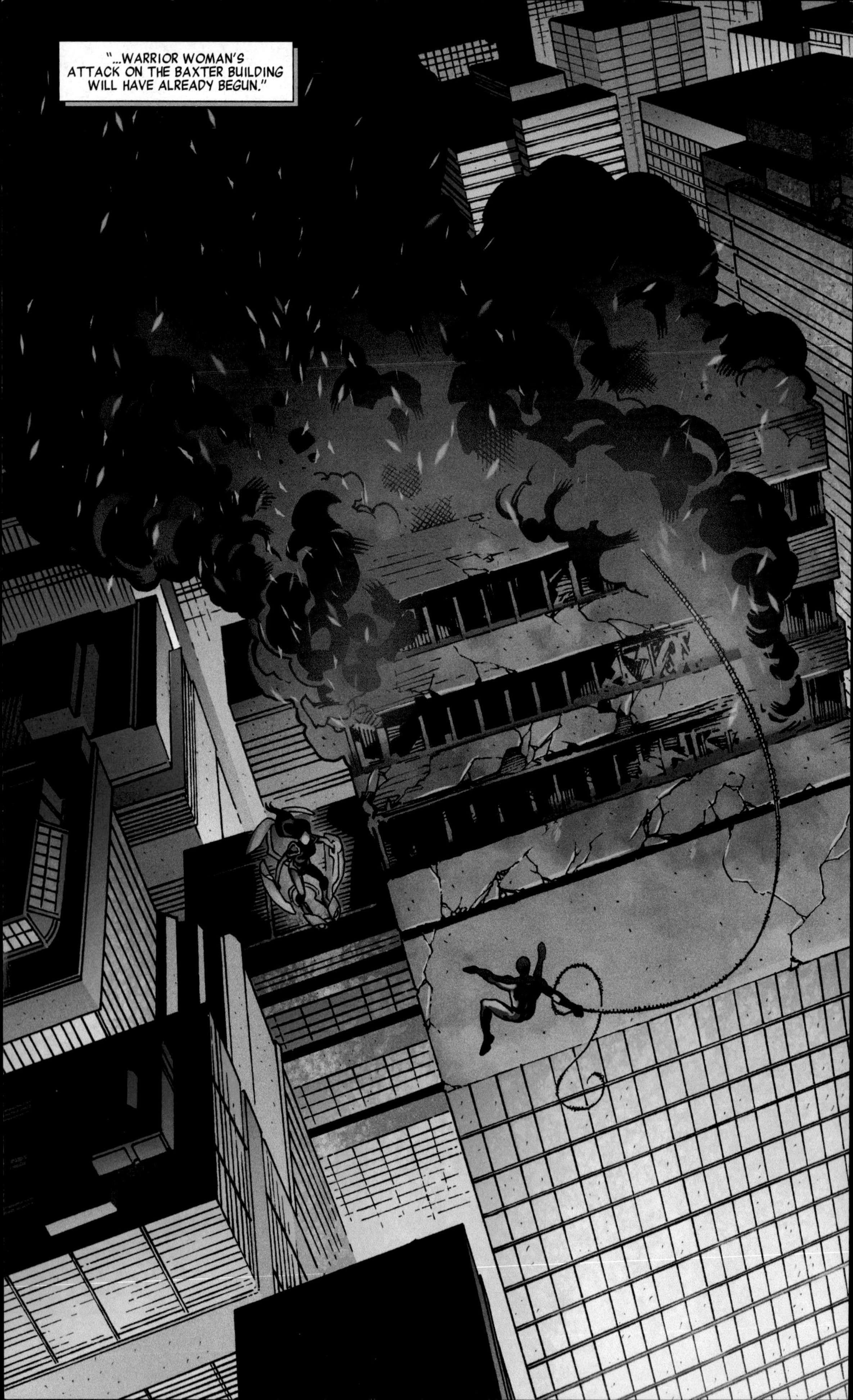
"...WARRIOR WOMAN'S ATTACK ON THE BAXTER BUILDING WILL HAVE ALREADY BEGUN."

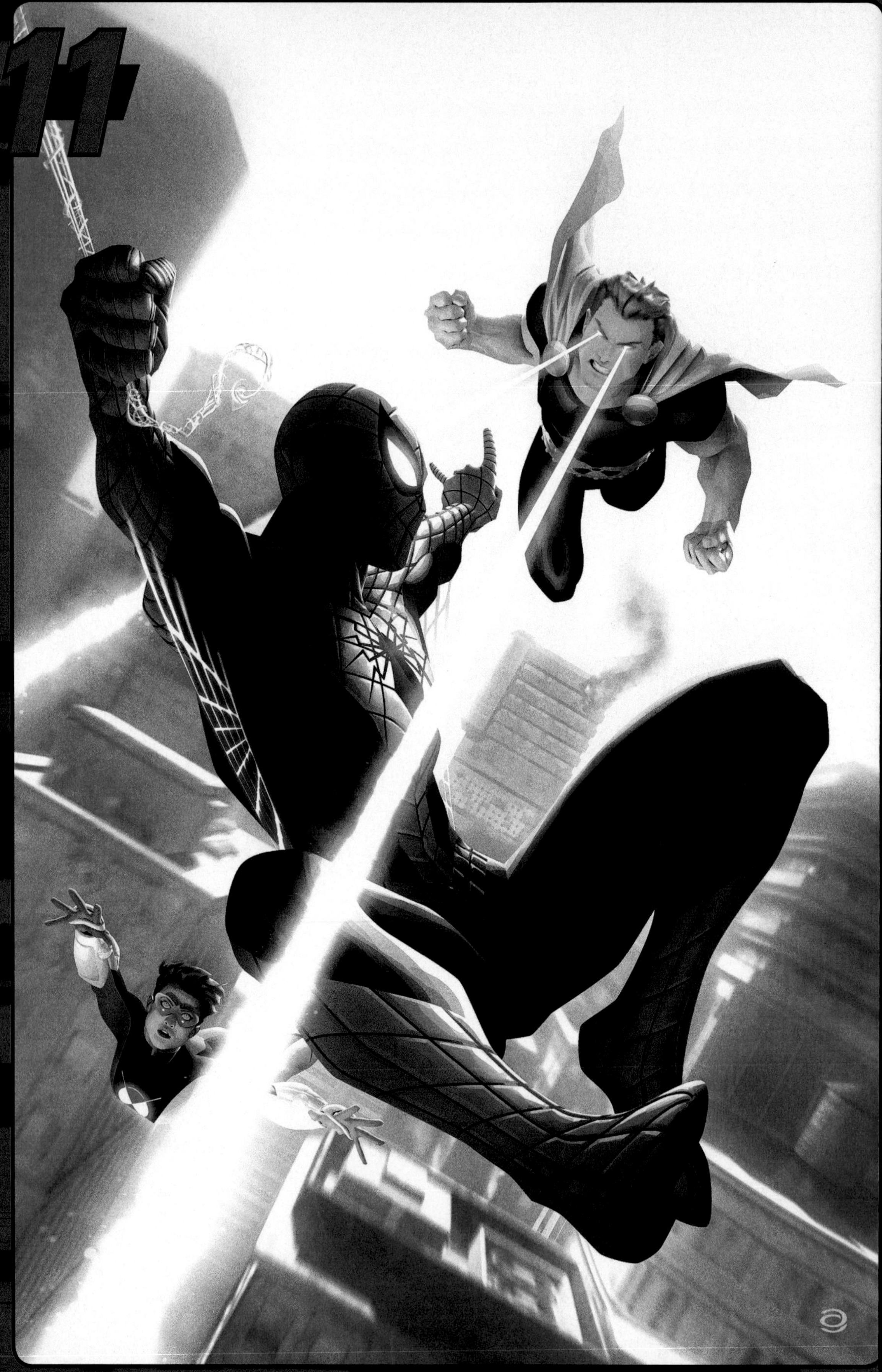
11

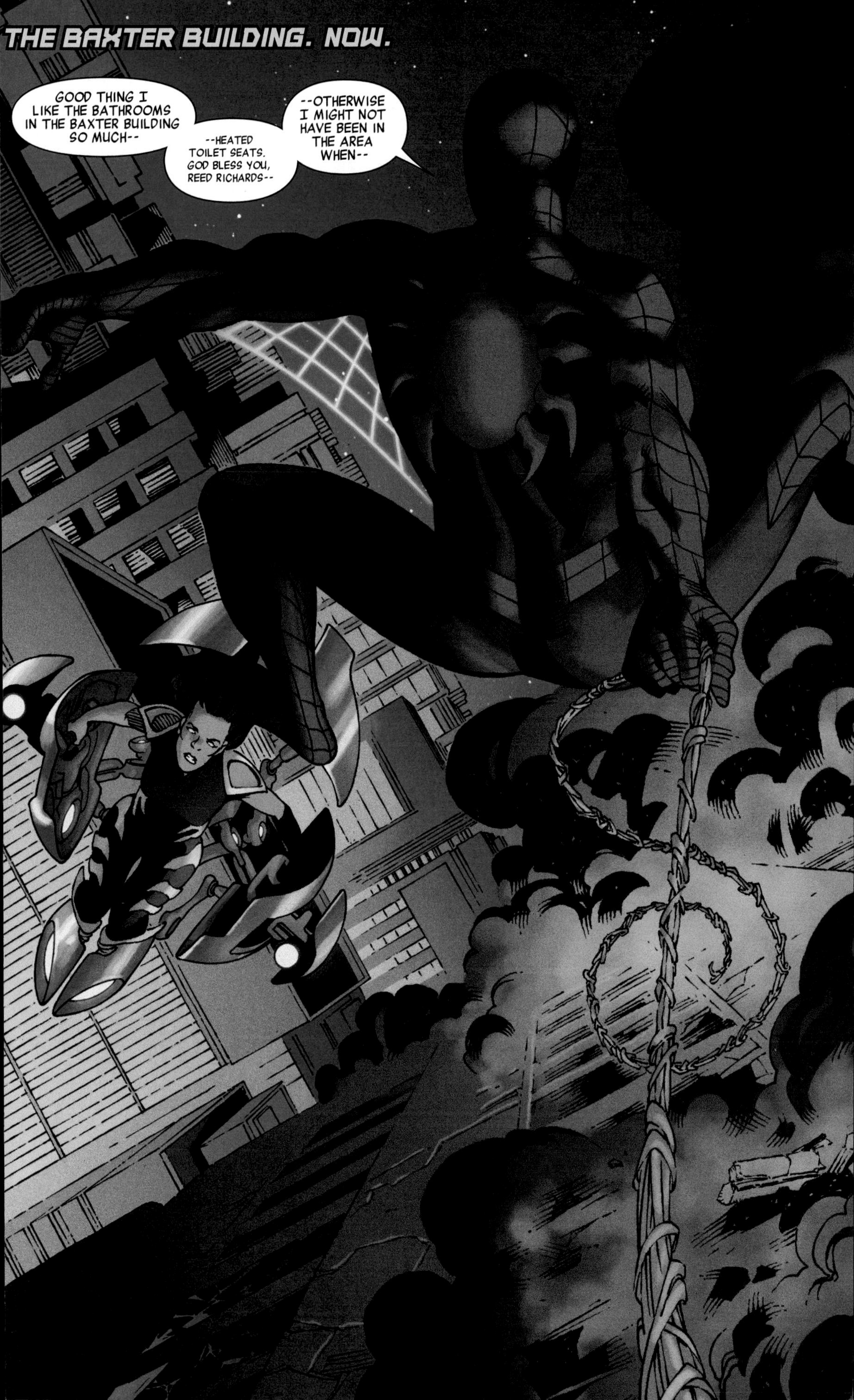
THE BAXTER BUILDING. NOW.
GOOD THING I LIKE THE BATHROOMS IN THE BAXTER BUILDING SO MUCH--
--HEATED TOILET SEATS. GOD BLESS YOU, REED RICHARDS--
--OTHERWISE I MIGHT NOT HAVE BEEN IN THE AREA WHEN--

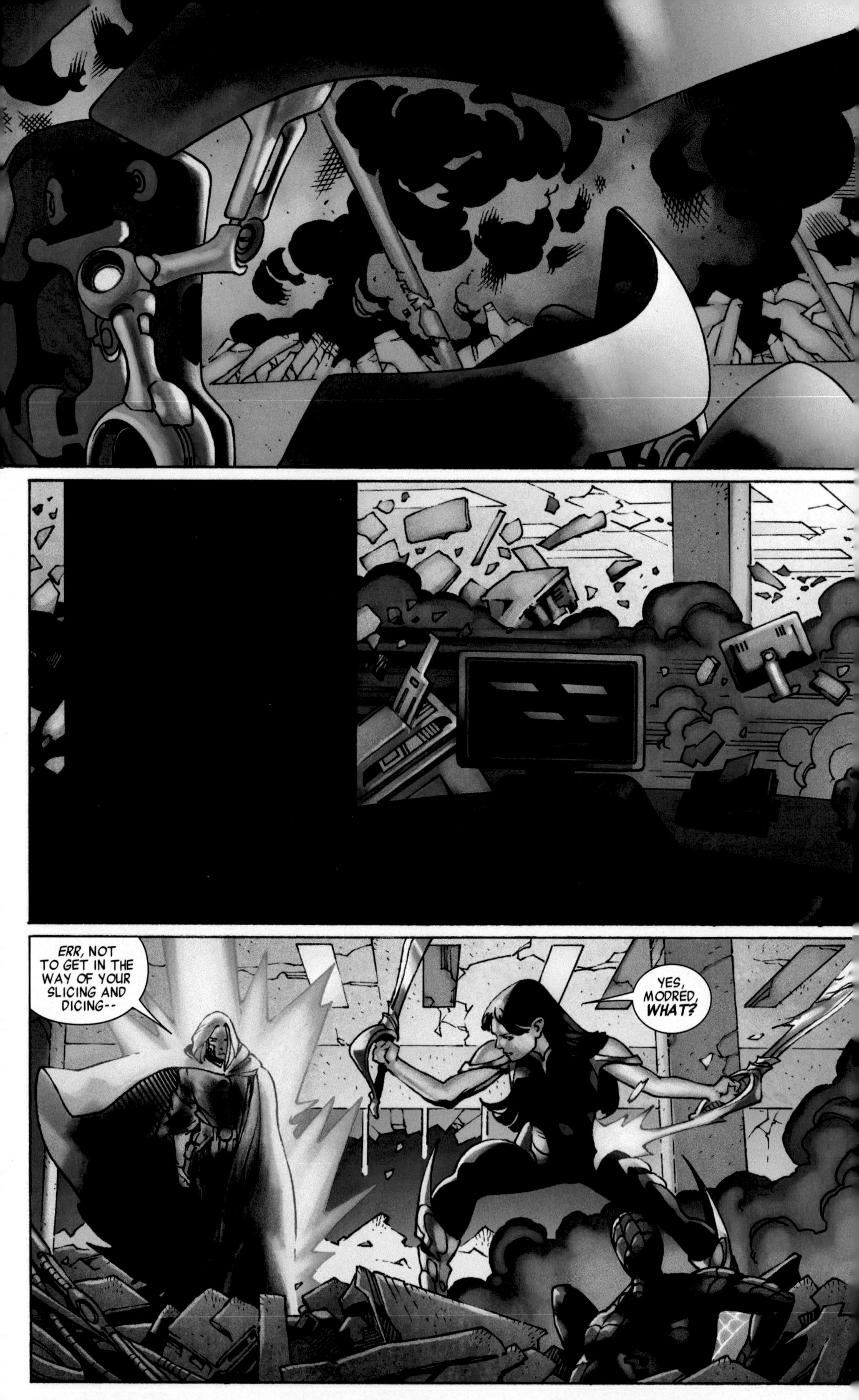

ERR, NOT TO GET IN THE WAY OF YOUR SLICING AND DICING--
YES, MODRED, ***WHAT?***

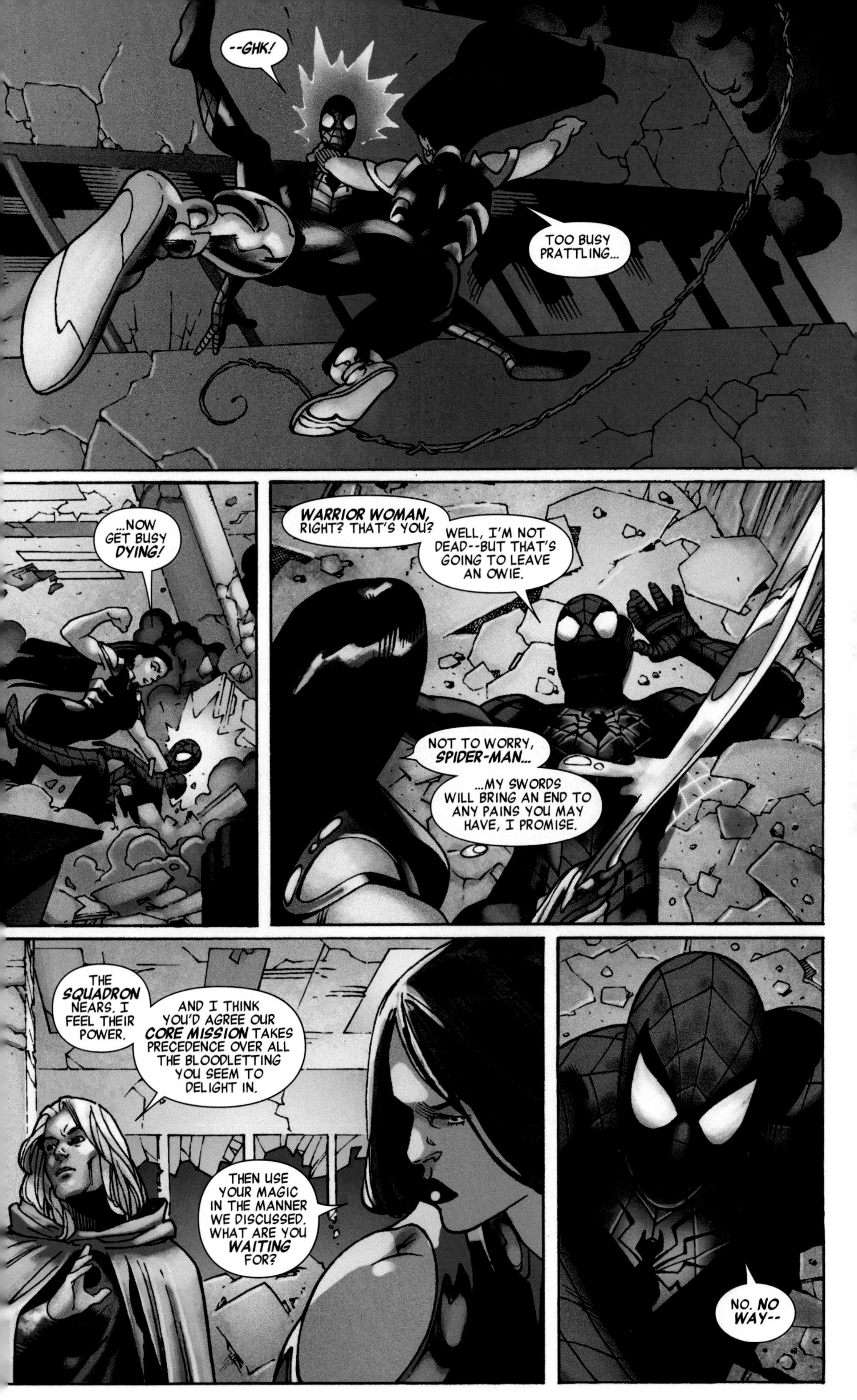
--GHK!
TOO BUSY PRATTLING...
...NOW GET BUSY DYING!
WARRIOR WOMAN, RIGHT? THAT'S YOU?
WELL, I'M NOT DEAD--BUT THAT'S GOING TO LEAVE AN OWIE.
NOT TO WORRY, SPIDER-MAN...
...MY SWORDS WILL BRING AN END TO ANY PAINS YOU MAY HAVE, I PROMISE.
THE SQUADRON NEARS. I FEEL THEIR POWER.
AND I THINK YOU'D AGREE OUR CORE MISSION TAKES PRECEDENCE OVER ALL THE BLOODLETTING YOU SEEM TO DELIGHT IN.
THEN USE YOUR MAGIC IN THE MANNER WE DISCUSSED. WHAT ARE YOU WAITING FOR?
NO. NO WAY--

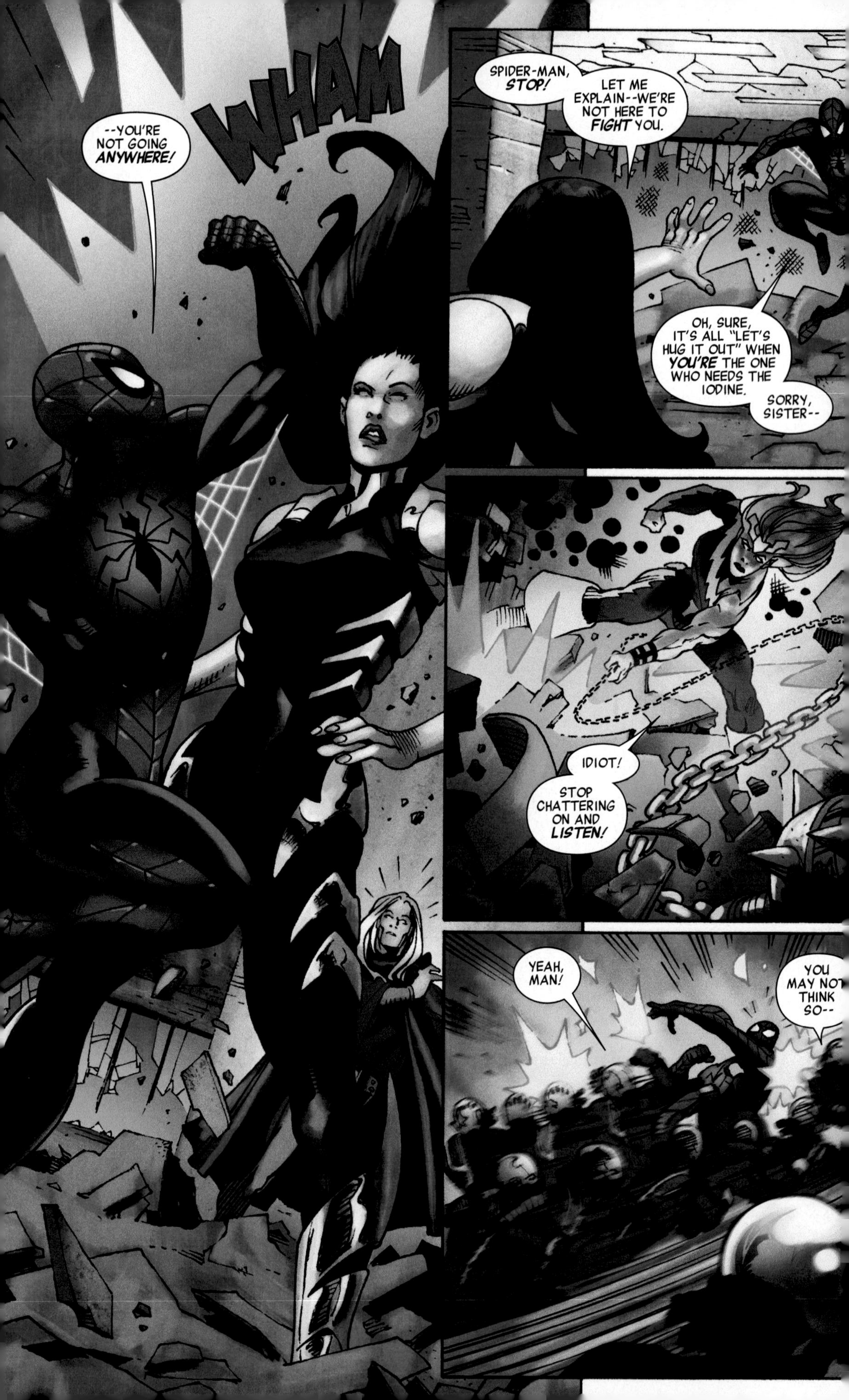

WHAM
--YOU'RE NOT GOING ANYWHERE!
SPIDER-MAN, STOP!
LET ME EXPLAIN--WE'RE NOT HERE TO FIGHT YOU.
OH, SURE, IT'S ALL "LET'S HUG IT OUT" WHEN YOU'RE THE ONE WHO NEEDS THE IODINE.
SORRY, SISTER--
IDIOT!
STOP CHATTERING ON AND LISTEN!
YEAH, MAN!
YOU MAY NOT THINK SO--

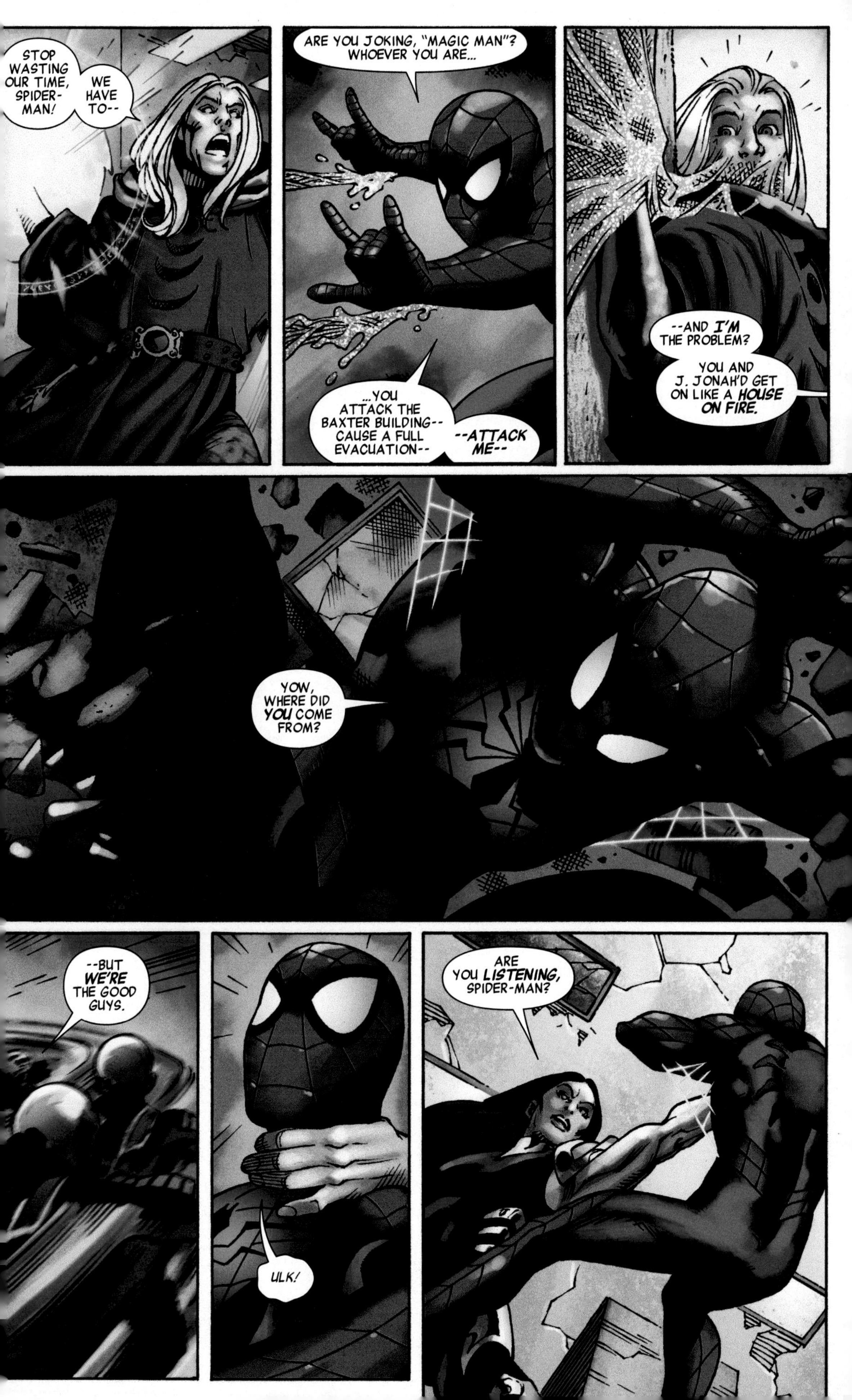
STOP WASTING OUR TIME, SPIDER-MAN!
WE HAVE TO--
ARE YOU JOKING, "MAGIC MAN"? WHOEVER YOU ARE...
...YOU ATTACK THE BAXTER BUILDING-- CAUSE A FULL EVACUATION--
--ATTACK ME--
--AND I'M THE PROBLEM?
YOU AND J. JONAH'D GET ON LIKE A HOUSE ON FIRE.
YOW, WHERE DID YOU COME FROM?
--BUT WE'RE THE GOOD GUYS.
ULK!
ARE YOU LISTENING, SPIDER-MAN?

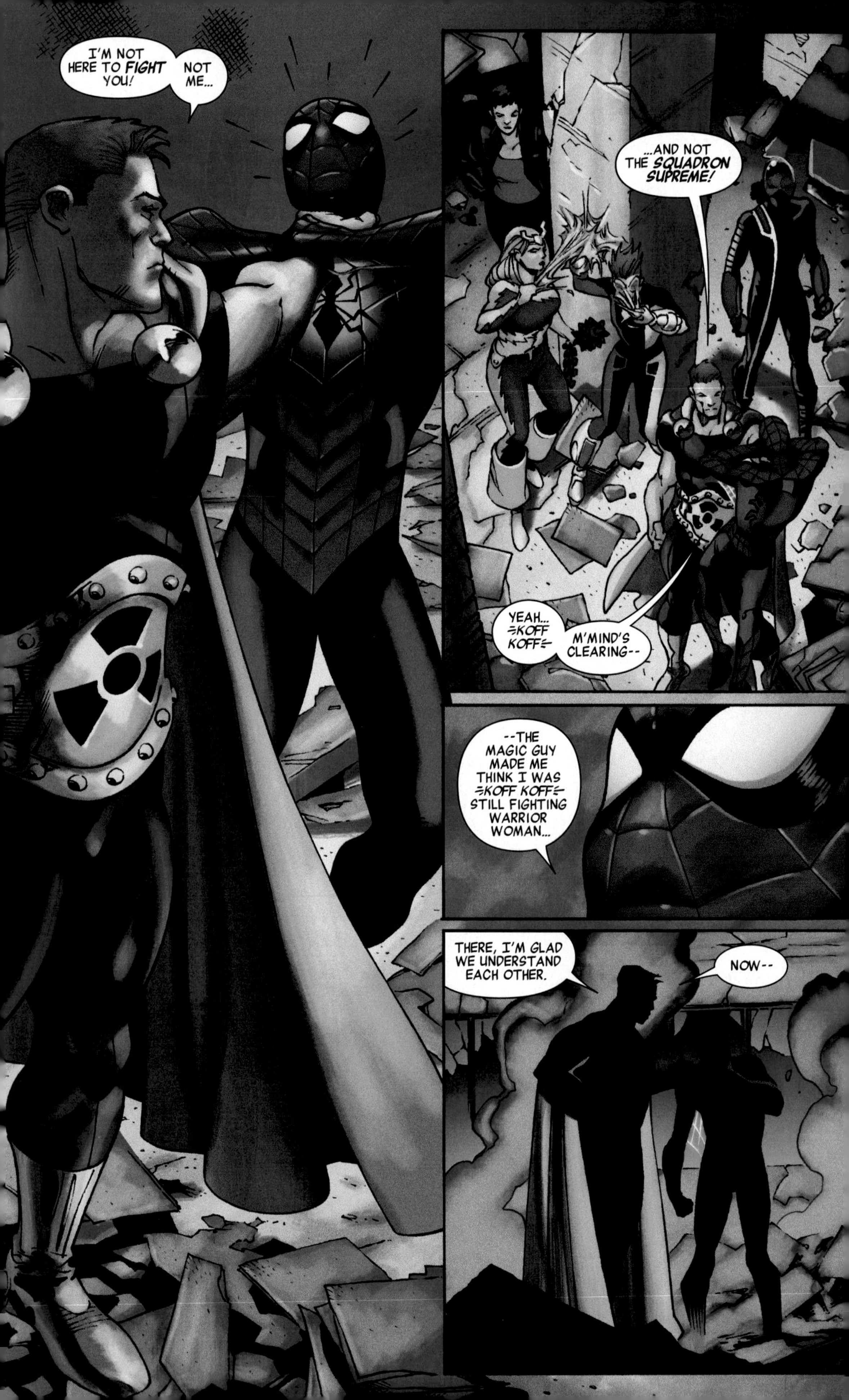

I'M NOT HERE TO **FIGHT** YOU!
NOT ME...
...AND NOT THE ***SQUADRON SUPREME!***
YEAH... ≠KOFF KOFF≠
M'MIND'S CLEARING--
--THE MAGIC GUY MADE ME THINK I WAS ≠KOFF KOFF≠ STILL FIGHTING WARRIOR WOMAN...
THERE, I'M GLAD WE UNDERSTAND EACH OTHER.
NOW--

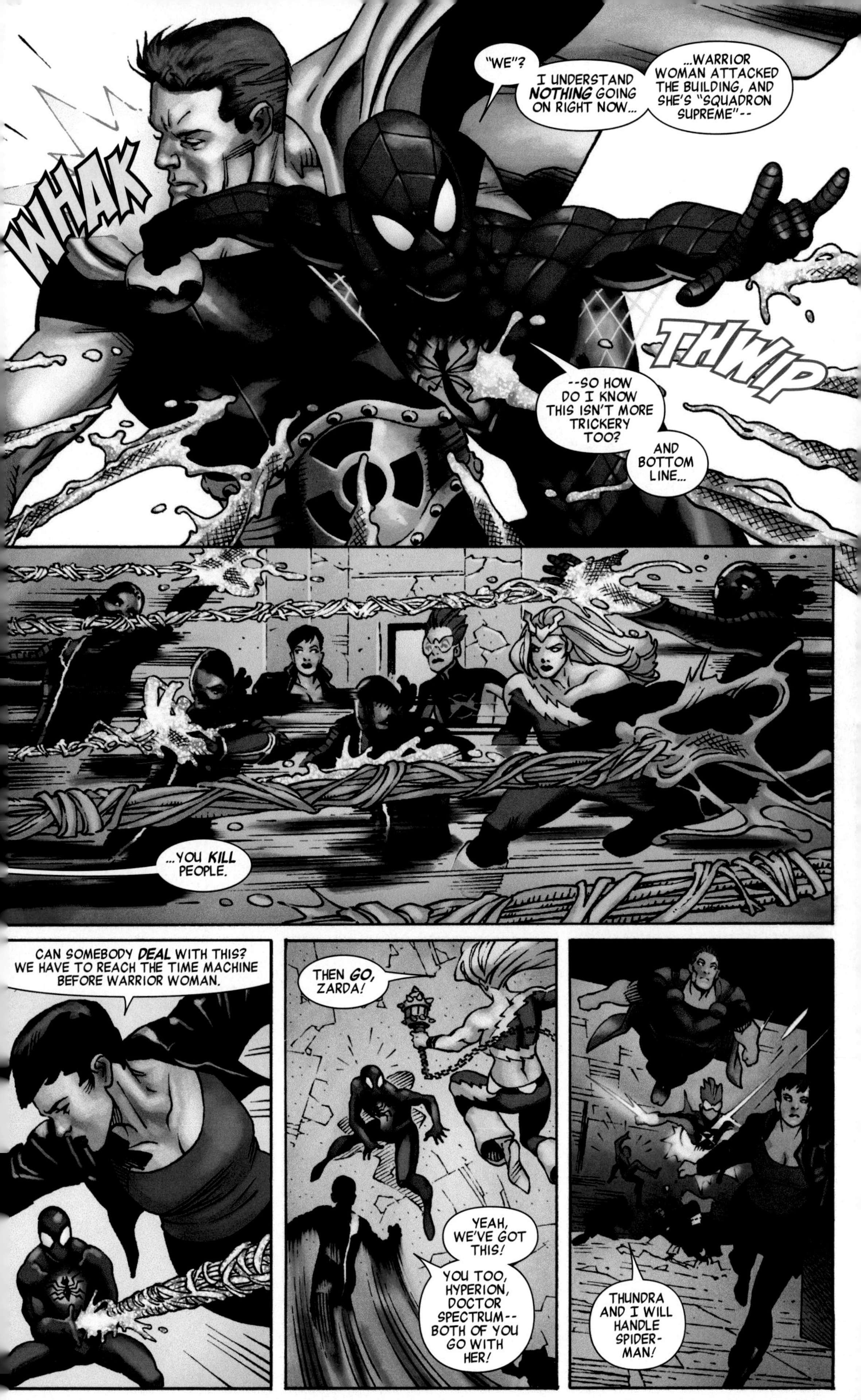
WHAK
"WE"?
I UNDERSTAND NOTHING GOING ON RIGHT NOW...
...WARRIOR WOMAN ATTACKED THE BUILDING, AND SHE'S "SQUADRON SUPREME"--
THWIP
--SO HOW DO I KNOW THIS ISN'T MORE TRICKERY TOO?
AND BOTTOM LINE...
...YOU KILL PEOPLE.
CAN SOMEBODY DEAL WITH THIS? WE HAVE TO REACH THE TIME MACHINE BEFORE WARRIOR WOMAN.
THEN GO, ZARDA!
YEAH, WE'VE GOT THIS!
YOU TOO, HYPERION, DOCTOR SPECTRUM--BOTH OF YOU GO WITH HER!
THUNDRA AND I WILL HANDLE SPIDER-MAN!

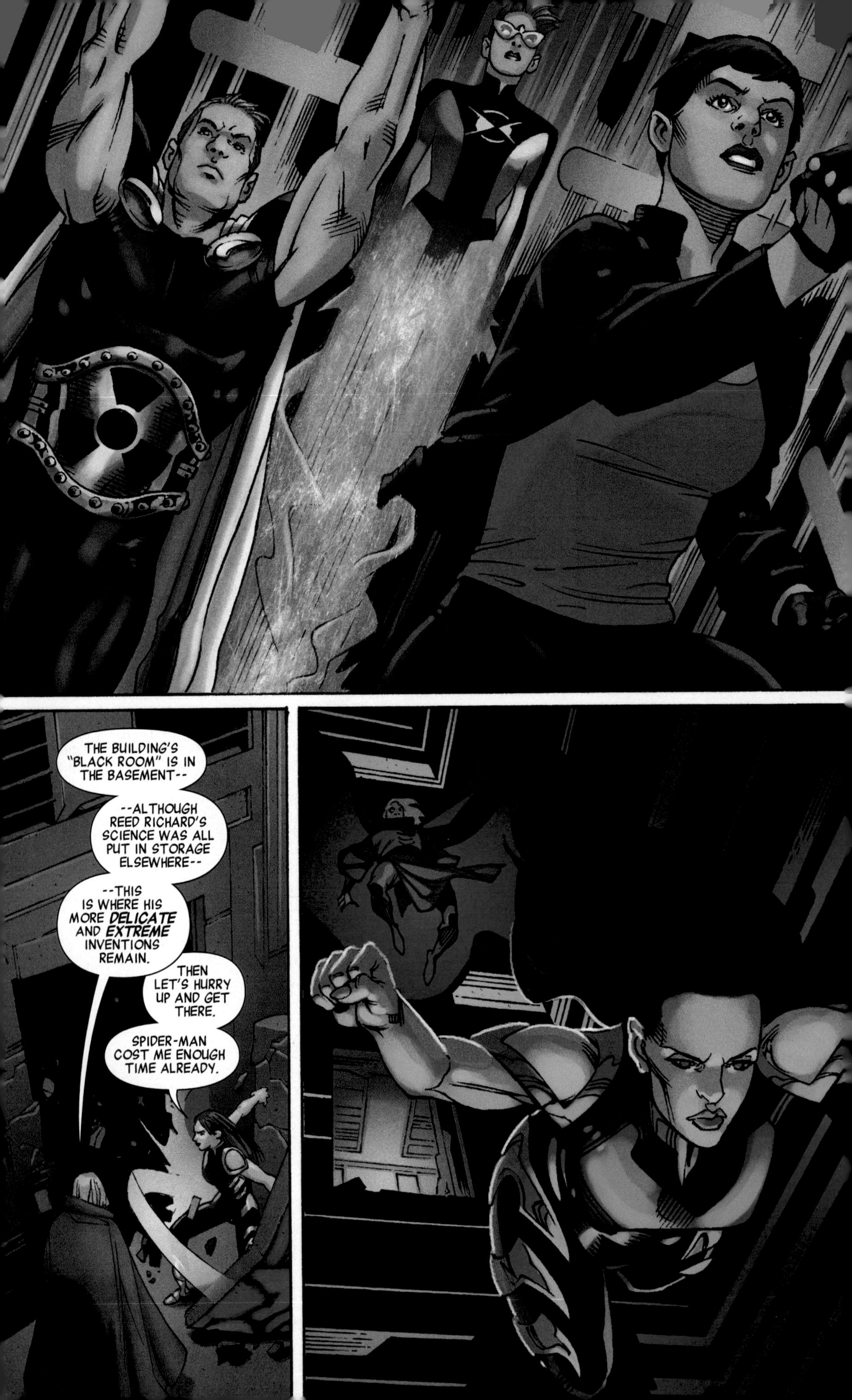
THE BUILDING'S "BLACK ROOM" IS IN THE BASEMENT--
--ALTHOUGH REED RICHARD'S SCIENCE WAS ALL PUT IN STORAGE ELSEWHERE--
--THIS IS WHERE HIS MORE ***DELICATE*** AND ***EXTREME*** INVENTIONS REMAIN.
THEN LET'S HURRY UP AND GET THERE.
SPIDER-MAN COST ME ENOUGH TIME ALREADY.

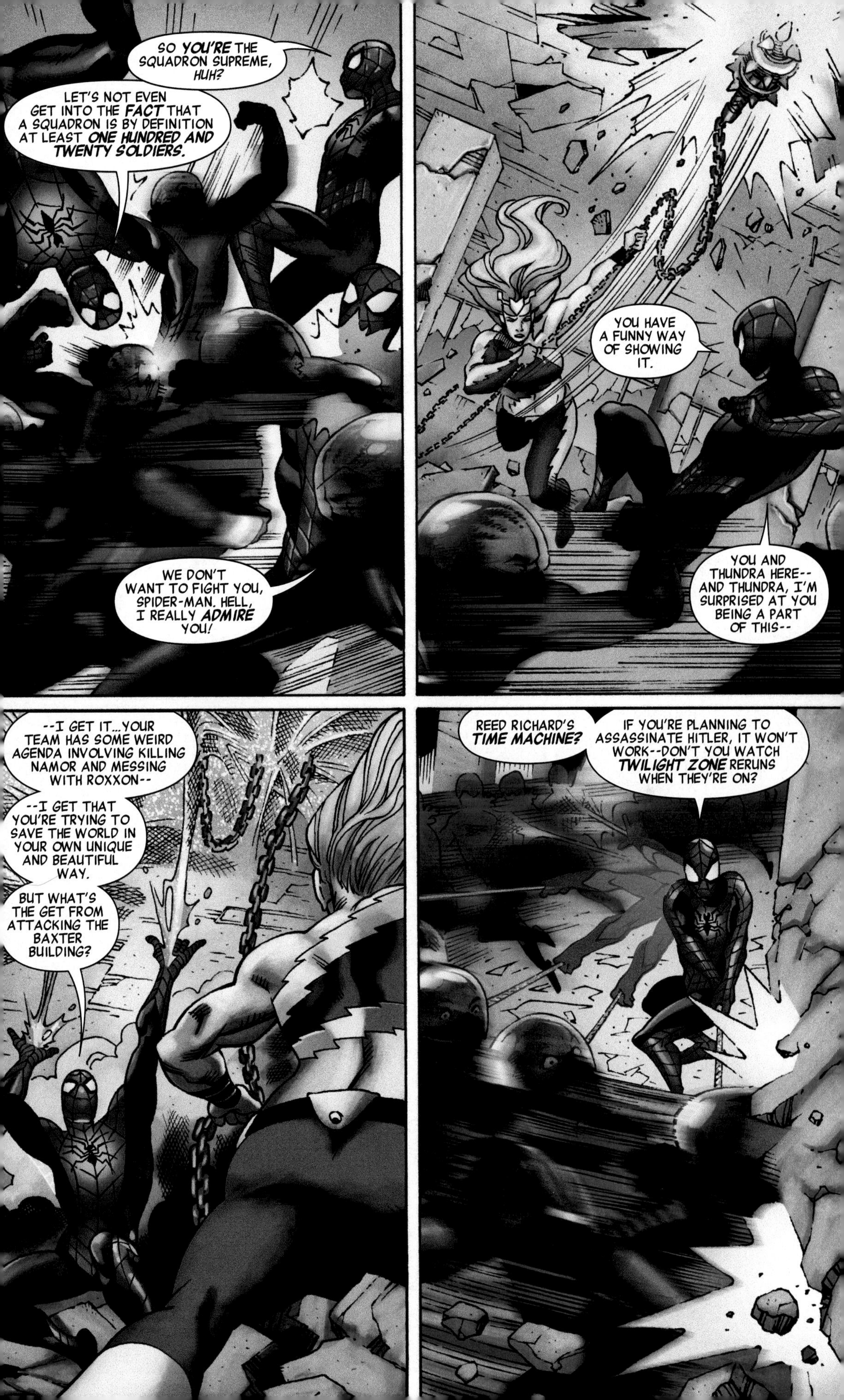
SO **YOU'RE** THE SQUADRON SUPREME, HUH?
LET'S NOT EVEN GET INTO THE **FACT** THAT A SQUADRON IS BY DEFINITION AT LEAST **ONE HUNDRED AND TWENTY SOLDIERS.**
WE DON'T WANT TO FIGHT YOU, SPIDER-MAN. HELL, I REALLY **ADMIRE** YOU!
YOU HAVE A FUNNY WAY OF SHOWING IT.
YOU AND THUNDRA HERE--AND THUNDRA, I'M SURPRISED AT YOU BEING A PART OF THIS--
--I GET IT...YOUR TEAM HAS SOME WEIRD AGENDA INVOLVING KILLING NAMOR AND MESSING WITH ROXXON--
--I GET THAT YOU'RE TRYING TO SAVE THE WORLD IN YOUR OWN UNIQUE AND BEAUTIFUL WAY.
BUT WHAT'S THE GET FROM ATTACKING THE BAXTER BUILDING?
REED RICHARD'S **TIME MACHINE?**
IF YOU'RE PLANNING TO ASSASSINATE HITLER, IT WON'T WORK--DON'T YOU WATCH **TWILIGHT ZONE** RERUNS WHEN THEY'RE ON?

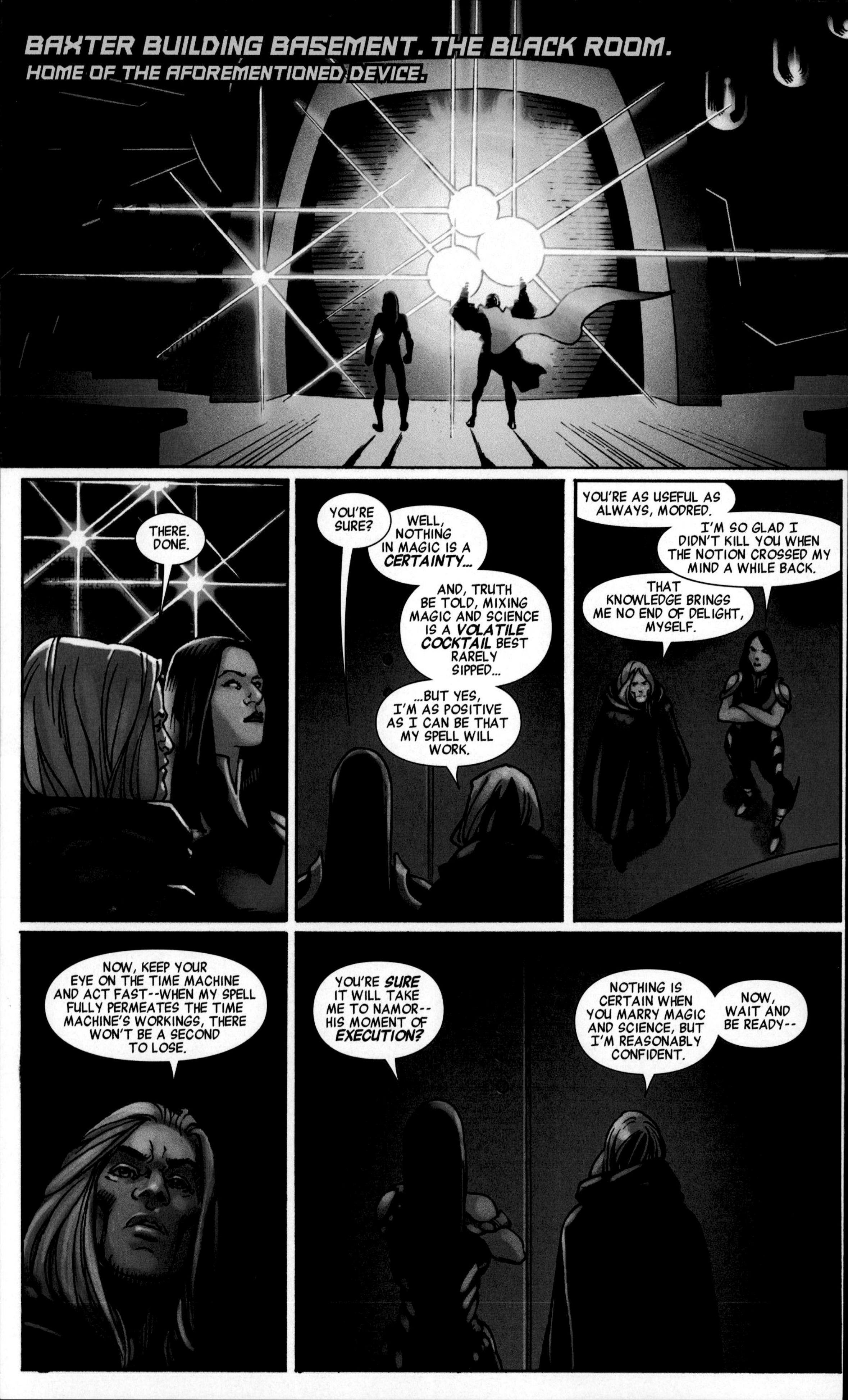
BAXTER BUILDING BASEMENT. THE BLACK ROOM.
HOME OF THE AFOREMENTIONED DEVICE.
THERE. DONE.
YOU'RE SURE?
WELL, NOTHING IN MAGIC IS A CERTAINTY...
AND, TRUTH BE TOLD, MIXING MAGIC AND SCIENCE IS A VOLATILE COCKTAIL BEST RARELY SIPPED...
...BUT YES, I'M AS POSITIVE AS I CAN BE THAT MY SPELL WILL WORK.
YOU'RE AS USEFUL AS ALWAYS, MODRED.
I'M SO GLAD I DIDN'T KILL YOU WHEN THE NOTION CROSSED MY MIND A WHILE BACK.
THAT KNOWLEDGE BRINGS ME NO END OF DELIGHT, MYSELF.
NOW, KEEP YOUR EYE ON THE TIME MACHINE AND ACT FAST--WHEN MY SPELL FULLY PERMEATES THE TIME MACHINE'S WORKINGS, THERE WON'T BE A SECOND TO LOSE.
YOU'RE SURE IT WILL TAKE ME TO NAMOR--HIS MOMENT OF EXECUTION?
NOTHING IS CERTAIN WHEN YOU MARRY MAGIC AND SCIENCE, BUT I'M REASONABLY CONFIDENT.
NOW, WAIT AND BE READY--

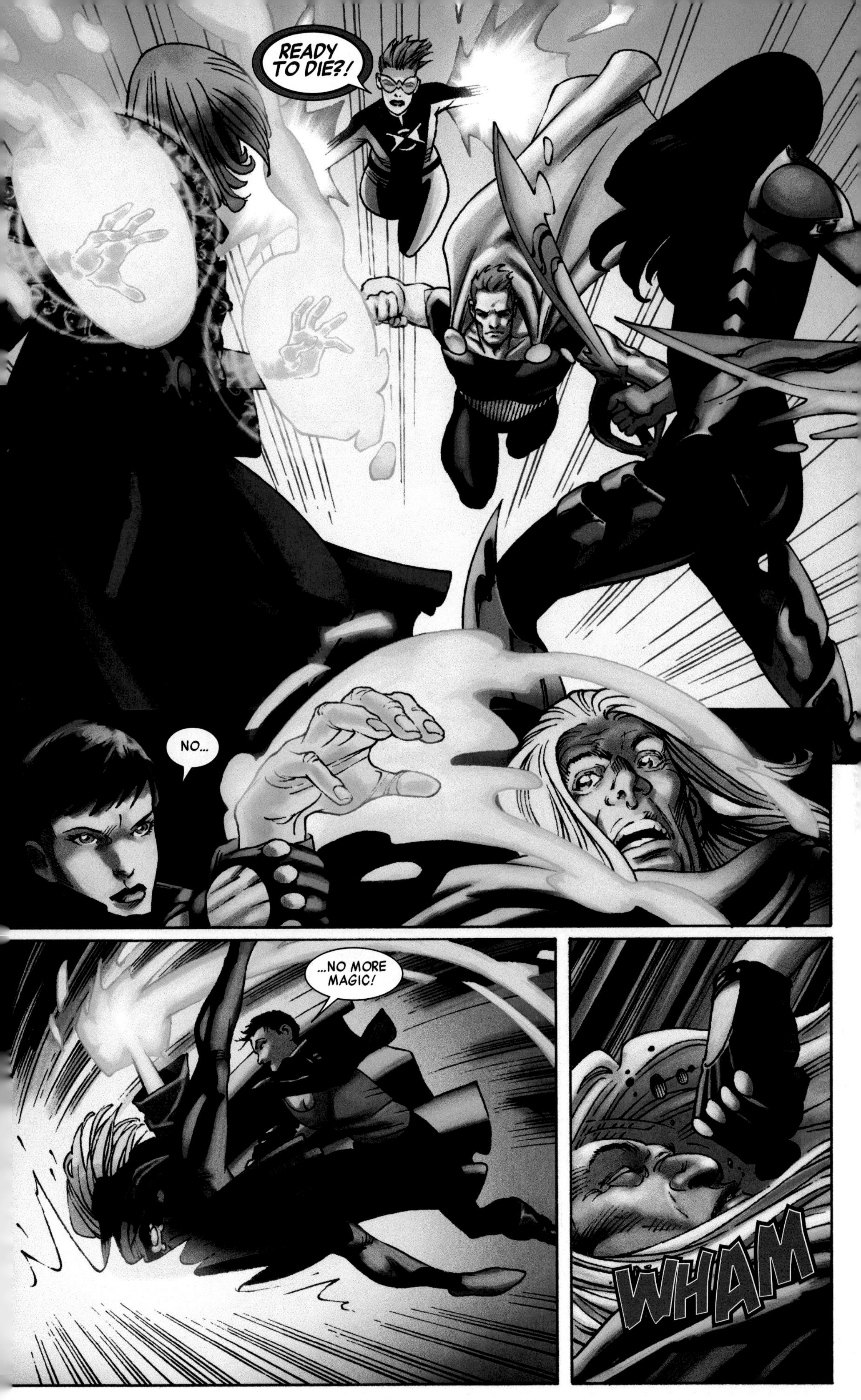
READY TO DIE?!
NO...
...NO MORE MAGIC!
WHAM

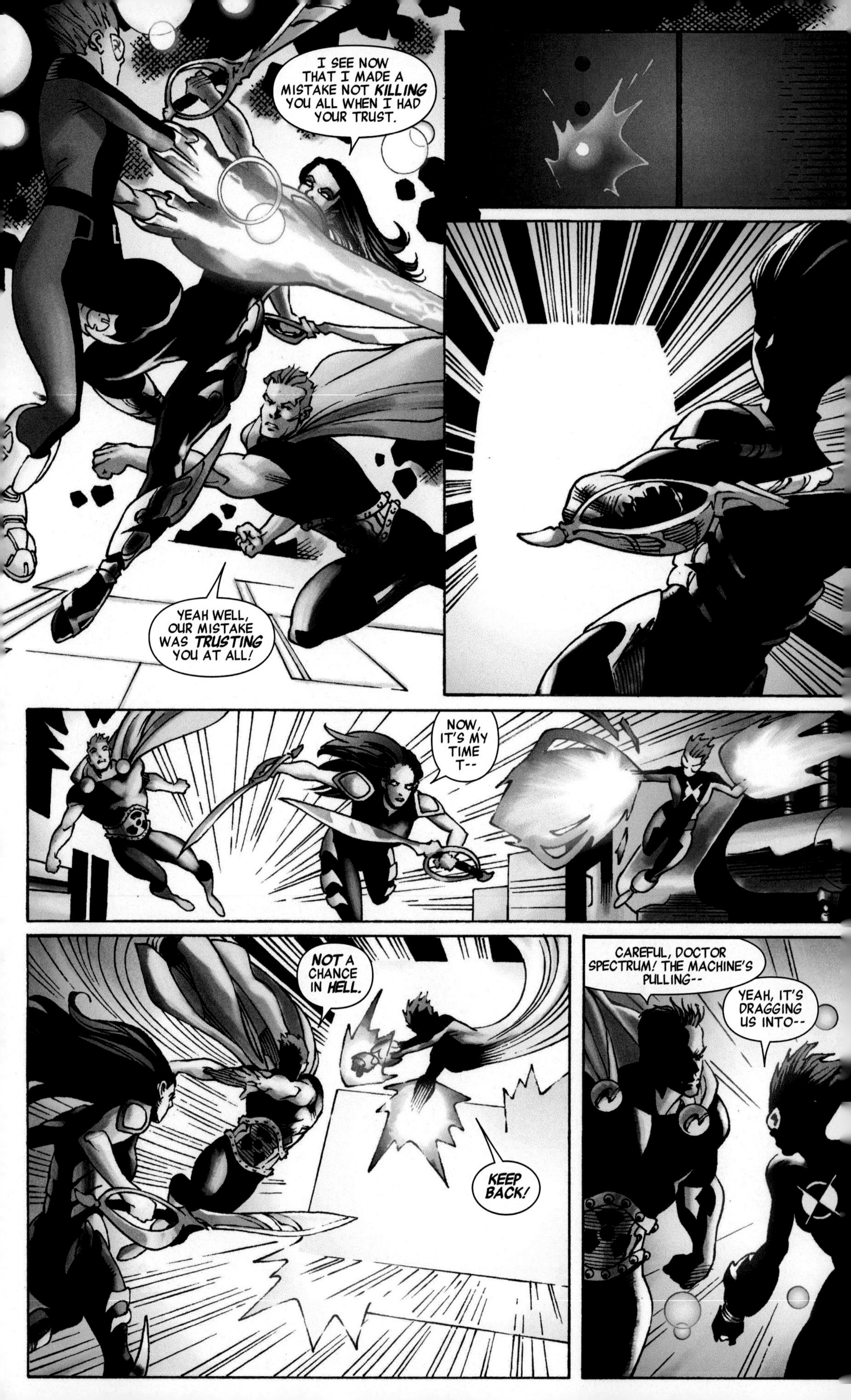
I SEE NOW THAT I MADE A MISTAKE NOT KILLING YOU ALL WHEN I HAD YOUR TRUST.
YEAH WELL, OUR MISTAKE WAS TRUSTING YOU AT ALL!
NOW, IT'S MY TIME T--
NOT A CHANCE IN HELL.
KEEP BACK!
CAREFUL, DOCTOR SPECTRUM! THE MACHINE'S PULLING--
YEAH, IT'S DRAGGING US INTO--

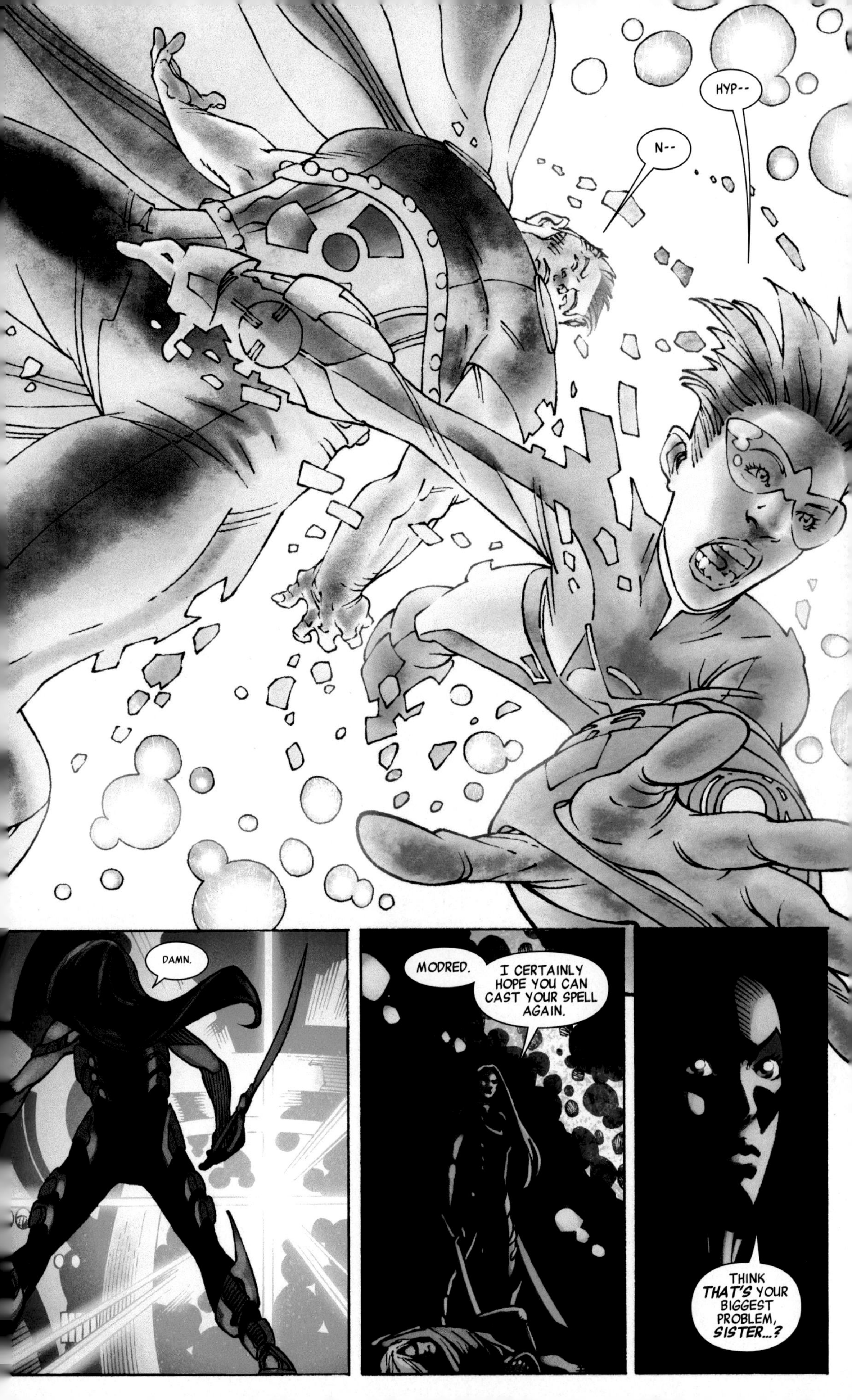
HYP--
N--
DAMN.
MODRED.
I CERTAINLY HOPE YOU CAN CAST YOUR SPELL AGAIN.
THINK THAT'S YOUR BIGGEST PROBLEM, SISTER...?

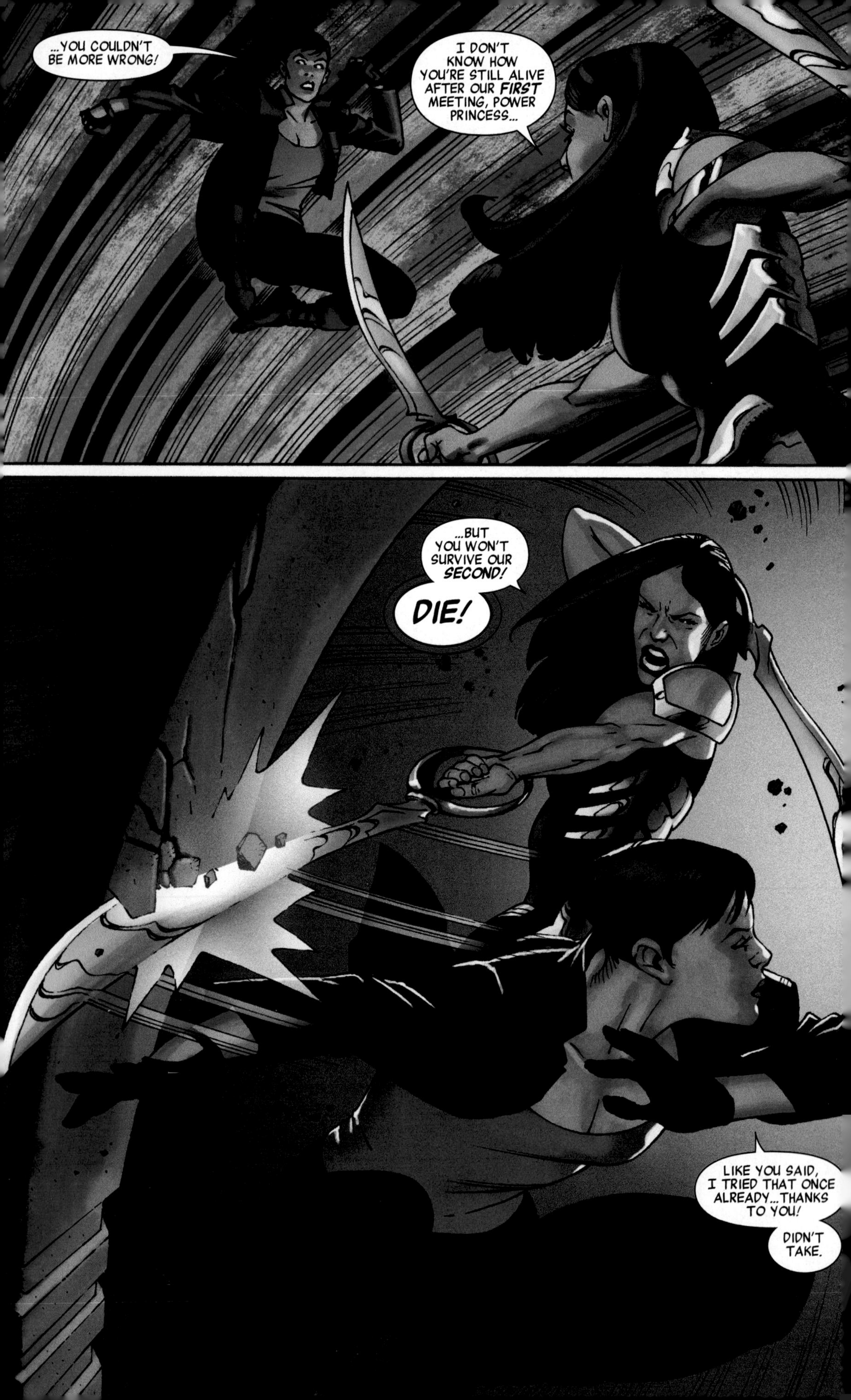
...YOU COULDN'T BE MORE WRONG!
I DON'T KNOW HOW YOU'RE STILL ALIVE AFTER OUR FIRST MEETING, POWER PRINCESS...
...BUT YOU WON'T SURVIVE OUR SECOND!
DIE!
LIKE YOU SAID, I TRIED THAT ONCE ALREADY...THANKS TO YOU!
DIDN'T TAKE.

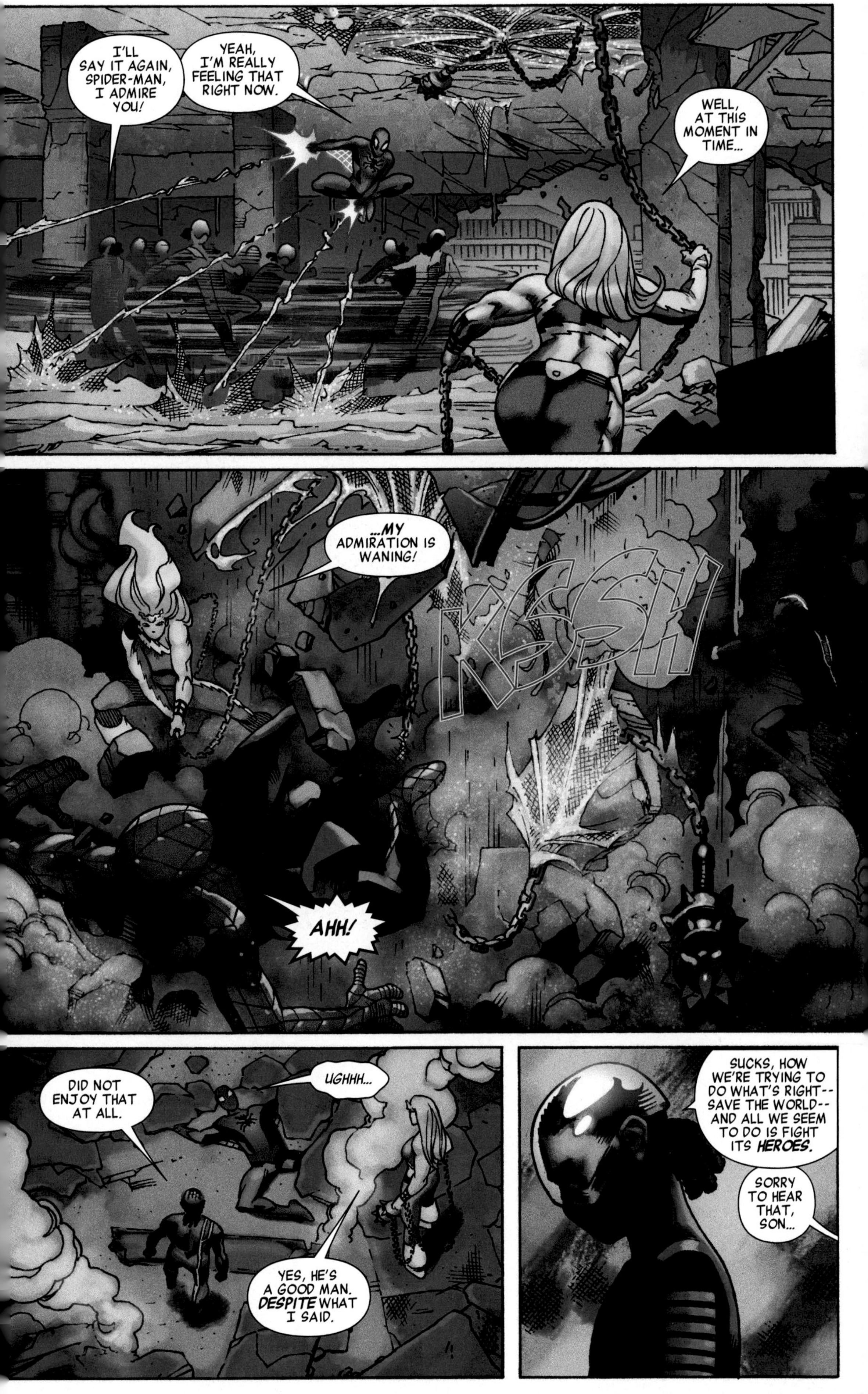
I'LL SAY IT AGAIN, SPIDER-MAN, I ADMIRE YOU!
YEAH, I'M REALLY FEELING THAT RIGHT NOW.
WELL, AT THIS MOMENT IN TIME...
...MY ADMIRATION IS WANING!
KSSH
AHH!
DID NOT ENJOY THAT AT ALL.
UGHHH...
YES, HE'S A GOOD MAN. DESPITE WHAT I SAID.
SUCKS, HOW WE'RE TRYING TO DO WHAT'S RIGHT-- SAVE THE WORLD-- AND ALL WE SEEM TO DO IS FIGHT ITS HEROES.
SORRY TO HEAR THAT, SON...

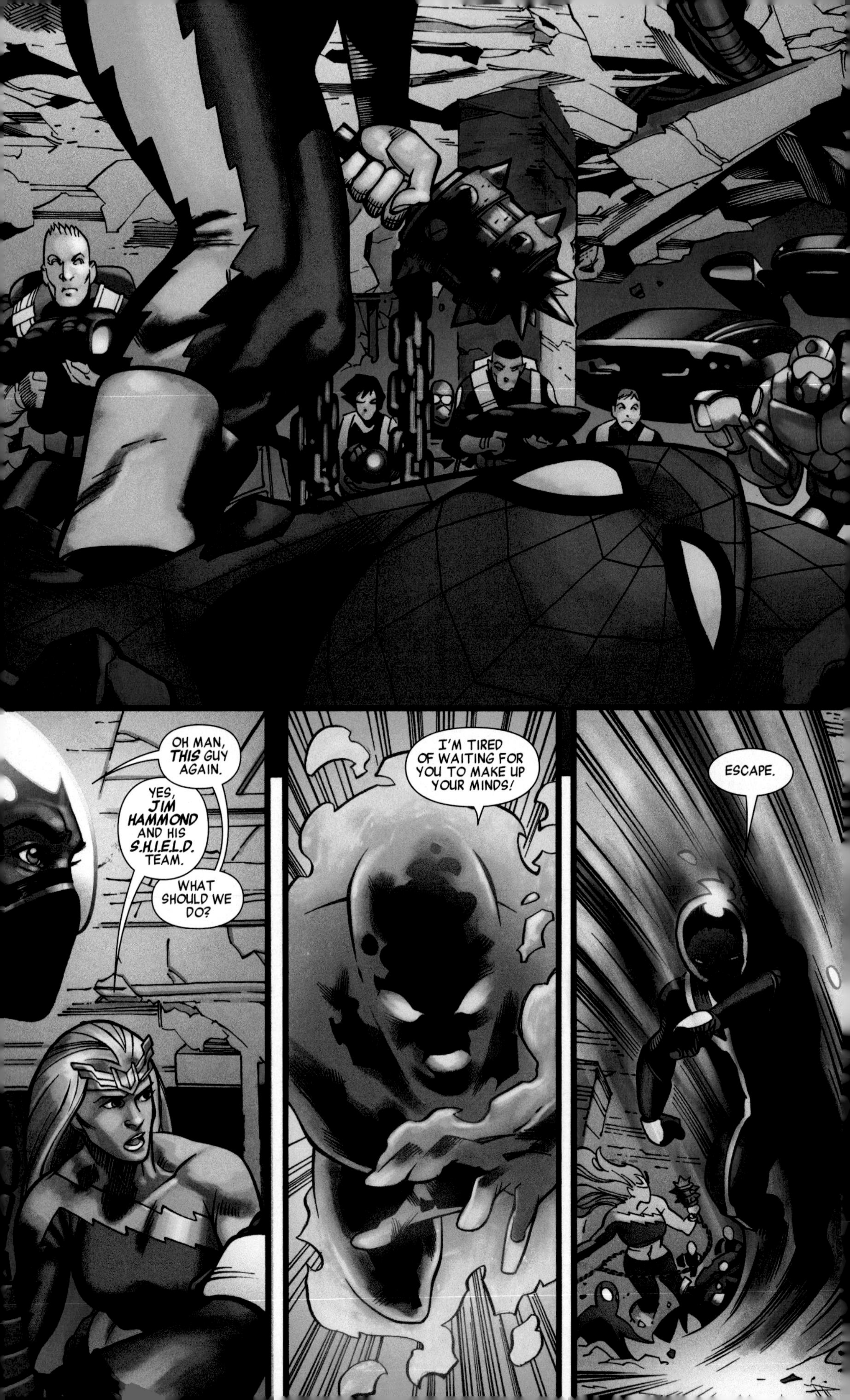
OH MAN, THIS GUY AGAIN.
YES, JIM HAMMOND AND HIS S.H.I.E.L.D. TEAM.
WHAT SHOULD WE DO?
I'M TIRED OF WAITING FOR YOU TO MAKE UP YOUR MINDS!
ESCAPE.

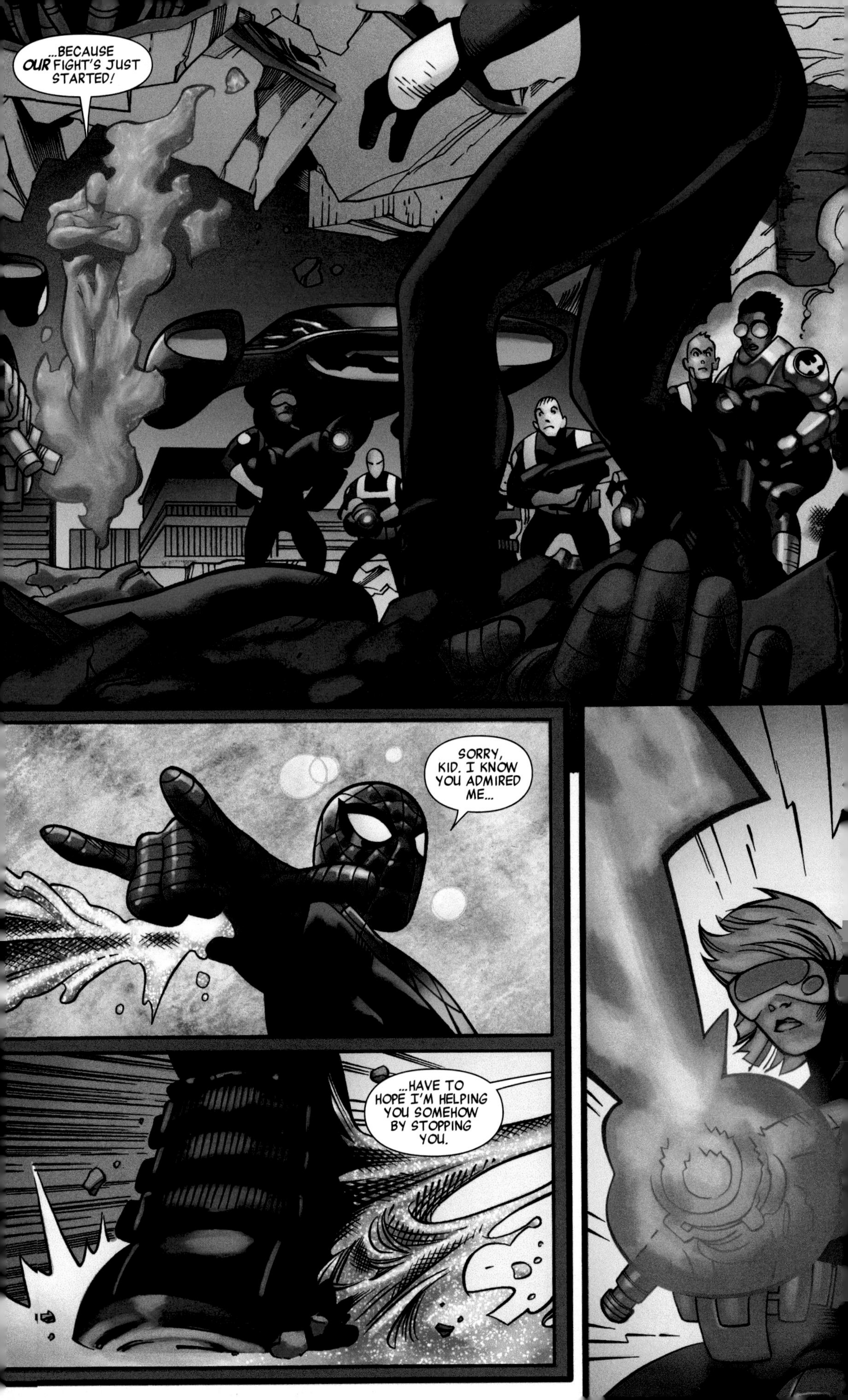
...BECAUSE OUR FIGHT'S JUST STARTED!
SORRY, KID. I KNOW YOU ADMIRED ME...
...HAVE TO HOPE I'M HELPING YOU SOMEHOW BY STOPPING YOU.

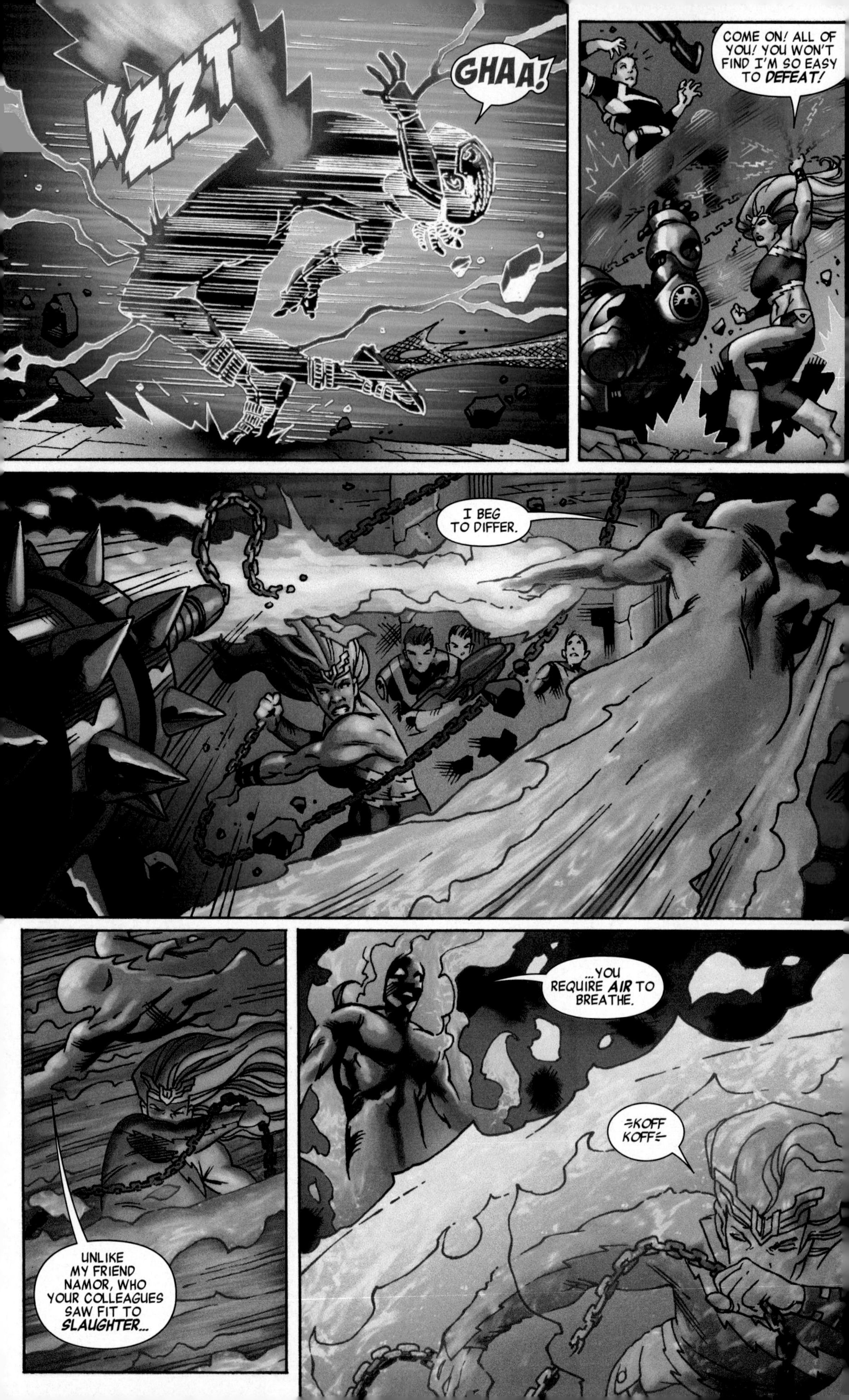
KZZT
GHAA!
COME ON! ALL OF YOU! YOU WON'T FIND I'M SO EASY TO DEFEAT!
I BEG TO DIFFER.
UNLIKE MY FRIEND NAMOR, WHO YOUR COLLEAGUES SAW FIT TO SLAUGHTER...
...YOU REQUIRE AIR TO BREATHE.
KOFF KOFF

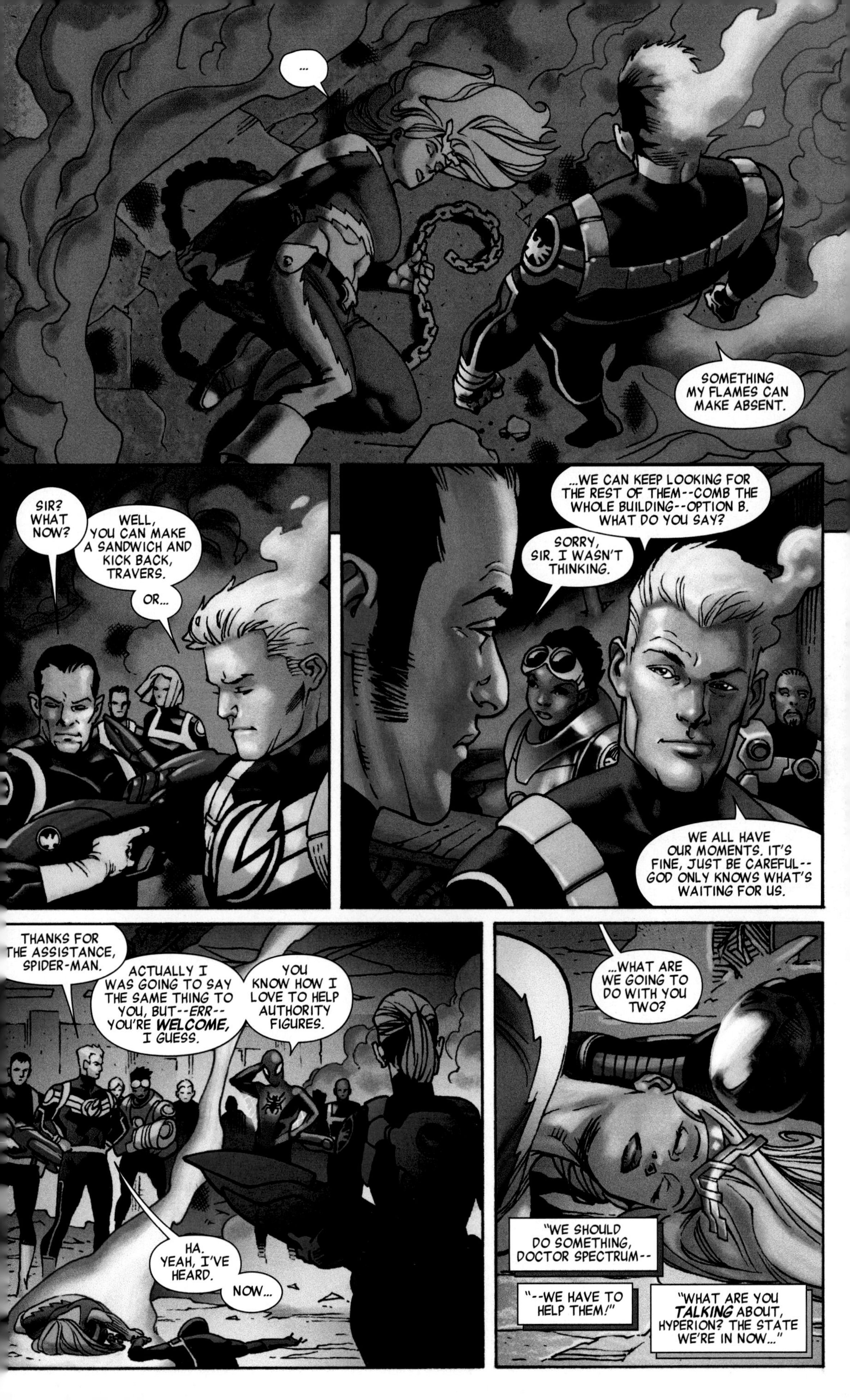
...
SOMETHING MY FLAMES CAN MAKE ABSENT.
SIR? WHAT NOW?
WELL, YOU CAN MAKE A SANDWICH AND KICK BACK, TRAVERS.
OR...
...WE CAN KEEP LOOKING FOR THE REST OF THEM--COMB THE WHOLE BUILDING--OPTION B. WHAT DO YOU SAY?
SORRY, SIR. I WASN'T THINKING.
WE ALL HAVE OUR MOMENTS. IT'S FINE, JUST BE CAREFUL--GOD ONLY KNOWS WHAT'S WAITING FOR US.
THANKS FOR THE ASSISTANCE, SPIDER-MAN.
ACTUALLY I WAS GOING TO SAY THE SAME THING TO YOU, BUT--ERR--YOU'RE WELCOME, I GUESS.
YOU KNOW HOW I LOVE TO HELP AUTHORITY FIGURES.
HA. YEAH, I'VE HEARD.
NOW...
...WHAT ARE WE GOING TO DO WITH YOU TWO?
"WE SHOULD DO SOMETHING, DOCTOR SPECTRUM--
"--WE HAVE TO HELP THEM!"
"WHAT ARE YOU TALKING ABOUT, HYPERION? THE STATE WE'RE IN NOW..."

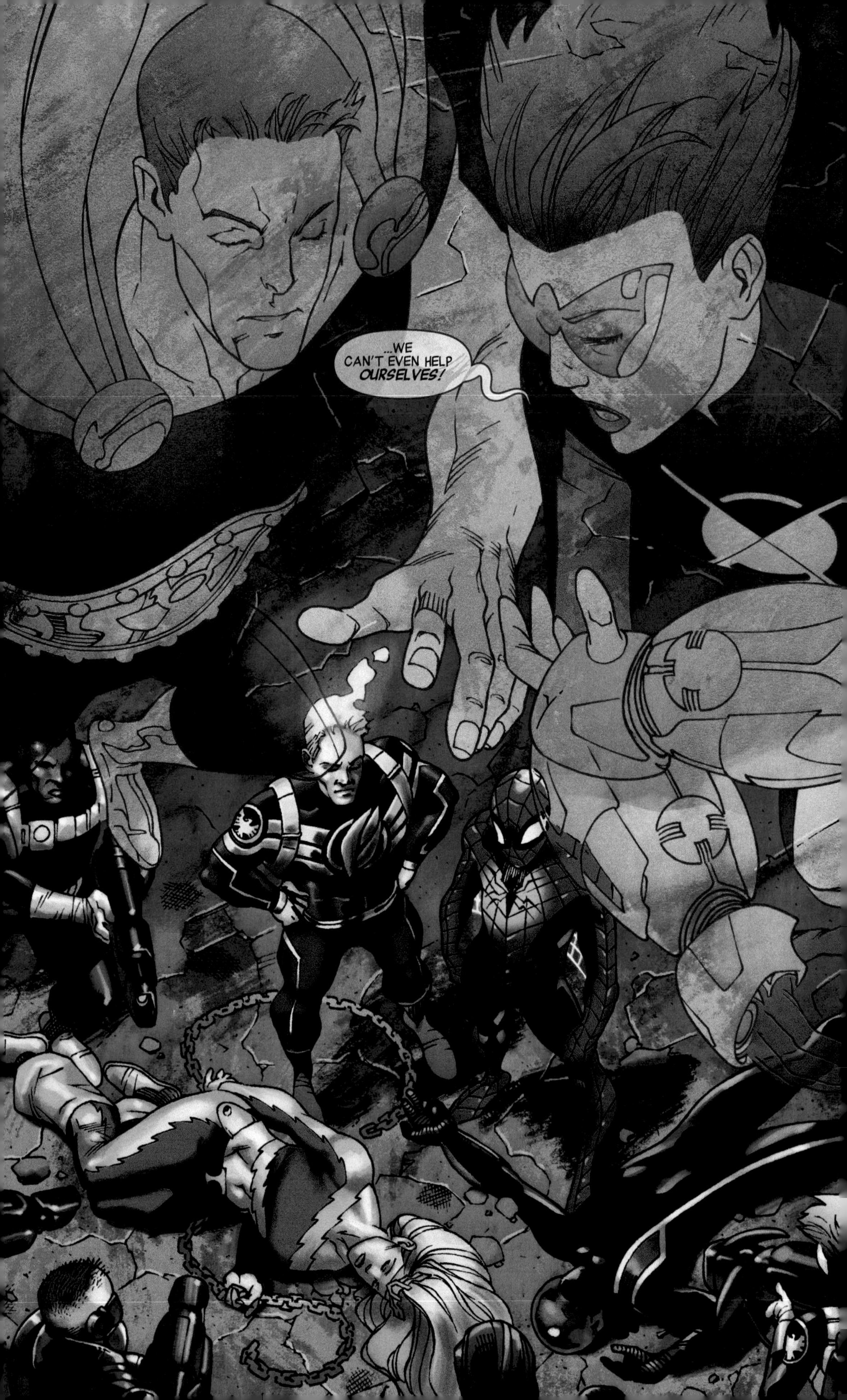
...WE CAN'T EVEN HELP *OURSELVES!*

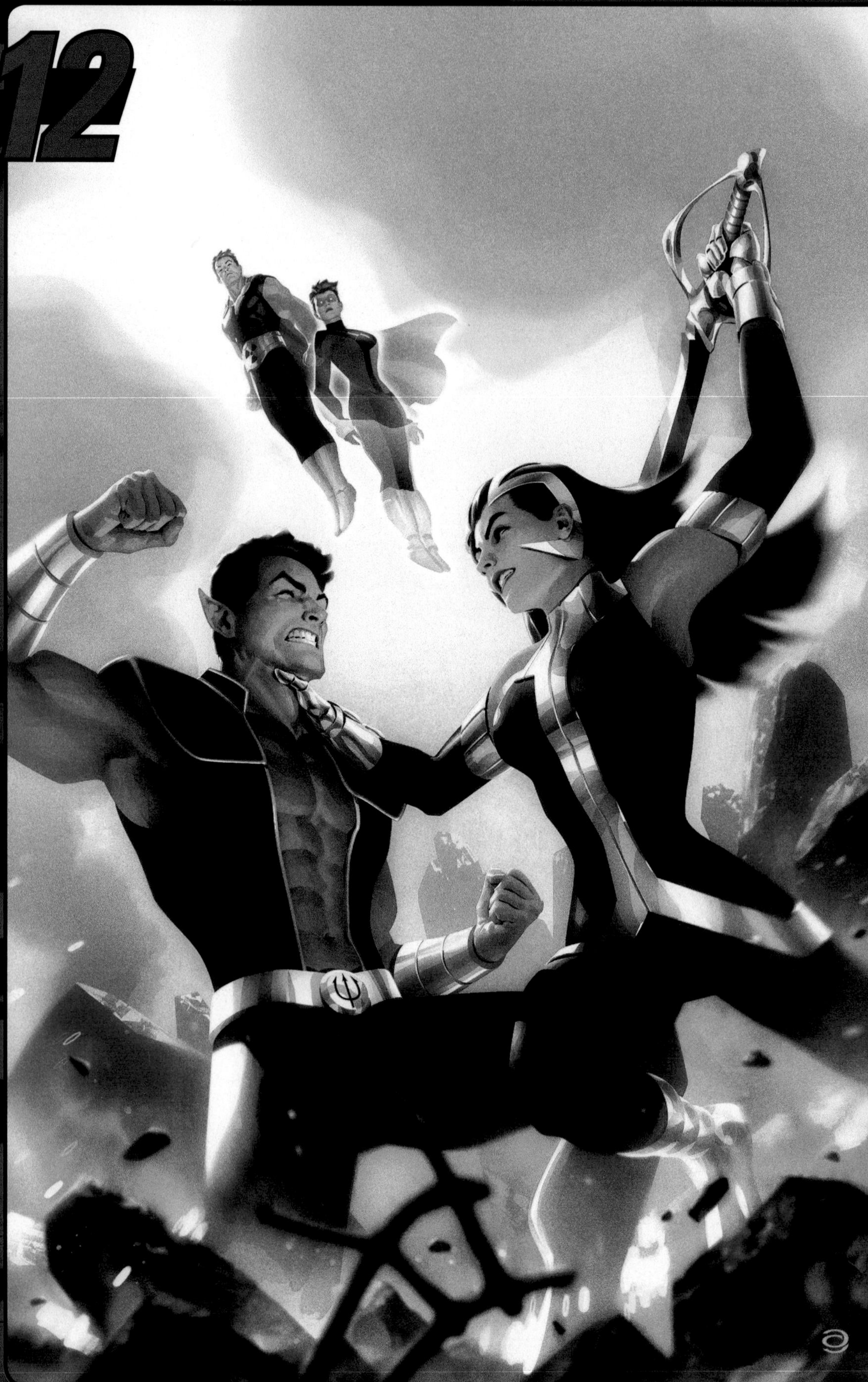
12

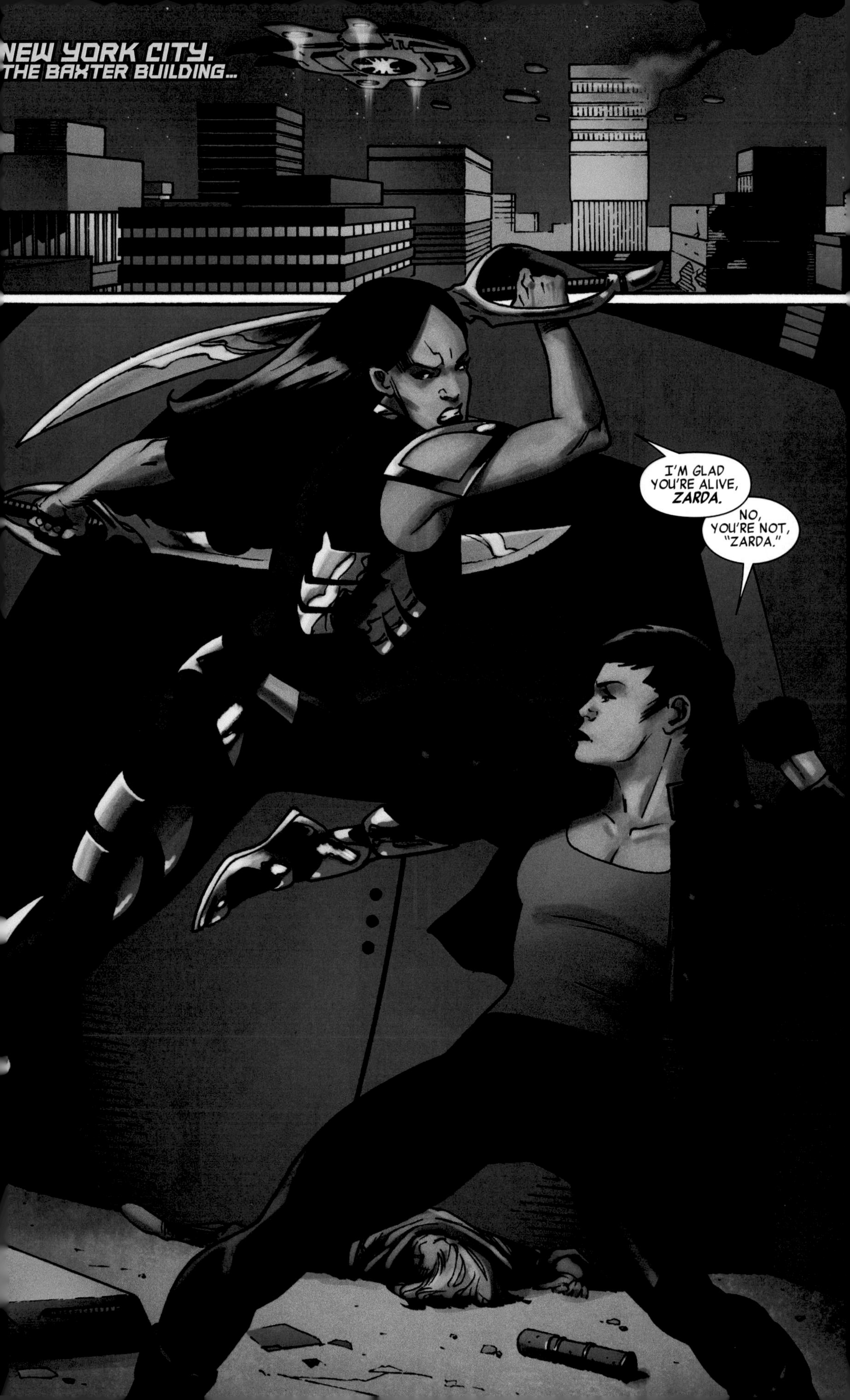
NEW YORK CITY.
THE BAXTER BUILDING...
I'M GLAD YOU'RE ALIVE, ZARDA.
NO, YOU'RE NOT, "ZARDA."

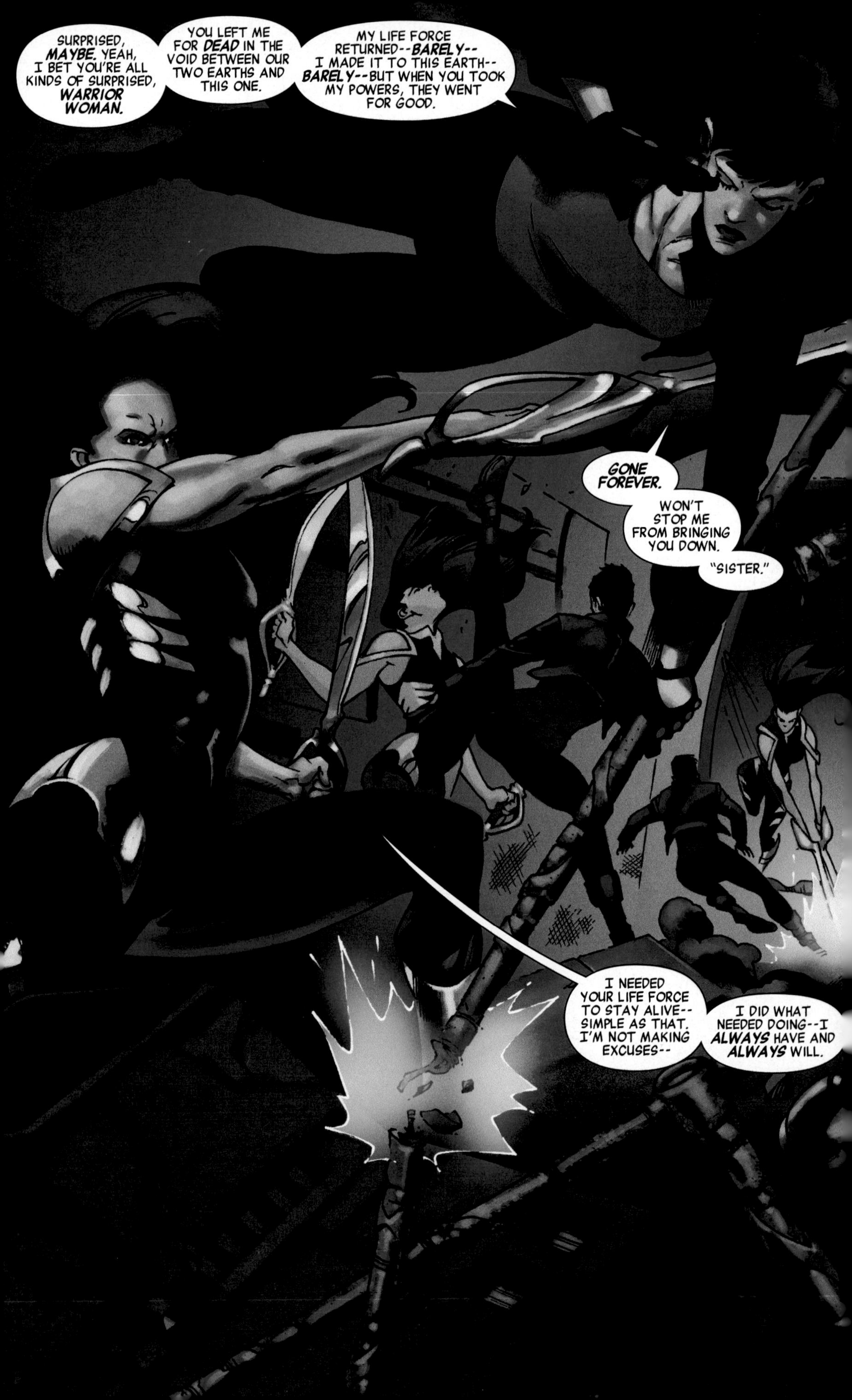
SURPRISED, **MAYBE**. YEAH, I BET YOU'RE ALL KINDS OF SURPRISED, **WARRIOR WOMAN.**
YOU LEFT ME FOR **DEAD** IN THE VOID BETWEEN OUR TWO EARTHS AND THIS ONE.
MY LIFE FORCE RETURNED--**BARELY**-- I MADE IT TO THIS EARTH-- **BARELY**--BUT WHEN YOU TOOK MY POWERS, THEY WENT FOR GOOD.
GONE FOREVER.
WON'T STOP ME FROM BRINGING YOU DOWN.
"SISTER."
I NEEDED YOUR LIFE FORCE TO STAY ALIVE-- SIMPLE AS THAT. I'M NOT MAKING EXCUSES--
I DID WHAT NEEDED DOING--I **ALWAYS** HAVE AND **ALWAYS** WILL.

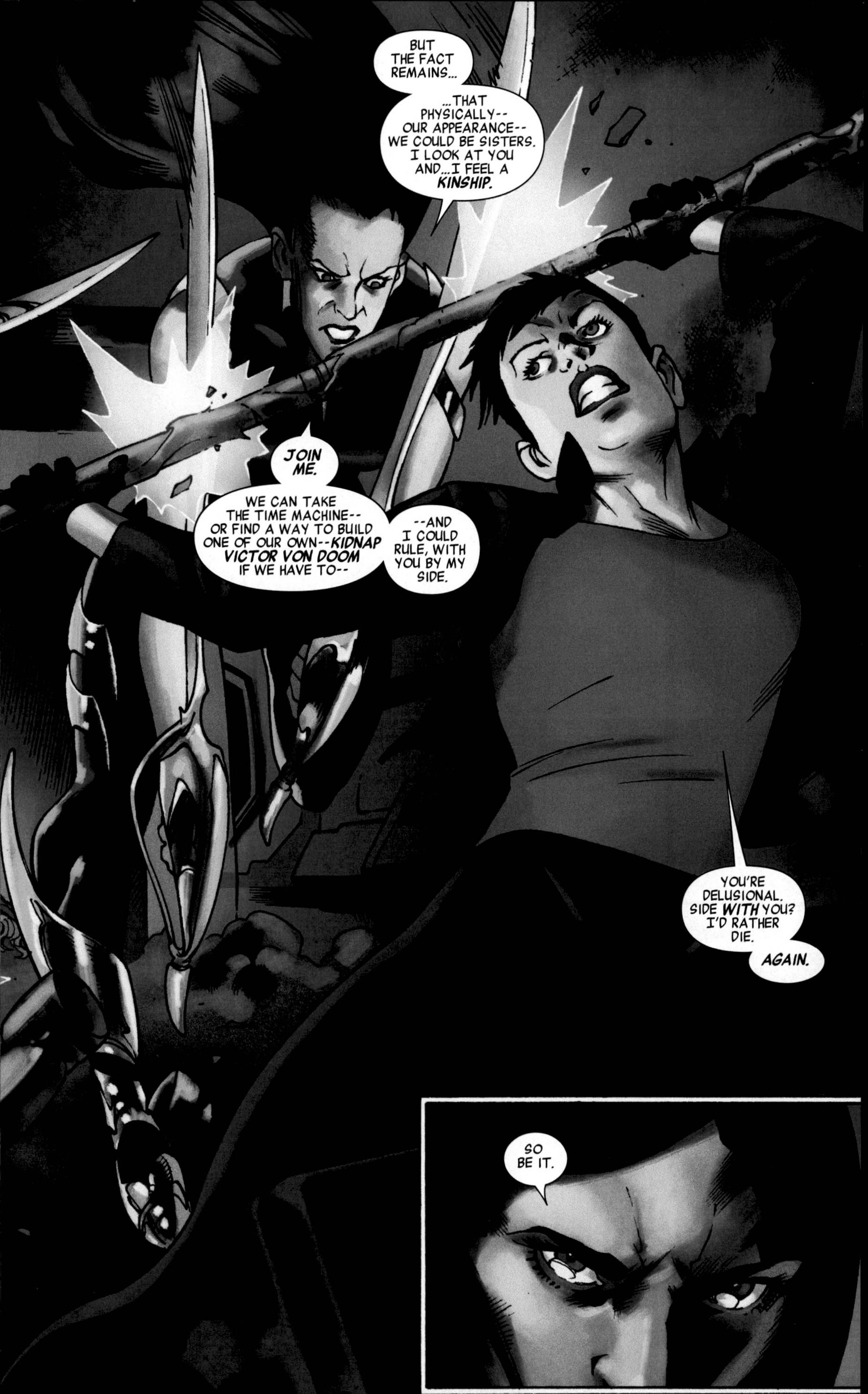
BUT THE FACT REMAINS...
...THAT PHYSICALLY-- OUR APPEARANCE-- WE COULD BE SISTERS. I LOOK AT YOU AND...I FEEL A KINSHIP.
JOIN ME.
WE CAN TAKE THE TIME MACHINE-- OR FIND A WAY TO BUILD ONE OF OUR OWN--KIDNAP VICTOR VON DOOM IF WE HAVE TO--
--AND I COULD RULE, WITH YOU BY MY SIDE.
YOU'RE DELUSIONAL. SIDE WITH YOU? I'D RATHER DIE.
AGAIN.
SO BE IT.

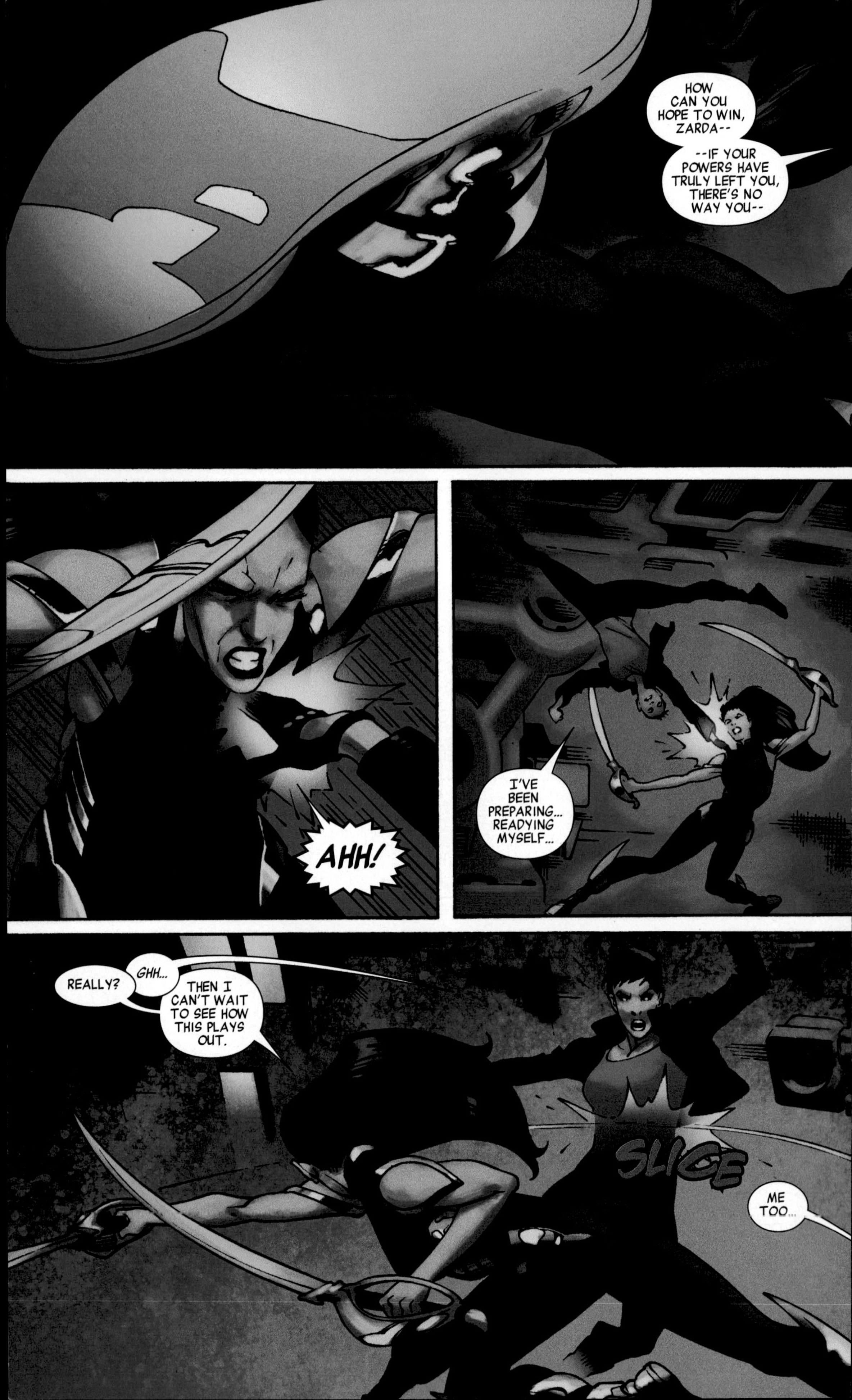
HOW CAN YOU HOPE TO WIN, ZARDA--
--IF YOUR POWERS HAVE TRULY LEFT YOU, THERE'S NO WAY YOU--
AHH!
I'VE BEEN PREPARING... READYING MYSELF...
REALLY?
GHH...
THEN I CAN'T WAIT TO SEE HOW THIS PLAYS OUT.
SLICE
ME TOO...

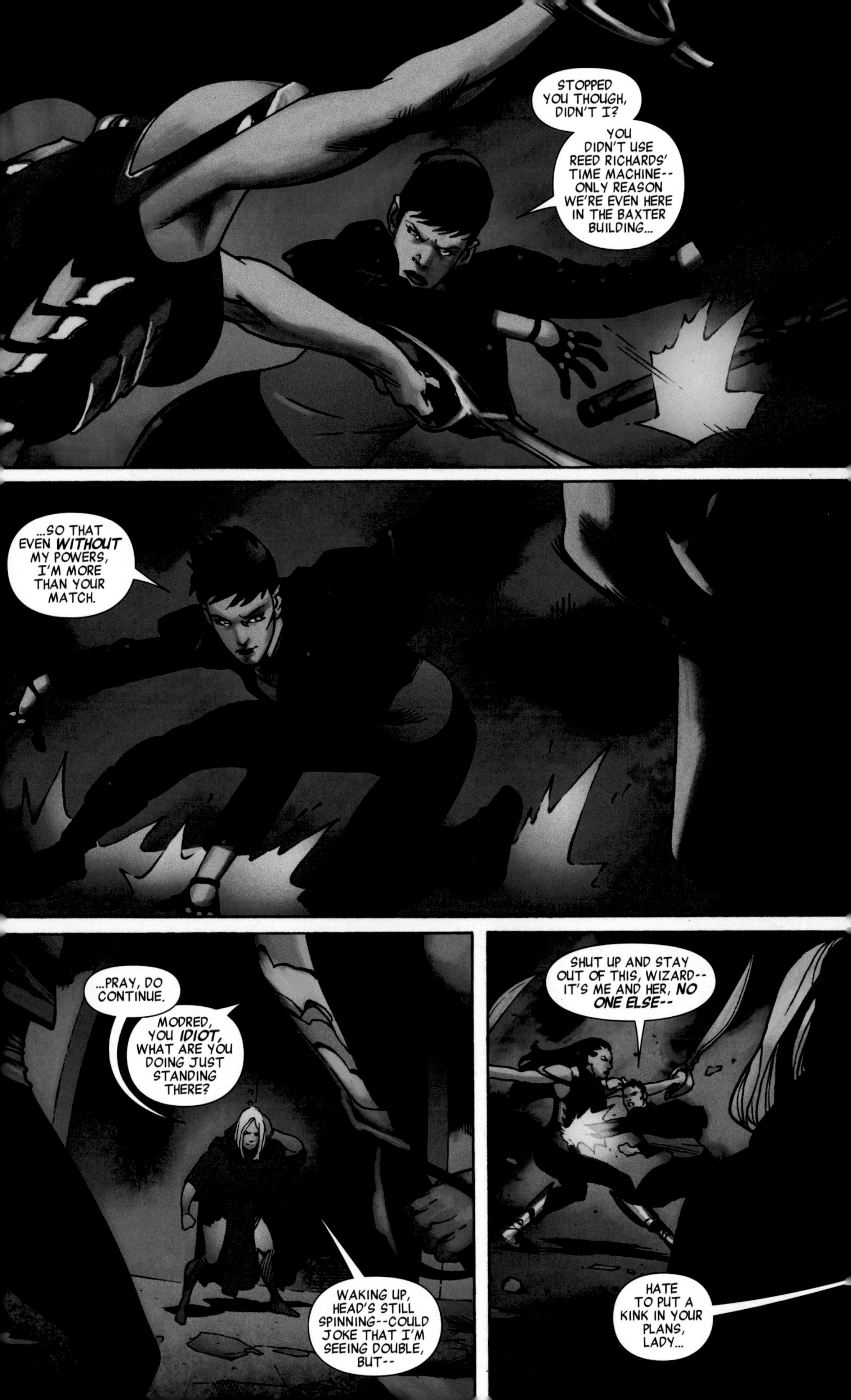
STOPPED YOU THOUGH, DIDN'T I?
YOU DIDN'T USE REED RICHARDS' TIME MACHINE--ONLY REASON WE'RE EVEN HERE IN THE BAXTER BUILDING...
...SO THAT EVEN **WITHOUT** MY POWERS, I'M MORE THAN YOUR MATCH.
...PRAY, DO CONTINUE.
MODRED, YOU **IDIOT,** WHAT ARE YOU DOING JUST STANDING THERE?
WAKING UP, HEAD'S STILL SPINNING--COULD JOKE THAT I'M SEEING DOUBLE, BUT--
SHUT UP AND STAY OUT OF THIS, WIZARD--IT'S ME AND HER, **NO ONE ELSE--**
HATE TO PUT A KINK IN YOUR PLANS, LADY...

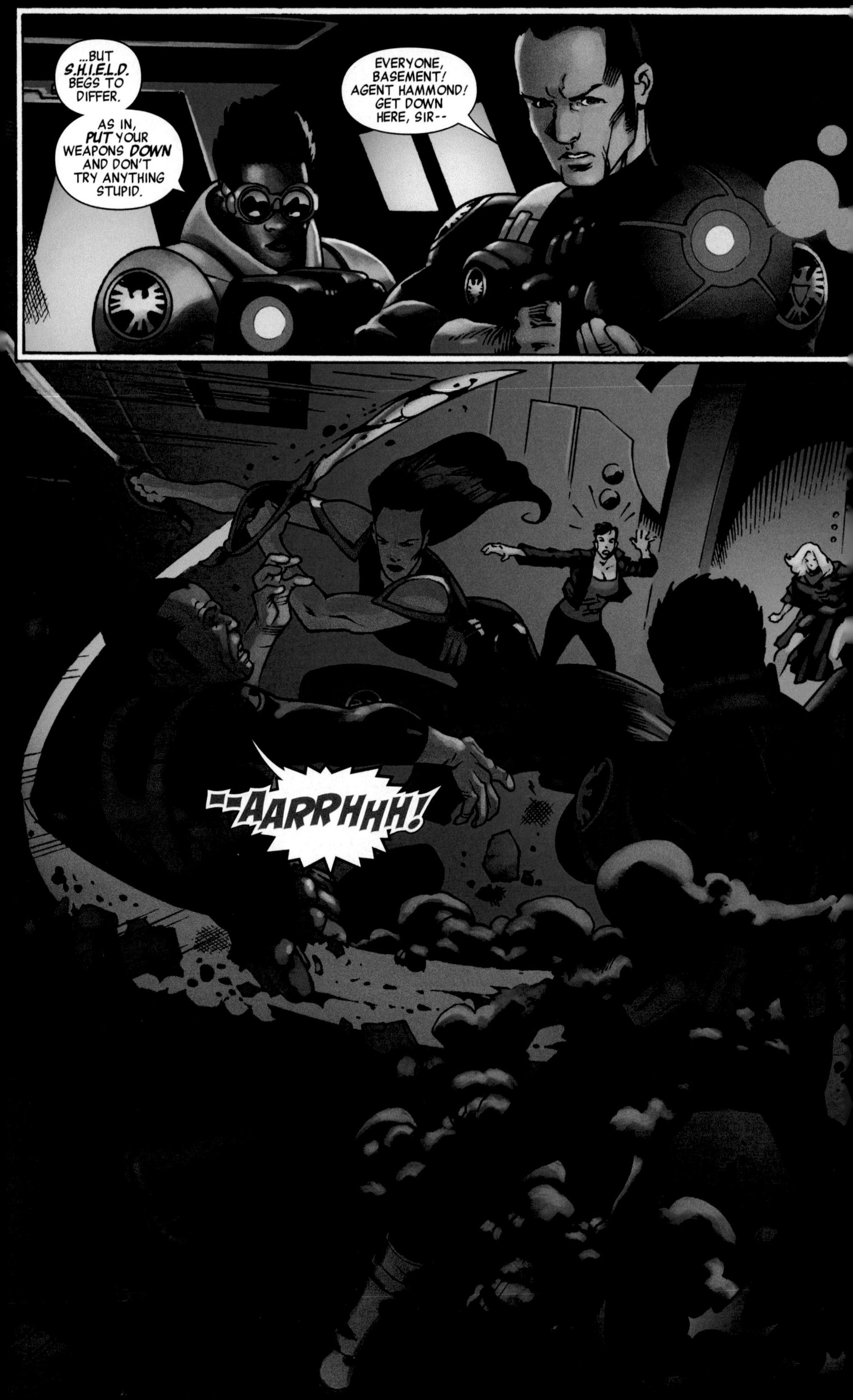
...BUT S.H.I.E.L.D. BEGS TO DIFFER.
AS IN, PUT YOUR WEAPONS DOWN AND DON'T TRY ANYTHING STUPID.
EVERYONE, BASEMENT! AGENT HAMMOND! GET DOWN HERE, SIR--
--AARRHHH!

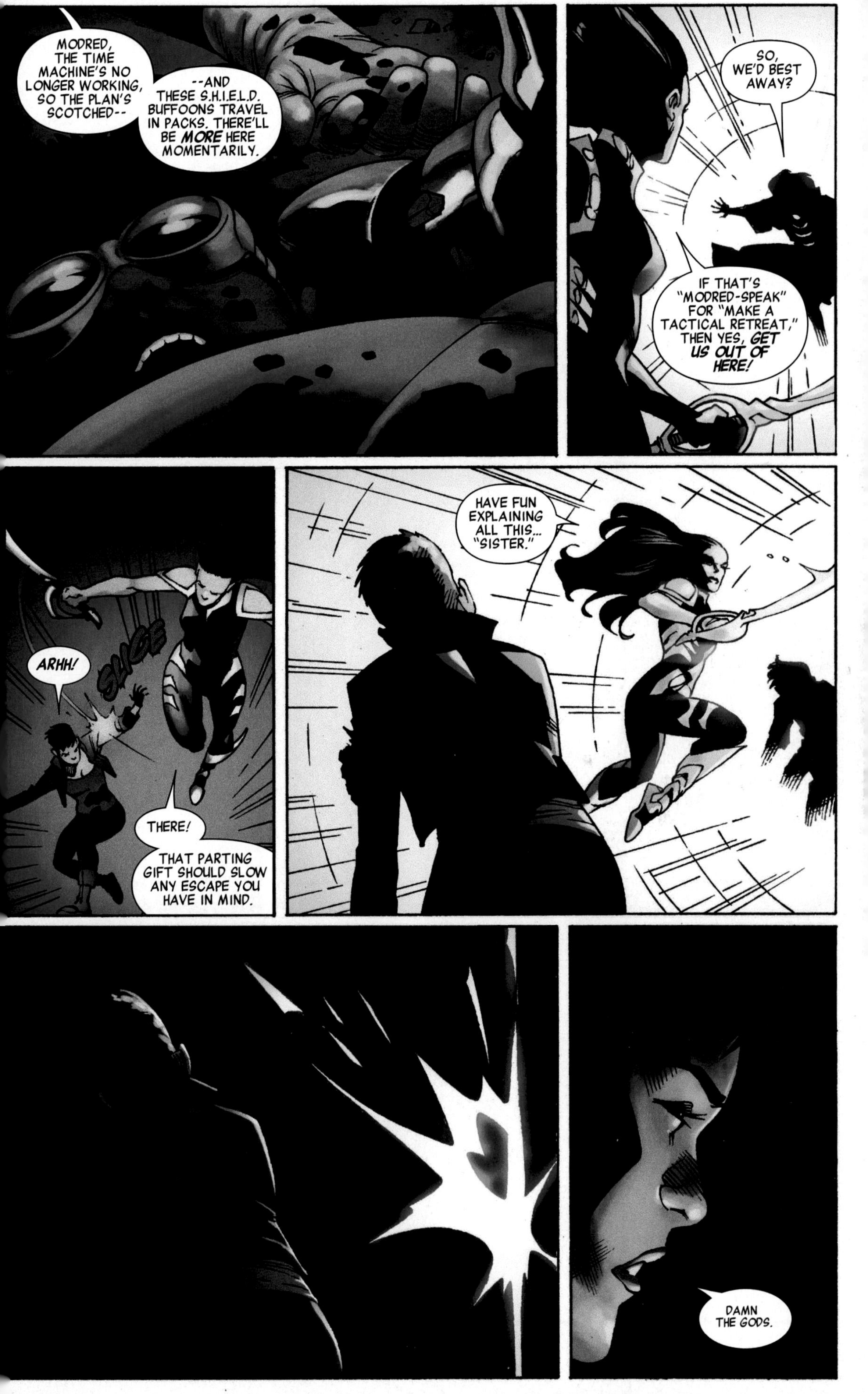
MODRED, THE TIME MACHINE'S NO LONGER WORKING, SO THE PLAN'S SCOTCHED--
--AND THESE S.H.I.E.L.D. BUFFOONS TRAVEL IN PACKS. THERE'LL BE **MORE** HERE MOMENTARILY.
SO, WE'D BEST AWAY?
IF THAT'S "MODRED-SPEAK" FOR "MAKE A TACTICAL RETREAT," THEN YES, **GET US OUT OF HERE!**
ARHH!
SLICE
THERE!
THAT PARTING GIFT SHOULD SLOW ANY ESCAPE YOU HAVE IN MIND.
HAVE FUN EXPLAINING ALL THIS... "SISTER."
DAMN THE GODS.

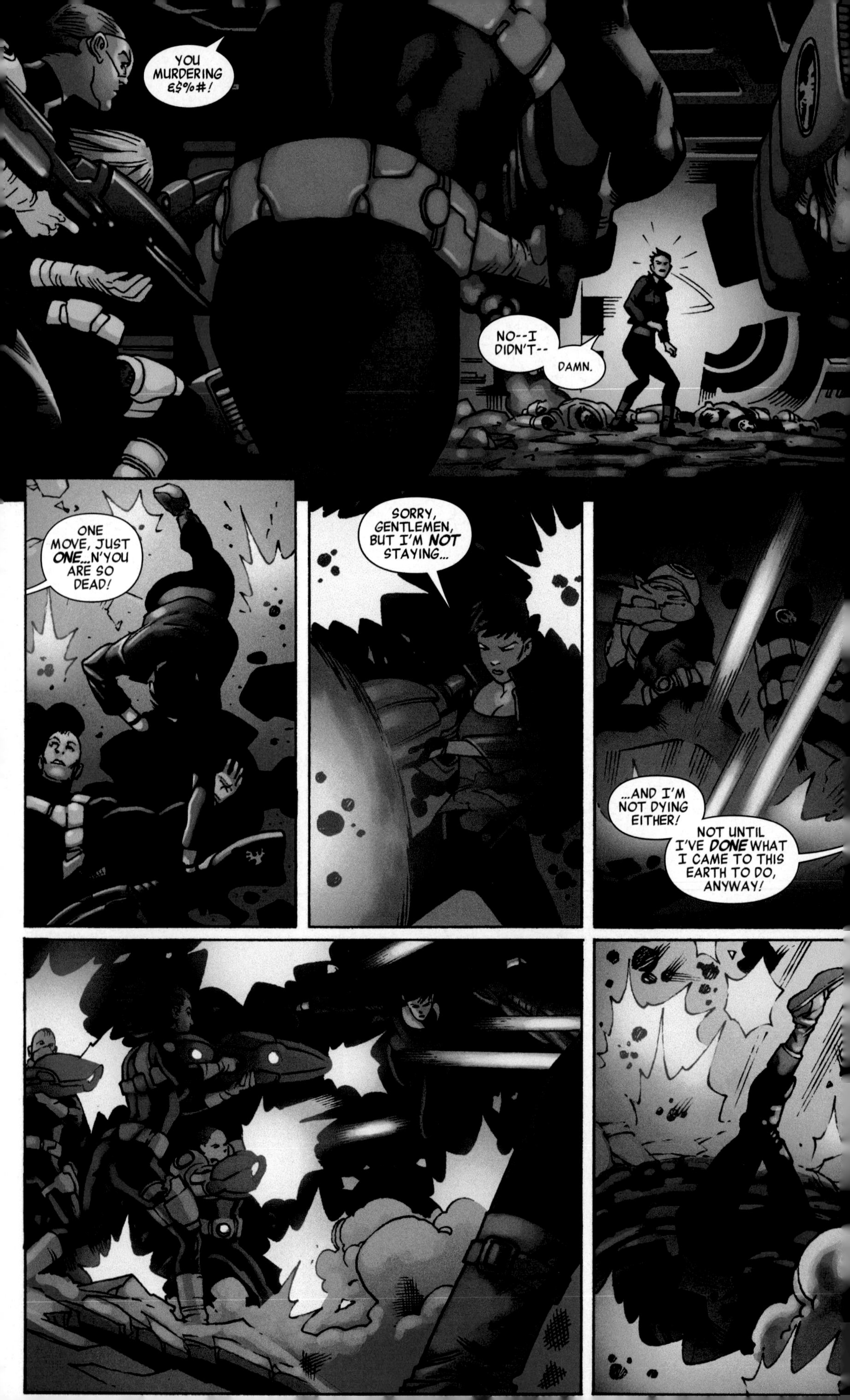

YOU MURDERING &$%#!
NO--I DIDN'T--
DAMN.
ONE MOVE, JUST ONE...N'YOU ARE SO DEAD!
SORRY, GENTLEMEN, BUT I'M NOT STAYING...
...AND I'M NOT DYING EITHER!
NOT UNTIL I'VE DONE WHAT I CAME TO THIS EARTH TO DO, ANYWAY!

AFTER HER!

GET THAT ^%$#!

GET OUT OF THE WAY! MOVE IT!

AND WATCH YOUR LANGUAGE.

AGENT HAMMOND!

SIR!

DAMMIT!

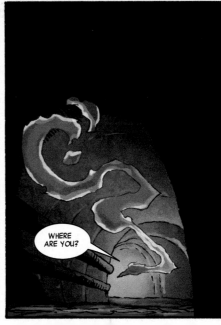

WHERE ARE YOU?

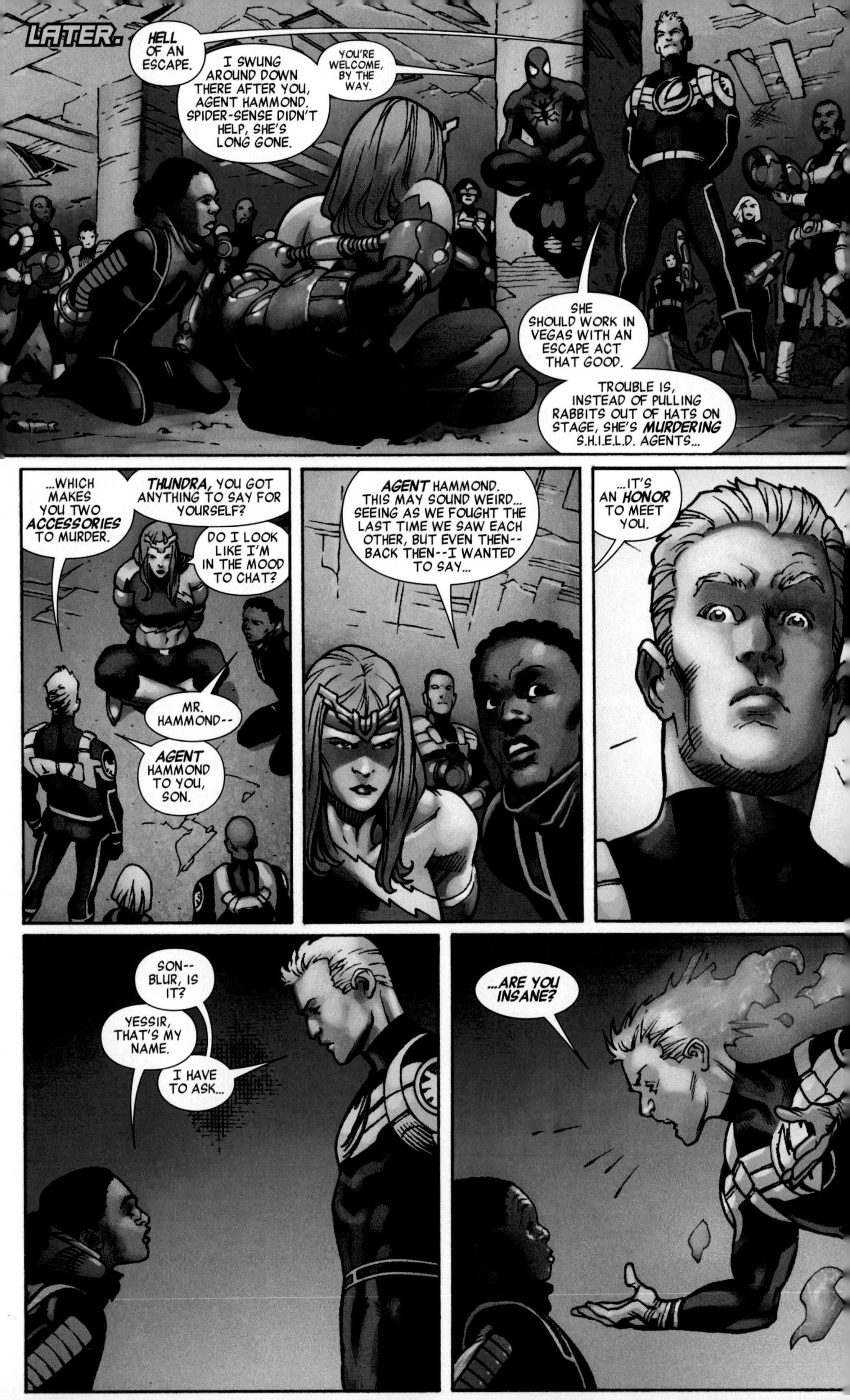
LATER.
HELL OF AN ESCAPE.
I SWUNG AROUND DOWN THERE AFTER YOU, AGENT HAMMOND. SPIDER-SENSE DIDN'T HELP, SHE'S LONG GONE.
YOU'RE WELCOME, BY THE WAY.
SHE SHOULD WORK IN VEGAS WITH AN ESCAPE ACT THAT GOOD.
TROUBLE IS, INSTEAD OF PULLING RABBITS OUT OF HATS ON STAGE, SHE'S MURDERING S.H.I.E.L.D. AGENTS...
...WHICH MAKES YOU TWO ACCESSORIES TO MURDER.
THUNDRA, YOU GOT ANYTHING TO SAY FOR YOURSELF?
DO I LOOK LIKE I'M IN THE MOOD TO CHAT?
MR. HAMMOND--
AGENT HAMMOND TO YOU, SON.
AGENT HAMMOND. THIS MAY SOUND WEIRD... SEEING AS WE FOUGHT THE LAST TIME WE SAW EACH OTHER, BUT EVEN THEN-- BACK THEN--I WANTED TO SAY...
...IT'S AN HONOR TO MEET YOU.
SON-- BLUR, IS IT?
YESSIR, THAT'S MY NAME.
I HAVE TO ASK...
...ARE YOU INSANE?

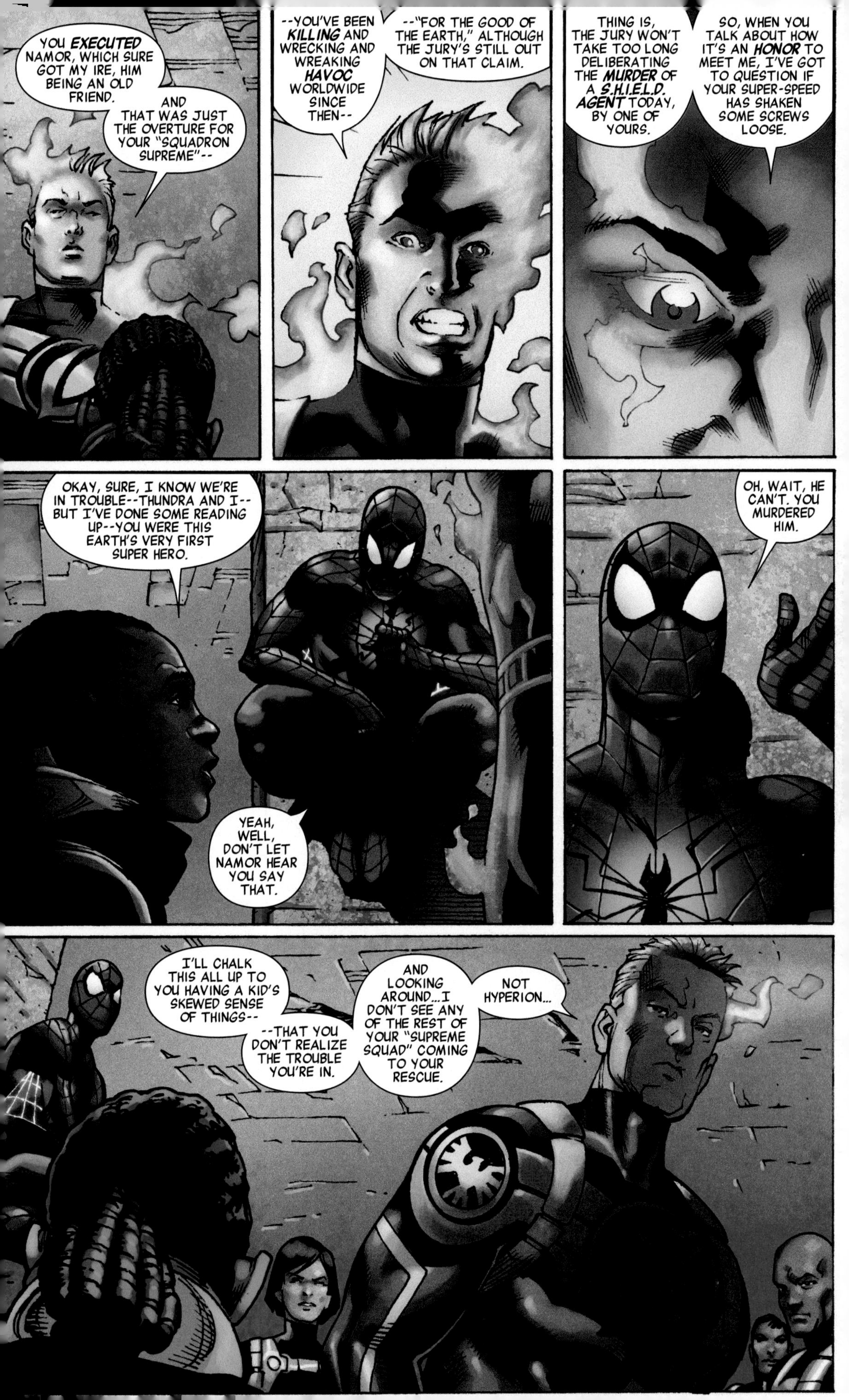
YOU EXECUTED NAMOR, WHICH SURE GOT MY IRE, HIM BEING AN OLD FRIEND.
AND THAT WAS JUST THE OVERTURE FOR YOUR "SQUADRON SUPREME"--
--YOU'VE BEEN KILLING AND WRECKING AND WREAKING HAVOC WORLDWIDE SINCE THEN--
--"FOR THE GOOD OF THE EARTH," ALTHOUGH THE JURY'S STILL OUT ON THAT CLAIM.
THING IS, THE JURY WON'T TAKE TOO LONG DELIBERATING THE MURDER OF A S.H.I.E.L.D. AGENT TODAY, BY ONE OF YOURS.
SO, WHEN YOU TALK ABOUT HOW IT'S AN HONOR TO MEET ME, I'VE GOT TO QUESTION IF YOUR SUPER-SPEED HAS SHAKEN SOME SCREWS LOOSE.
OKAY, SURE, I KNOW WE'RE IN TROUBLE--THUNDRA AND I--BUT I'VE DONE SOME READING UP--YOU WERE THIS EARTH'S VERY FIRST SUPER HERO.
YEAH, WELL, DON'T LET NAMOR HEAR YOU SAY THAT.
OH, WAIT, HE CAN'T. YOU MURDERED HIM.
I'LL CHALK THIS ALL UP TO YOU HAVING A KID'S SKEWED SENSE OF THINGS--
--THAT YOU DON'T REALIZE THE TROUBLE YOU'RE IN.
AND LOOKING AROUND...I DON'T SEE ANY OF THE REST OF YOUR "SUPREME SQUAD" COMING TO YOUR RESCUE.
NOT HYPERION...

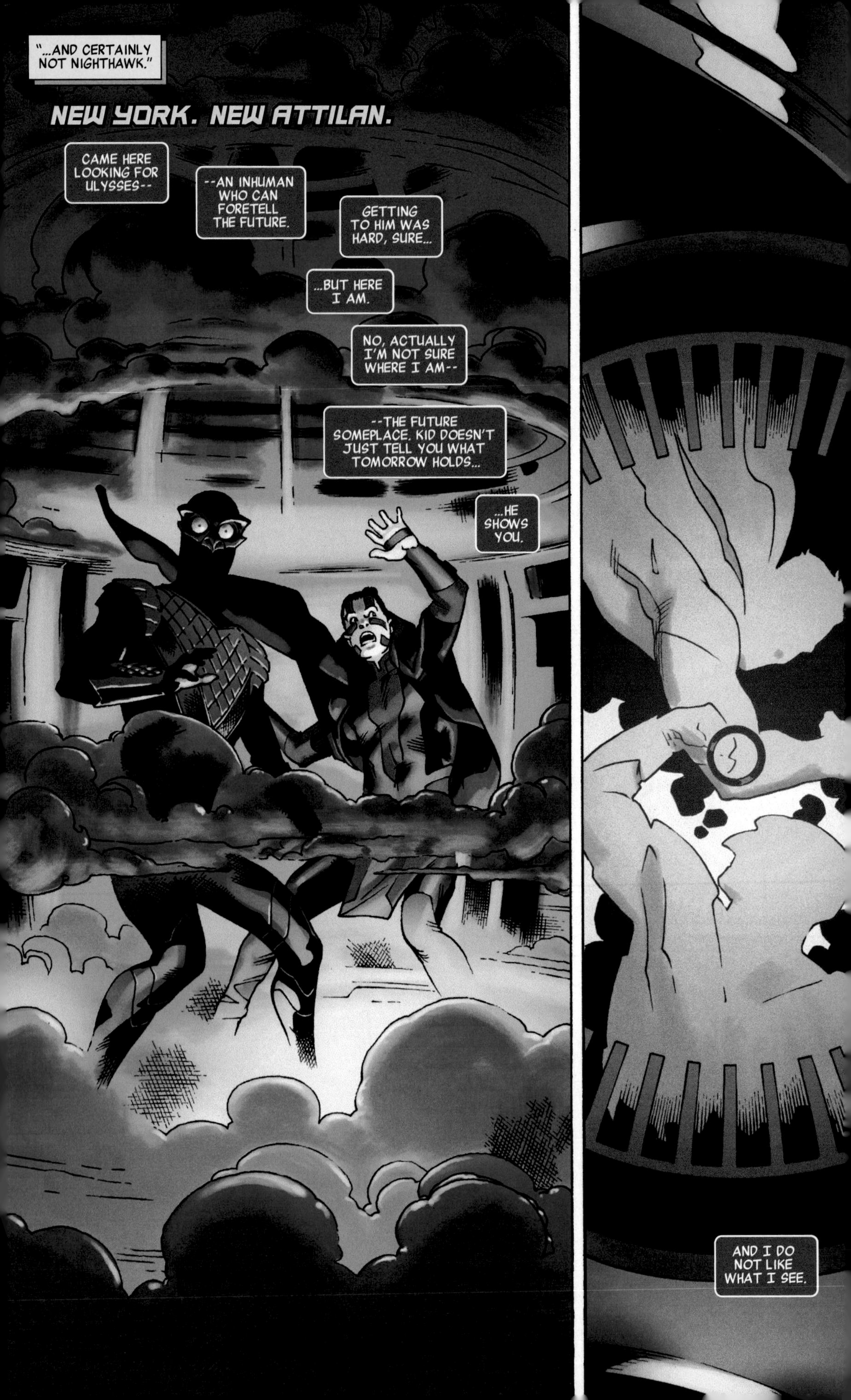
"...AND CERTAINLY NOT NIGHTHAWK."
NEW YORK. NEW ATTILAN.
CAME HERE LOOKING FOR ULYSSES--
--AN INHUMAN WHO CAN FORETELL THE FUTURE.
GETTING TO HIM WAS HARD, SURE...
...BUT HERE I AM.
NO, ACTUALLY I'M NOT SURE WHERE I AM--
--THE FUTURE SOMEPLACE. KID DOESN'T JUST TELL YOU WHAT TOMORROW HOLDS...
...HE SHOWS YOU.
AND I DO NOT LIKE WHAT I SEE.

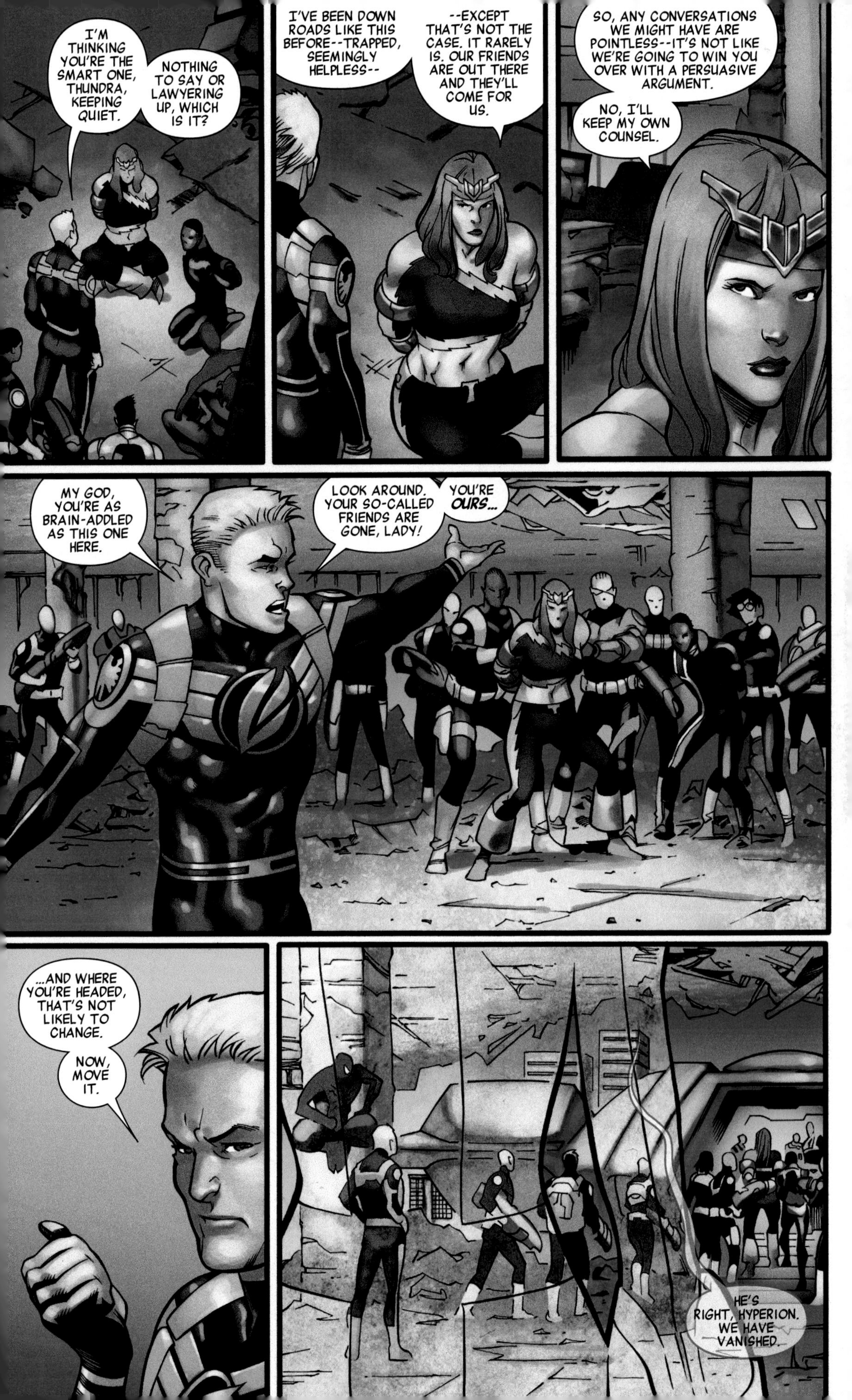

I'M THINKING YOU'RE THE SMART ONE, THUNDRA, KEEPING QUIET.
NOTHING TO SAY OR LAWYERING UP, WHICH IS IT?
I'VE BEEN DOWN ROADS LIKE THIS BEFORE--TRAPPED, SEEMINGLY HELPLESS--
--EXCEPT THAT'S NOT THE CASE. IT RARELY IS. OUR FRIENDS ARE OUT THERE AND THEY'LL COME FOR US.
SO, ANY CONVERSATIONS WE MIGHT HAVE ARE POINTLESS--IT'S NOT LIKE WE'RE GOING TO WIN YOU OVER WITH A PERSUASIVE ARGUMENT.
NO, I'LL KEEP MY OWN COUNSEL.
MY GOD, YOU'RE AS BRAIN-ADDLED AS THIS ONE HERE.
LOOK AROUND. YOUR SO-CALLED FRIENDS ARE GONE, LADY!
YOU'RE ***OURS...***
...AND WHERE YOU'RE HEADED, THAT'S NOT LIKELY TO CHANGE.
NOW, MOVE IT.
HE'S RIGHT, HYPERION. WE HAVE VANISHED.

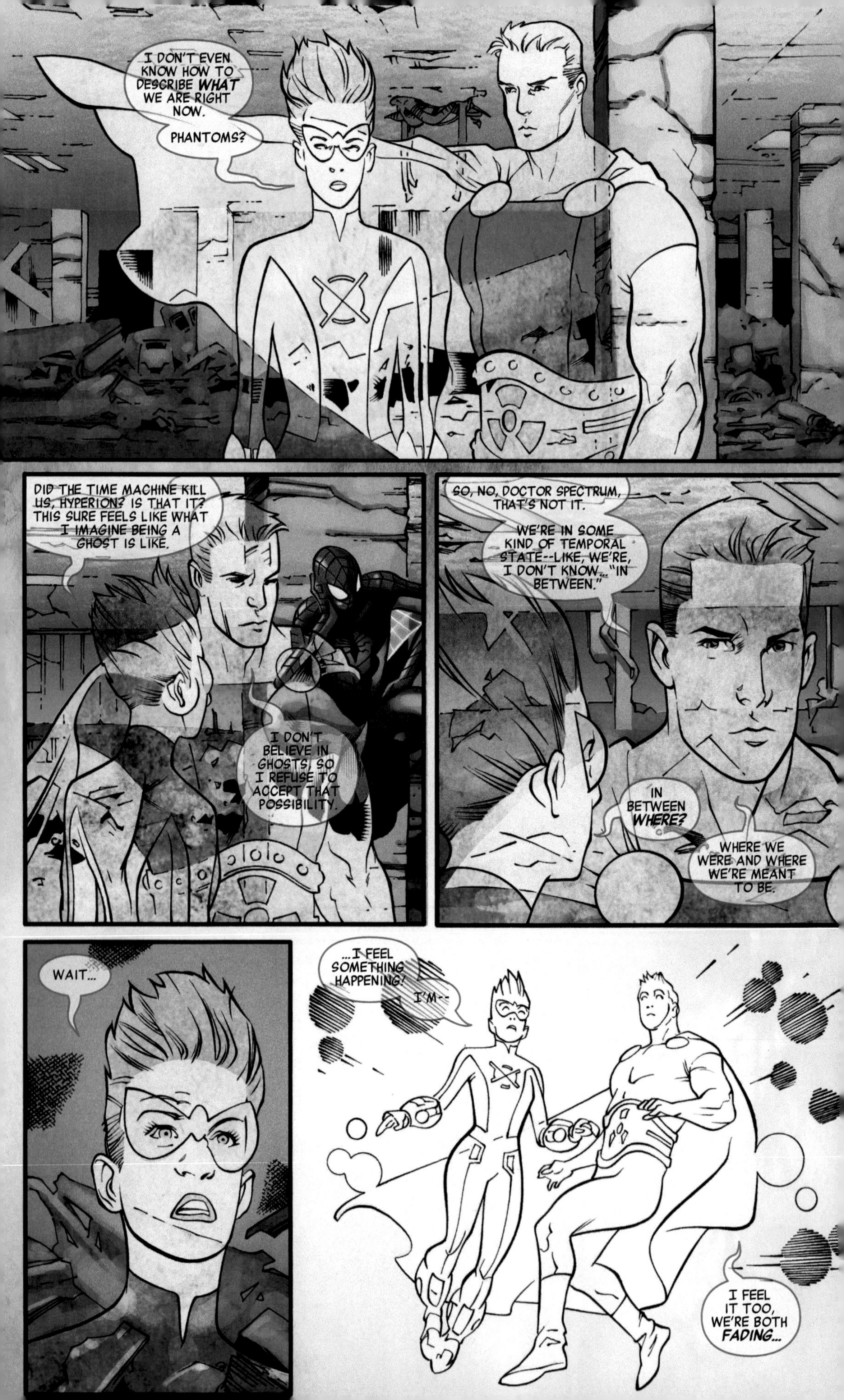
I DON'T EVEN KNOW HOW TO DESCRIBE **WHAT** WE ARE RIGHT NOW.
PHANTOMS?
DID THE TIME MACHINE KILL US, HYPERION? IS THAT IT? THIS SURE FEELS LIKE WHAT I IMAGINE BEING A GHOST IS LIKE.
I DON'T BELIEVE IN GHOSTS, SO I REFUSE TO ACCEPT THAT POSSIBILITY.
SO, NO, DOCTOR SPECTRUM, THAT'S NOT IT.
WE'RE IN SOME KIND OF TEMPORAL STATE--LIKE, WE'RE, I DON'T KNOW... "IN BETWEEN."
IN BETWEEN **WHERE?**
WHERE WE WERE AND WHERE WE'RE MEANT TO BE.
WAIT...
...I FEEL SOMETHING HAPPENING!
I'M--
I FEEL IT TOO, WE'RE BOTH **FADING...**

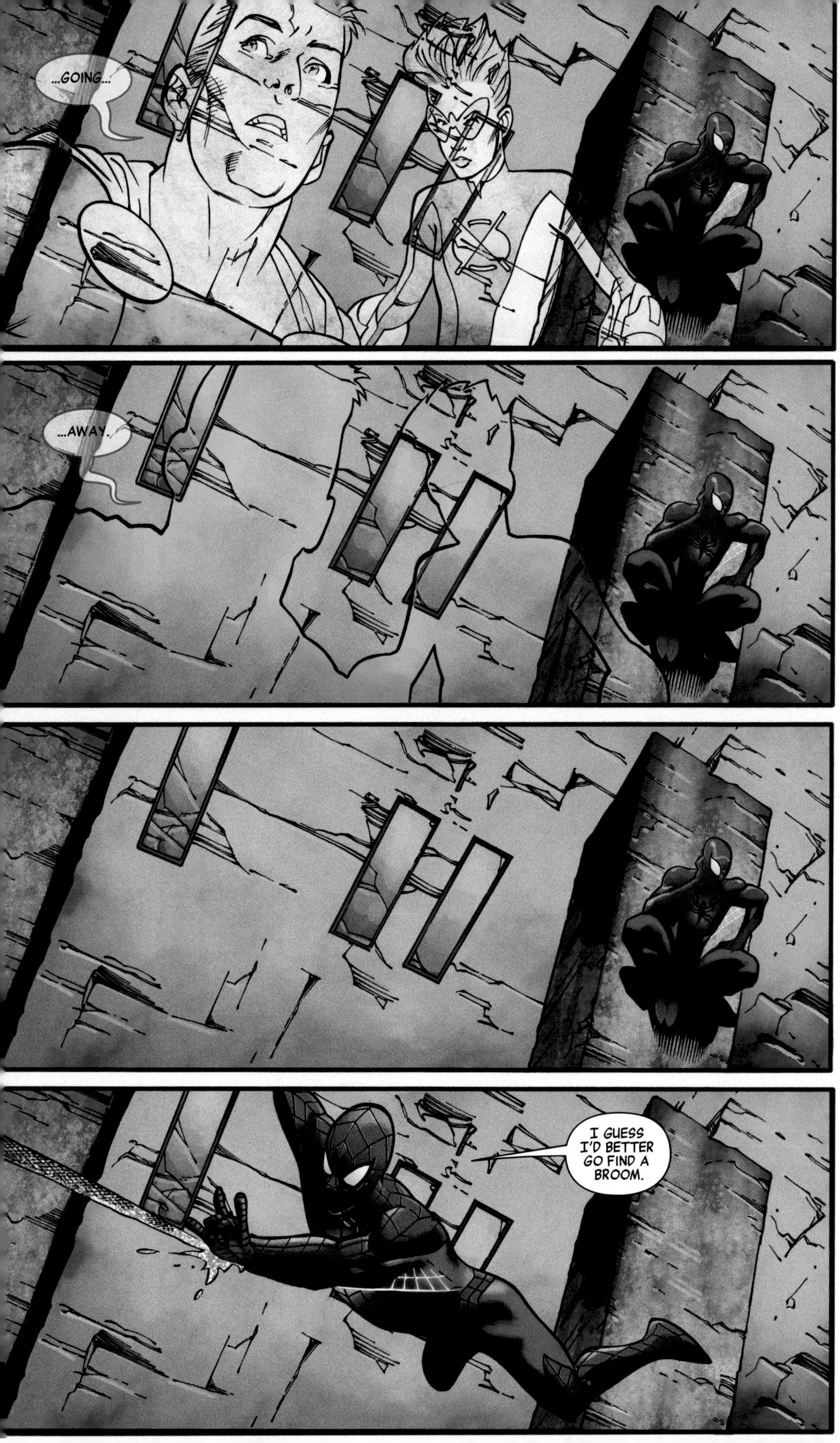
...GOING...
...AWAY.
I GUESS I'D BETTER GO FIND A BROOM.

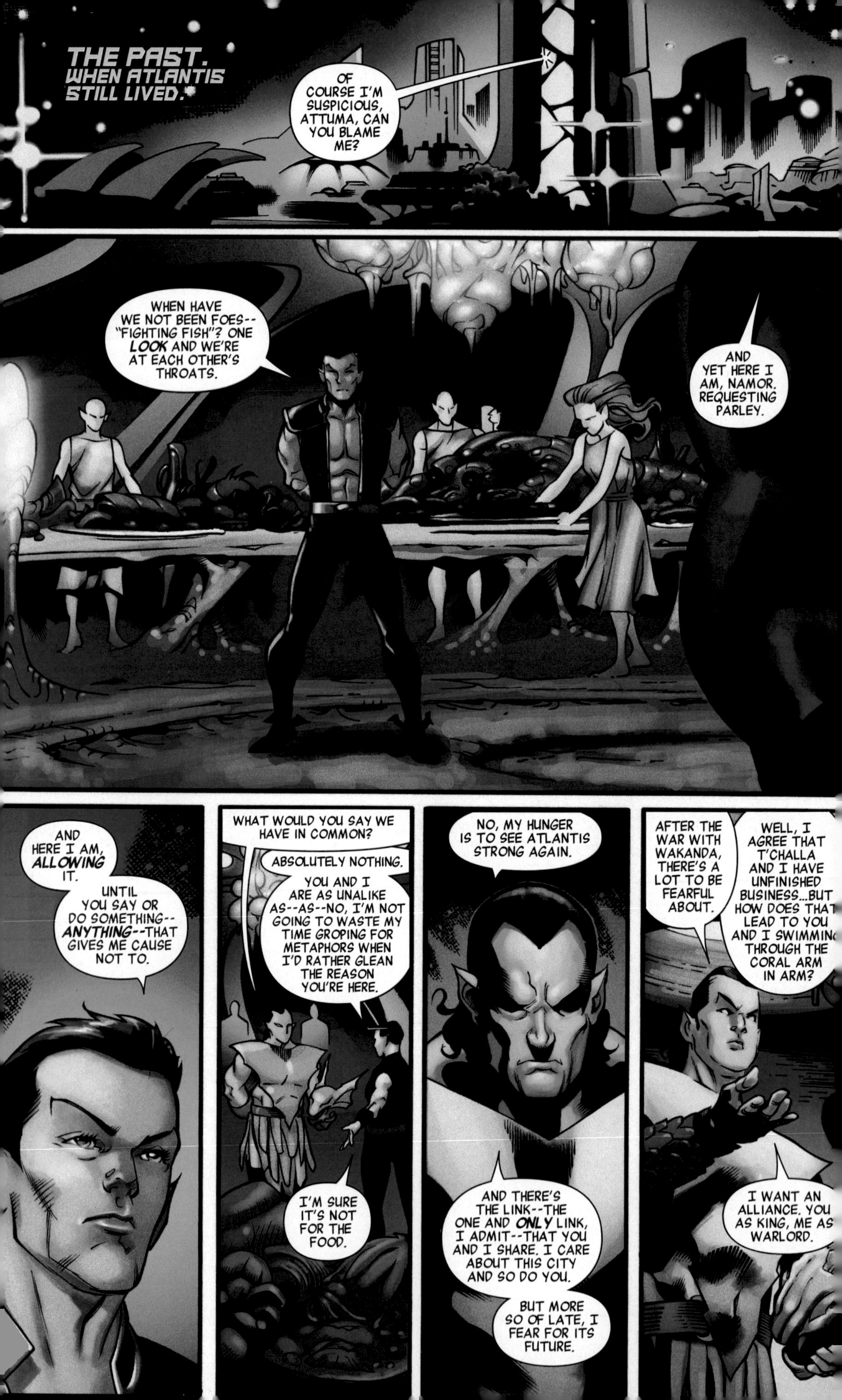
THE PAST. WHEN ATLANTIS STILL LIVED.
OF COURSE I'M SUSPICIOUS, ATTUMA, CAN YOU BLAME ME?
WHEN HAVE WE NOT BEEN FOES--"FIGHTING FISH"? ONE LOOK AND WE'RE AT EACH OTHER'S THROATS.
AND YET HERE I AM, NAMOR. REQUESTING PARLEY.
AND HERE I AM, ALLOWING IT.
UNTIL YOU SAY OR DO SOMETHING--ANYTHING--THAT GIVES ME CAUSE NOT TO.
WHAT WOULD YOU SAY WE HAVE IN COMMON?
ABSOLUTELY NOTHING.
YOU AND I ARE AS UNALIKE AS--AS--NO, I'M NOT GOING TO WASTE MY TIME GROPING FOR METAPHORS WHEN I'D RATHER GLEAN THE REASON YOU'RE HERE.
I'M SURE IT'S NOT FOR THE FOOD.
NO, MY HUNGER IS TO SEE ATLANTIS STRONG AGAIN.
AND THERE'S THE LINK--THE ONE AND ONLY LINK, I ADMIT--THAT YOU AND I SHARE. I CARE ABOUT THIS CITY AND SO DO YOU.
BUT MORE SO OF LATE, I FEAR FOR ITS FUTURE.
AFTER THE WAR WITH WAKANDA, THERE'S A LOT TO BE FEARFUL ABOUT.
WELL, I AGREE THAT T'CHALLA AND I HAVE UNFINISHED BUSINESS...BUT HOW DOES THAT LEAD TO YOU AND I SWIMMING THROUGH THE CORAL ARM IN ARM?
I WANT AN ALLIANCE. YOU AS KING, ME AS WARLORD.

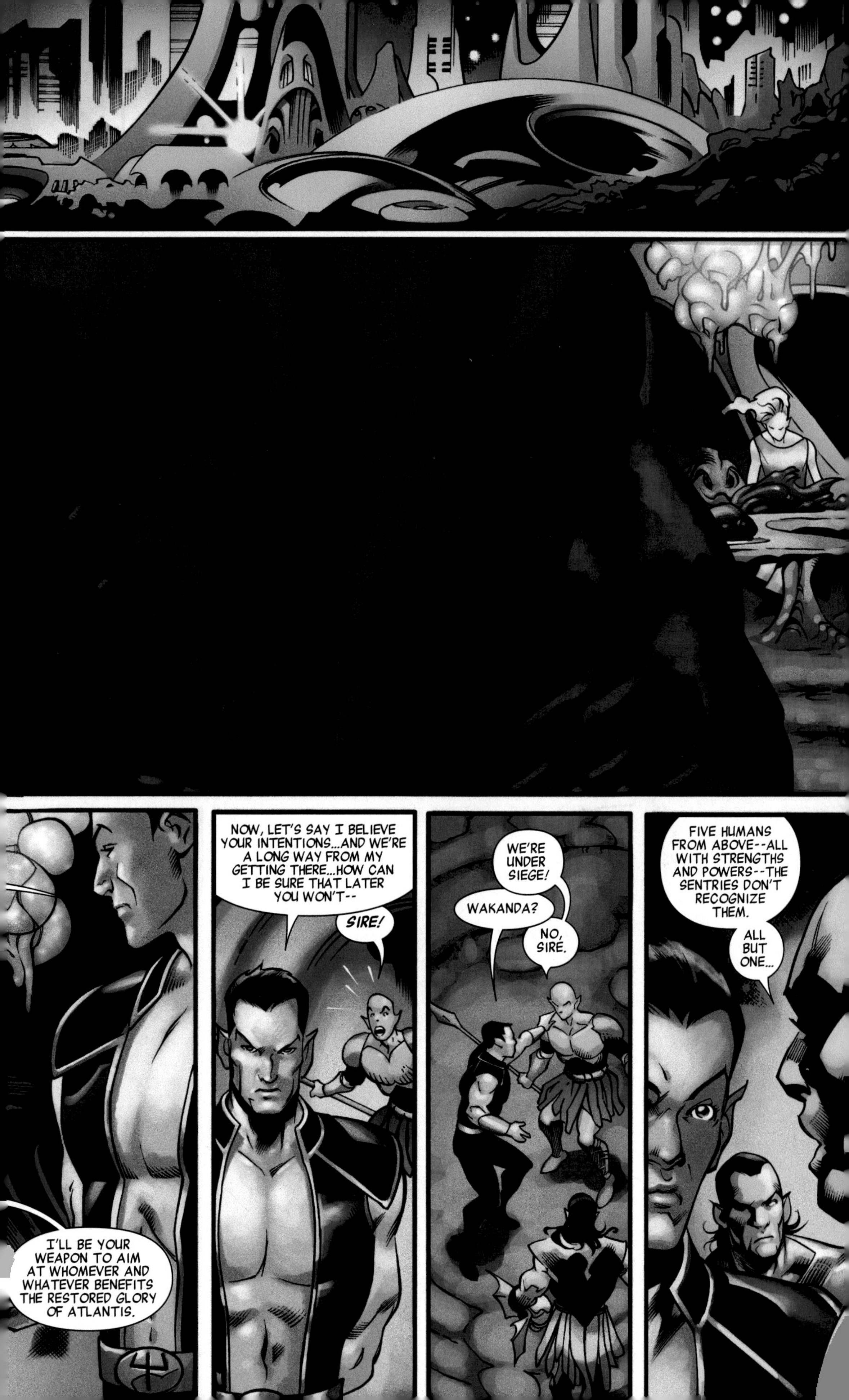
I'LL BE YOUR WEAPON TO AIM AT WHOMEVER AND WHATEVER BENEFITS THE RESTORED GLORY OF ATLANTIS.
NOW, LET'S SAY I BELIEVE YOUR INTENTIONS...AND WE'RE A LONG WAY FROM MY GETTING THERE...HOW CAN I BE SURE THAT LATER YOU WON'T--
SIRE!
WE'RE UNDER SIEGE!
WAKANDA?
NO, SIRE.
FIVE HUMANS FROM ABOVE--ALL WITH STRENGTHS AND POWERS--THE SENTRIES DON'T RECOGNIZE THEM.
ALL BUT ONE...

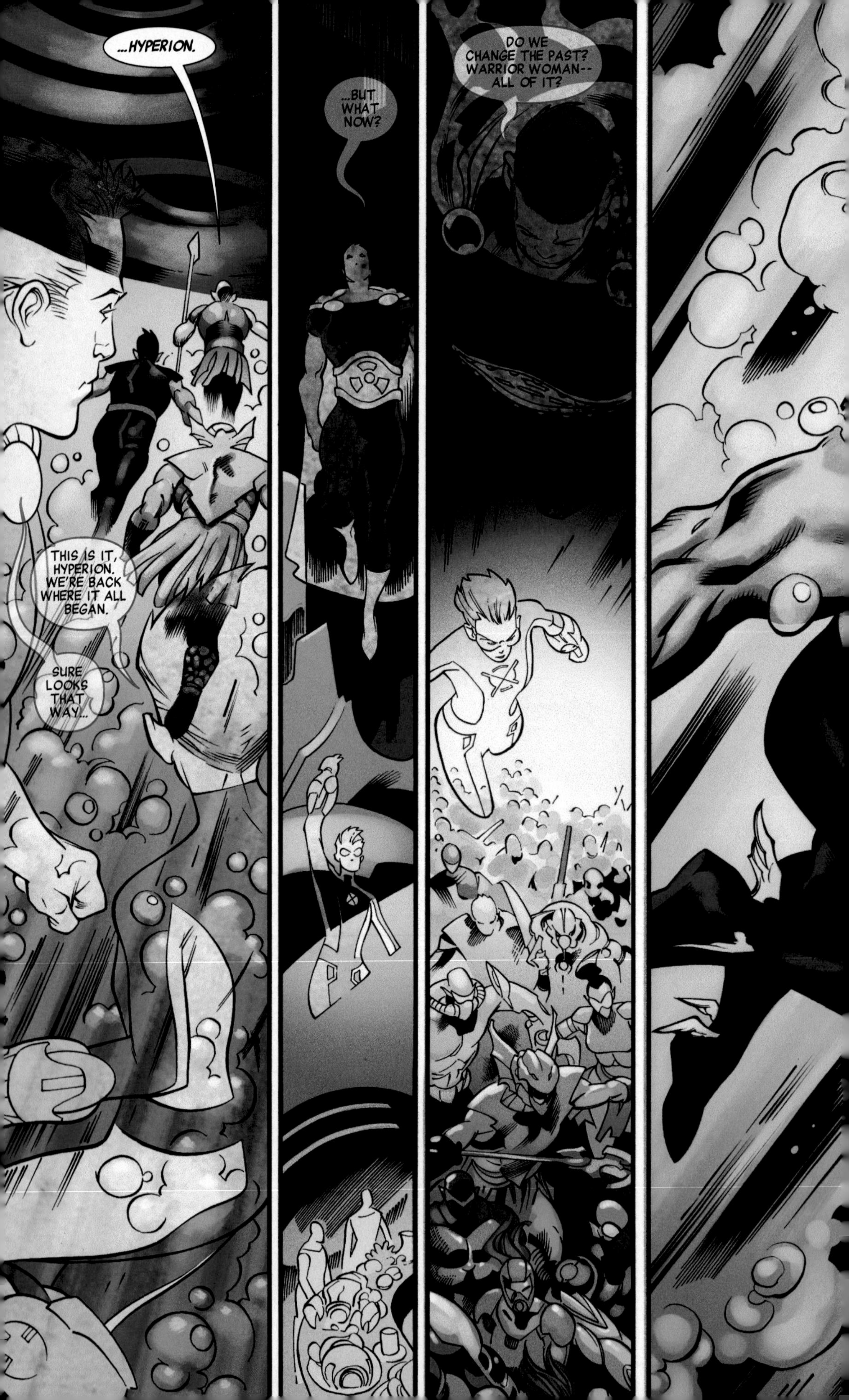
...HYPERION.
THIS IS IT, HYPERION. WE'RE BACK WHERE IT ALL BEGAN.
SURE LOOKS THAT WAY...
...BUT WHAT NOW?
DO WE CHANGE THE PAST? WARRIOR WOMAN-- ALL OF IT?

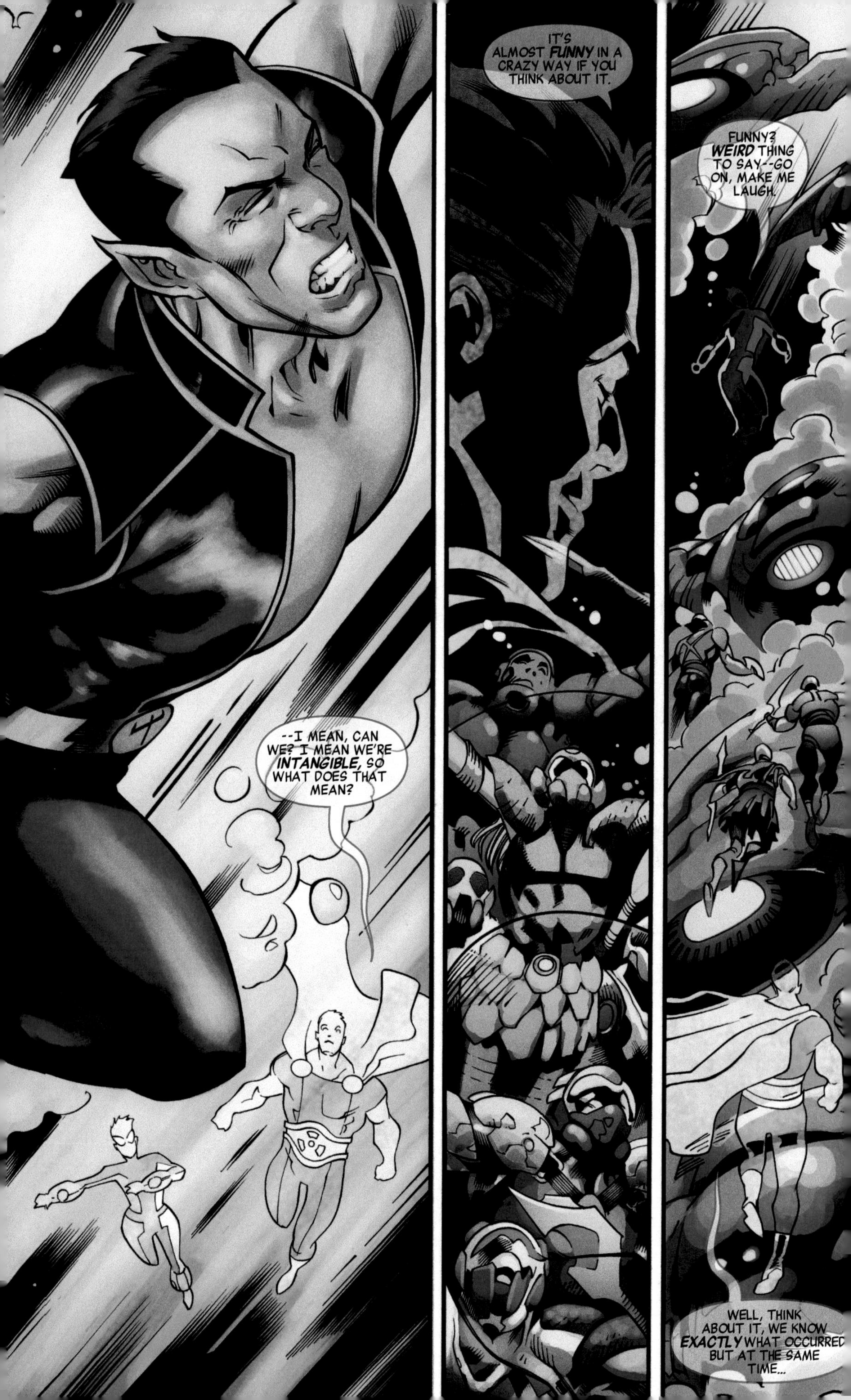
--I MEAN, CAN WE? I MEAN WE'RE INTANGIBLE, SO WHAT DOES THAT MEAN?
IT'S ALMOST FUNNY IN A CRAZY WAY IF YOU THINK ABOUT IT.
FUNNY? WEIRD THING TO SAY--GO ON, MAKE ME LAUGH.
WELL, THINK ABOUT IT, WE KNOW EXACTLY WHAT OCCURRED BUT AT THE SAME TIME...

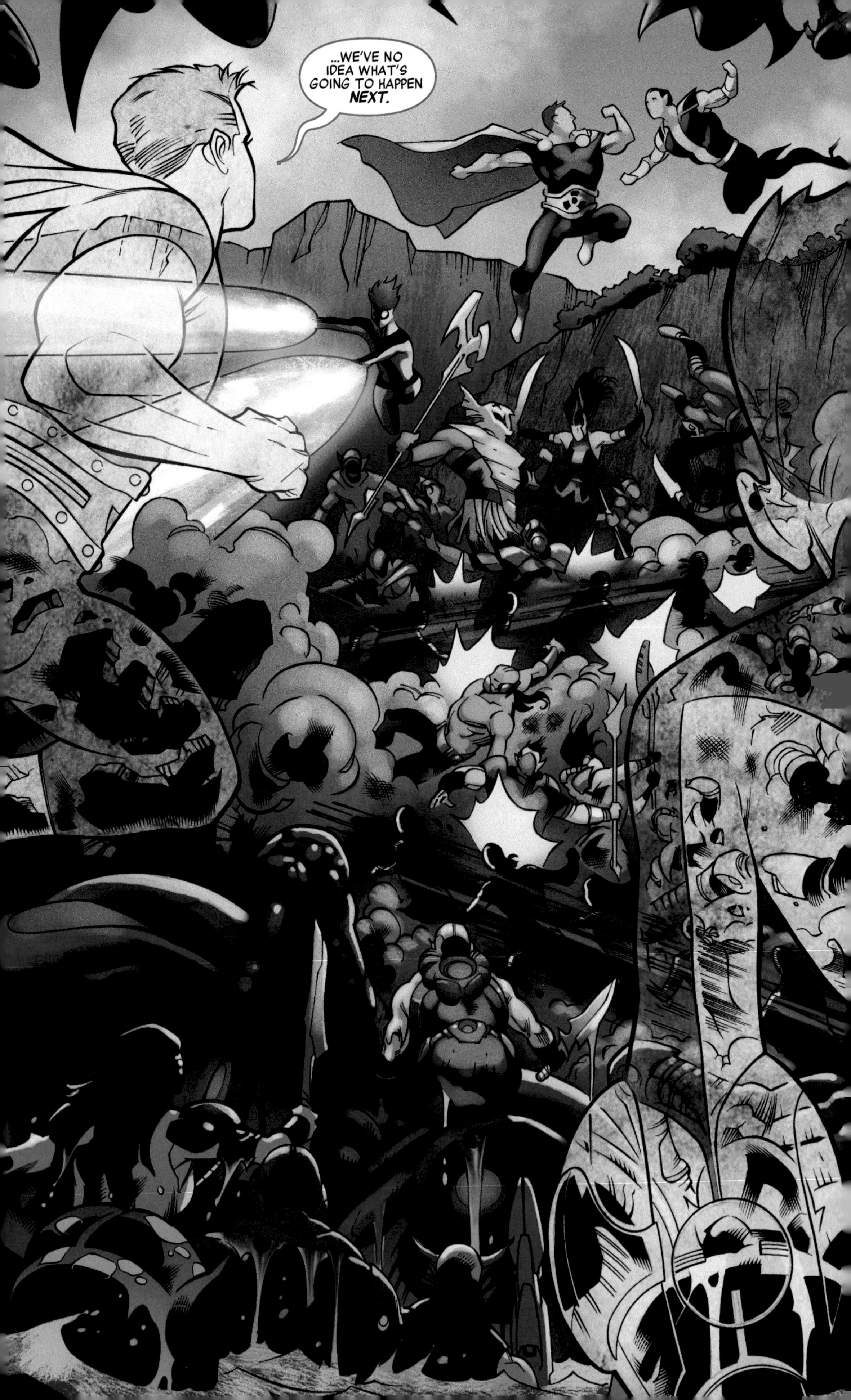
...WE'VE NO IDEA WHAT'S GOING TO HAPPEN **NEXT.**

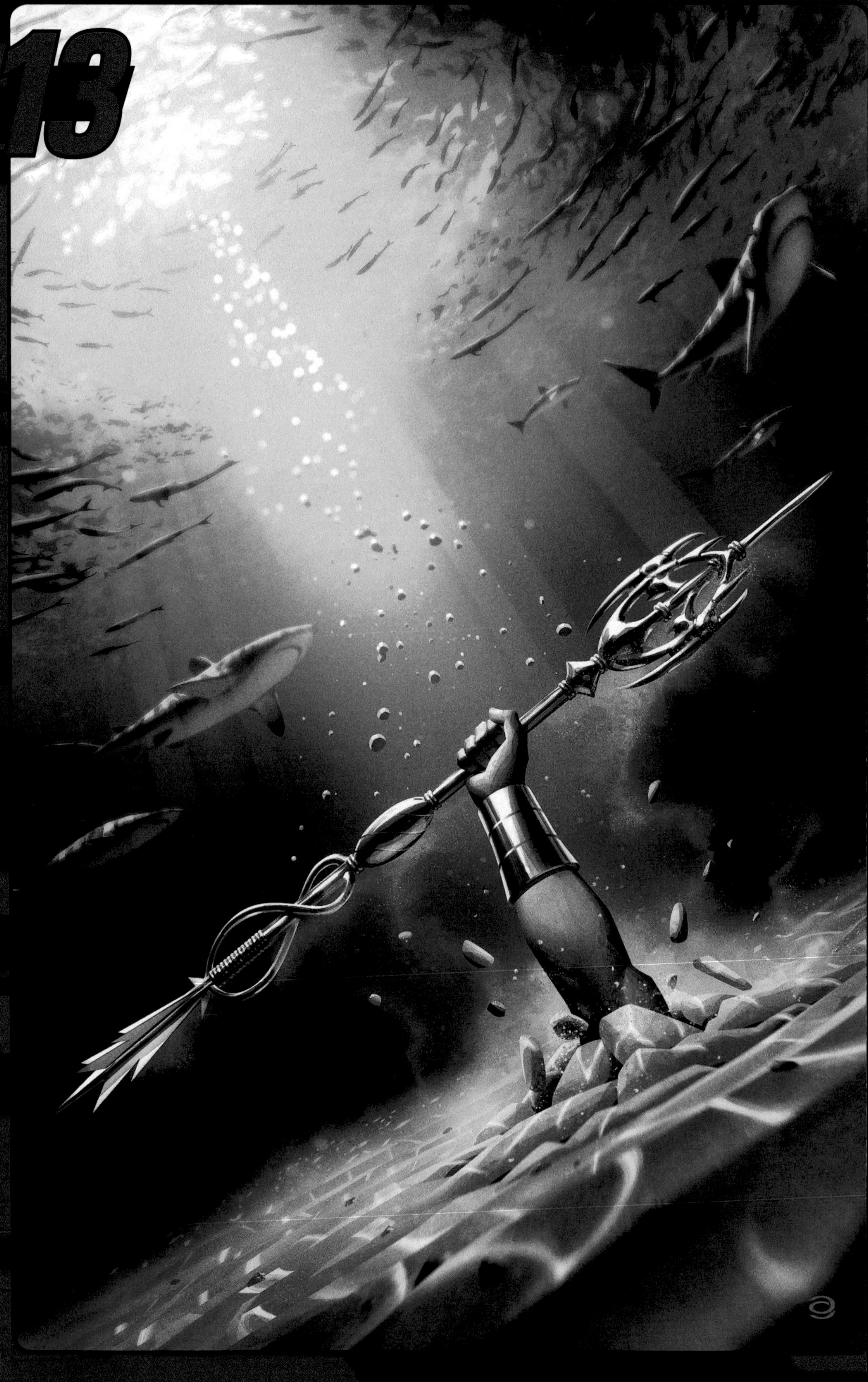
13

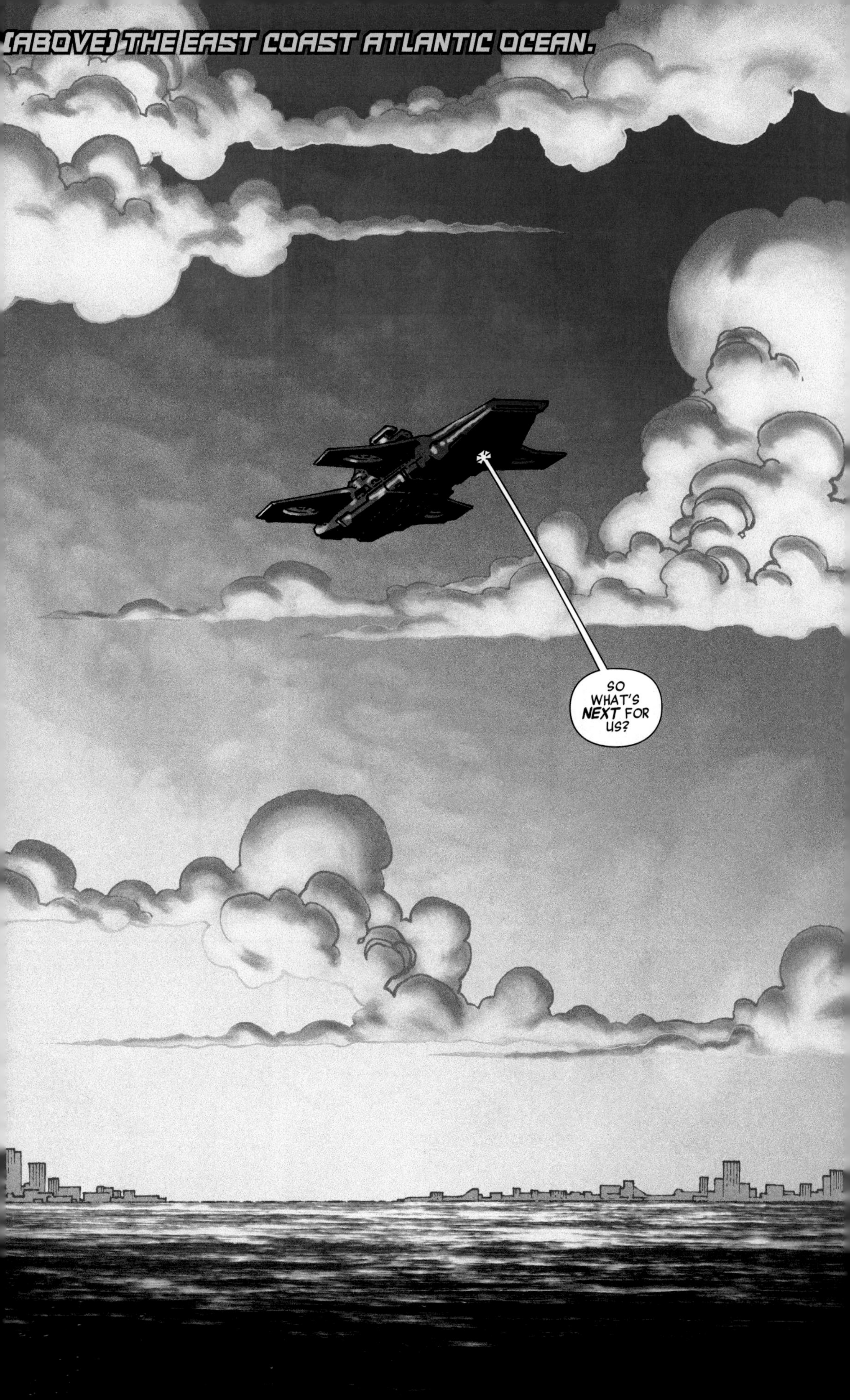
(ABOVE) THE EAST COAST ATLANTIC OCEAN.
SO WHAT'S NEXT FOR US?

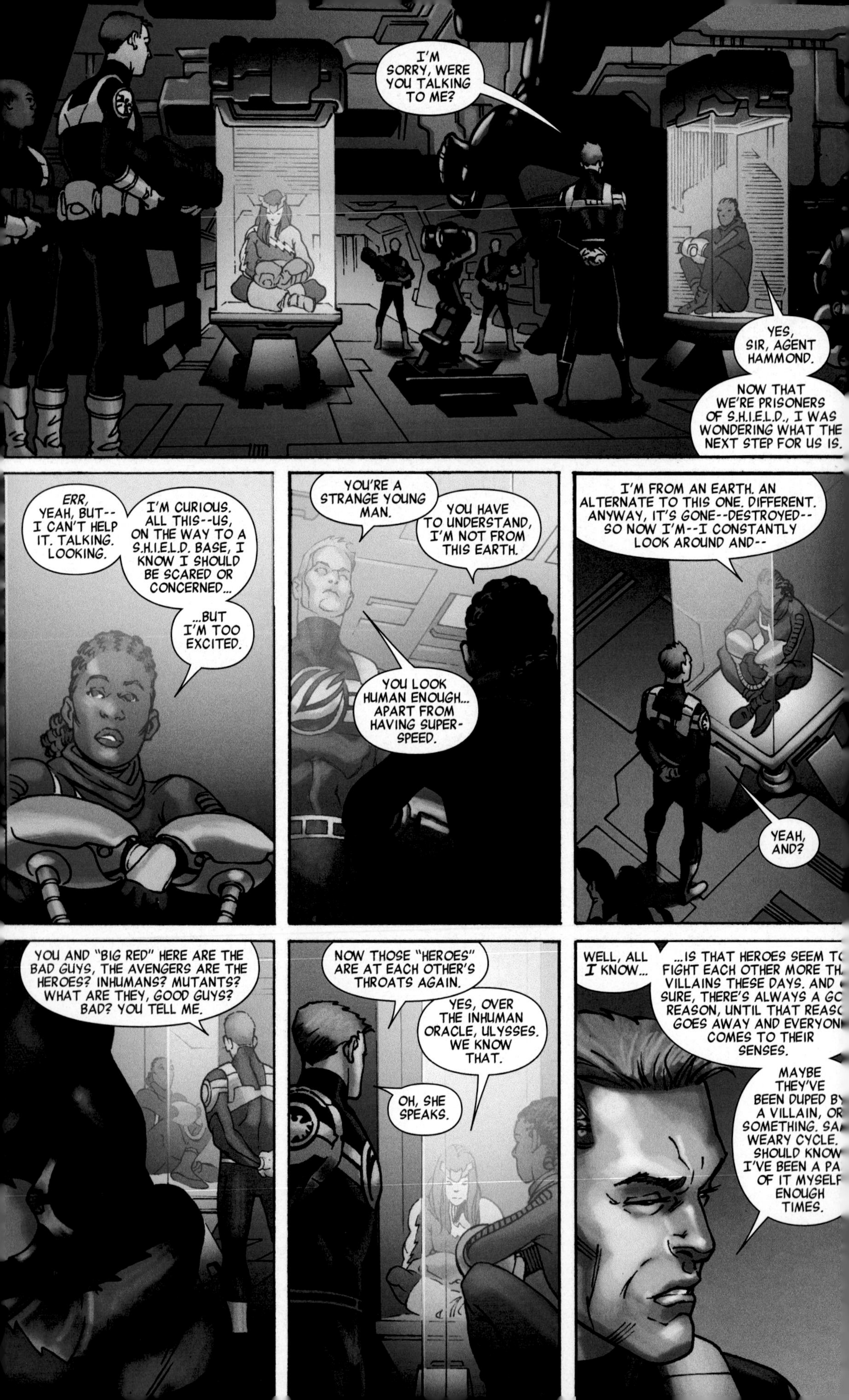

I'M SORRY, WERE YOU TALKING TO ME?
YES, SIR, AGENT HAMMOND.
NOW THAT WE'RE PRISONERS OF S.H.I.E.L.D., I WAS WONDERING WHAT THE NEXT STEP FOR US IS.
ERR, YEAH, BUT-- I CAN'T HELP IT. TALKING. LOOKING.
I'M CURIOUS. ALL THIS--US, ON THE WAY TO A S.H.I.E.L.D. BASE, I KNOW I SHOULD BE SCARED OR CONCERNED...
...BUT I'M TOO EXCITED.
YOU'RE A STRANGE YOUNG MAN.
YOU HAVE TO UNDERSTAND, I'M NOT FROM THIS EARTH.
YOU LOOK HUMAN ENOUGH... APART FROM HAVING SUPER-SPEED.
I'M FROM AN EARTH. AN ALTERNATE TO THIS ONE. DIFFERENT. ANYWAY, IT'S GONE--DESTROYED-- SO NOW I'M--I CONSTANTLY LOOK AROUND AND--
YEAH, AND?
YOU AND "BIG RED" HERE ARE THE BAD GUYS, THE AVENGERS ARE THE HEROES? INHUMANS? MUTANTS? WHAT ARE THEY, GOOD GUYS? BAD? YOU TELL ME.
NOW THOSE "HEROES" ARE AT EACH OTHER'S THROATS AGAIN.
YES, OVER THE INHUMAN ORACLE, ULYSSES. WE KNOW THAT.
OH, SHE SPEAKS.
WELL, ALL I KNOW...
...IS THAT HEROES SEEM T FIGHT EACH OTHER MORE TH VILLAINS THESE DAYS. AND SURE, THERE'S ALWAYS A G REASON, UNTIL THAT REAS GOES AWAY AND EVERYON COMES TO THEIR SENSES.
MAYBE THEY'VE BEEN DUPED BY A VILLAIN, OR SOMETHING. SA WEARY CYCLE. SHOULD KNOW I'VE BEEN A PA OF IT MYSELF ENOUGH TIMES.

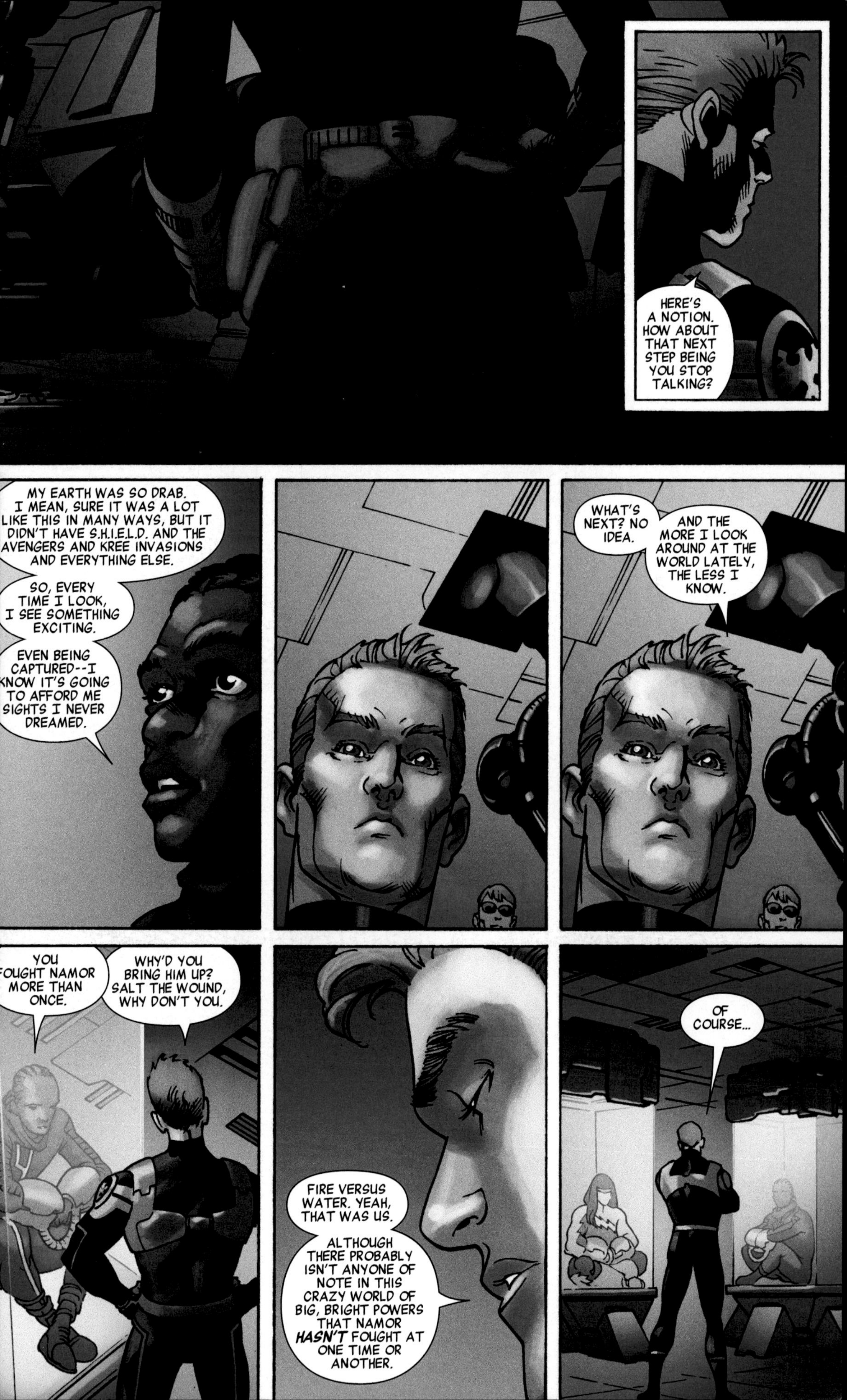
HERE'S A NOTION. HOW ABOUT THAT NEXT STEP BEING YOU STOP TALKING?
MY EARTH WAS SO DRAB. I MEAN, SURE IT WAS A LOT LIKE THIS IN MANY WAYS, BUT IT DIDN'T HAVE S.H.I.E.L.D. AND THE AVENGERS AND KREE INVASIONS AND EVERYTHING ELSE.
SO, EVERY TIME I LOOK, I SEE SOMETHING EXCITING.
EVEN BEING CAPTURED--I KNOW IT'S GOING TO AFFORD ME SIGHTS I NEVER DREAMED.
WHAT'S NEXT? NO IDEA.
AND THE MORE I LOOK AROUND AT THE WORLD LATELY, THE LESS I KNOW.
YOU FOUGHT NAMOR MORE THAN ONCE.
WHY'D YOU BRING HIM UP? SALT THE WOUND, WHY DON'T YOU.
FIRE VERSUS WATER. YEAH, THAT WAS US.
ALTHOUGH THERE PROBABLY ISN'T ANYONE OF NOTE IN THIS CRAZY WORLD OF BIG, BRIGHT POWERS THAT NAMOR ***HASN'T*** FOUGHT AT ONE TIME OR ANOTHER.
OF COURSE...

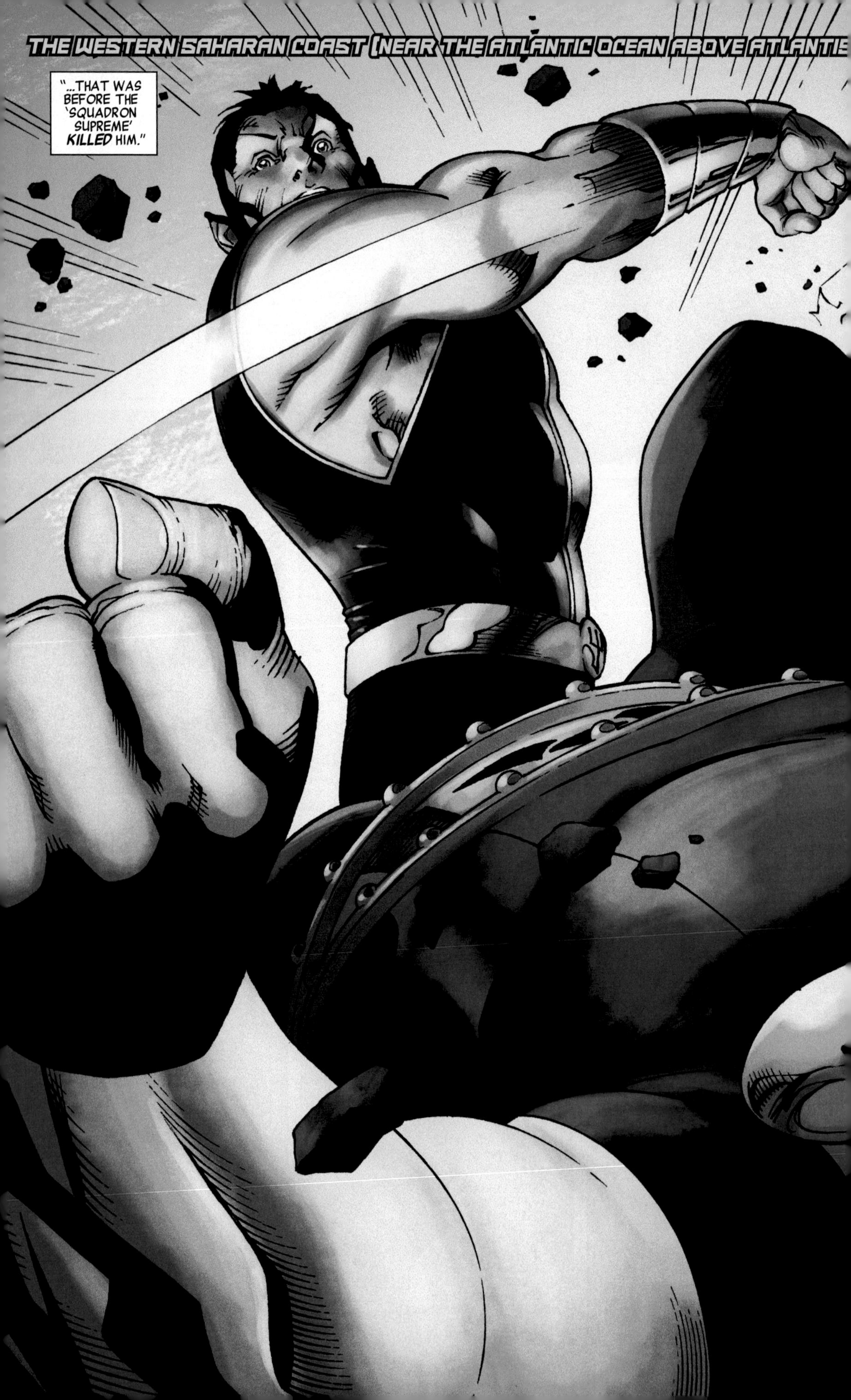
THE WESTERN SAHARAN COAST (NEAR THE ATLANTIC OCEAN ABOVE ATLANTIS
"...THAT WAS BEFORE THE 'SQUADRON SUPREME' KILLED HIM."

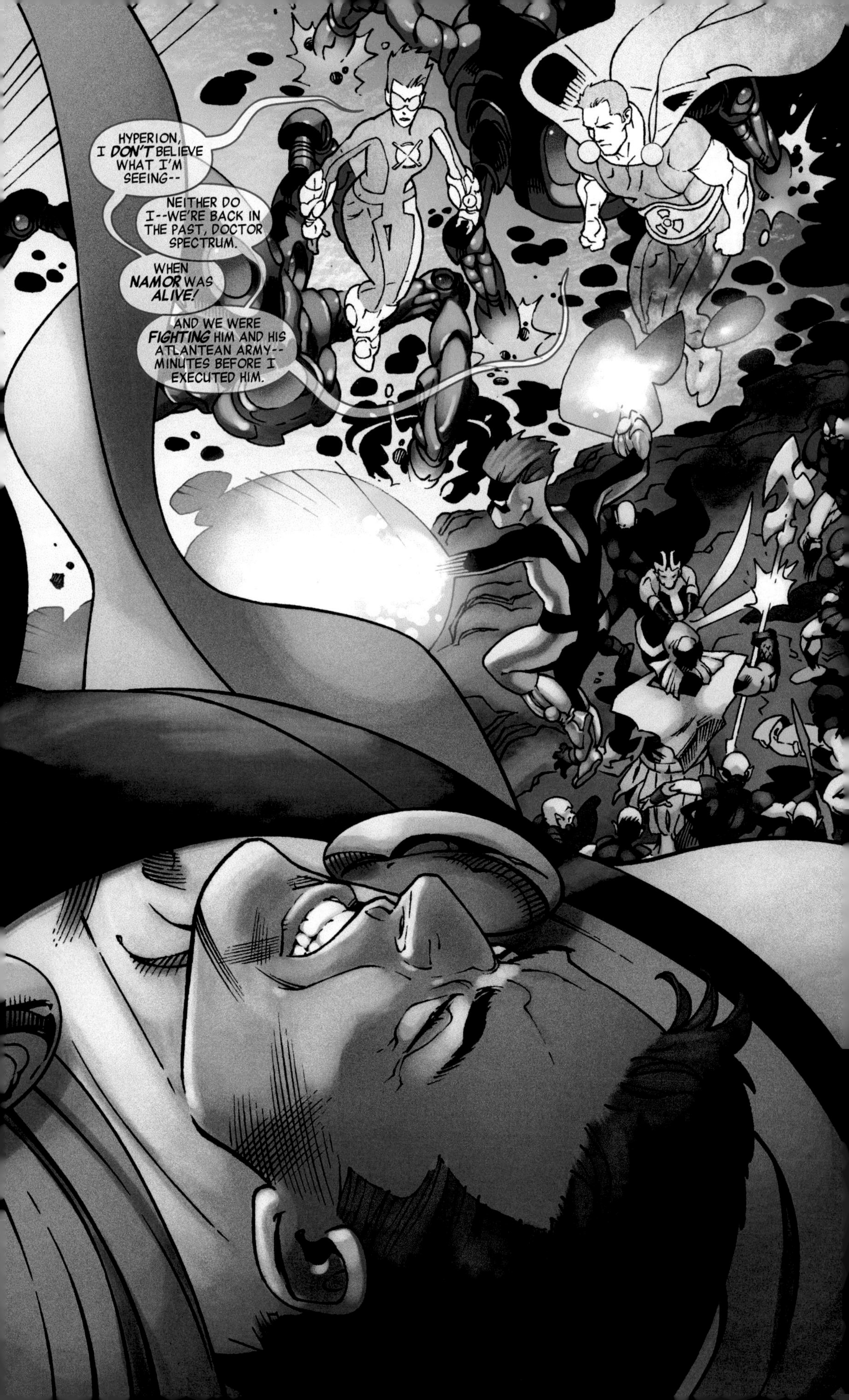
HYPERION, I DON'T BELIEVE WHAT I'M SEEING--
NEITHER DO I--WE'RE BACK IN THE PAST, DOCTOR SPECTRUM.
WHEN NAMOR WAS ALIVE!
AND WE WERE FIGHTING HIM AND HIS ATLANTEAN ARMY--MINUTES BEFORE I EXECUTED HIM.

I HAVE SO MANY QUESTIONS, DOCTOR SPECTRUM.

THEN IT'S LUCKY FOR BOTH OF US THAT I HAVE SOME OF THE ANSWERS...THANKS TO MODRED.

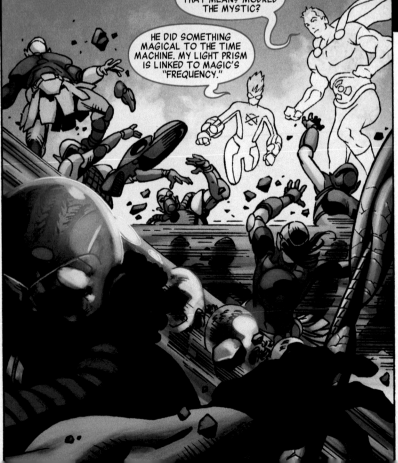

WHAT DOES THAT MEAN? MODRED THE MYSTIC?

HE DID SOMETHING MAGICAL TO THE TIME MACHINE. MY LIGHT PRISM IS LINKED TO MAGIC'S "FREQUENCY."

YOU REMEMBER IN WEIRDWORLD, HOW I WAS ABLE TO UNDERSTAND MAGIC--TRANSLATE IT, I GUESS IS A BETTER WAY TO SAY IT.

NOW THAT WE'RE HERE UNDER THE BLANKET OF MODRED'S SPELL, I UNDERSTAND EVERYTHING.

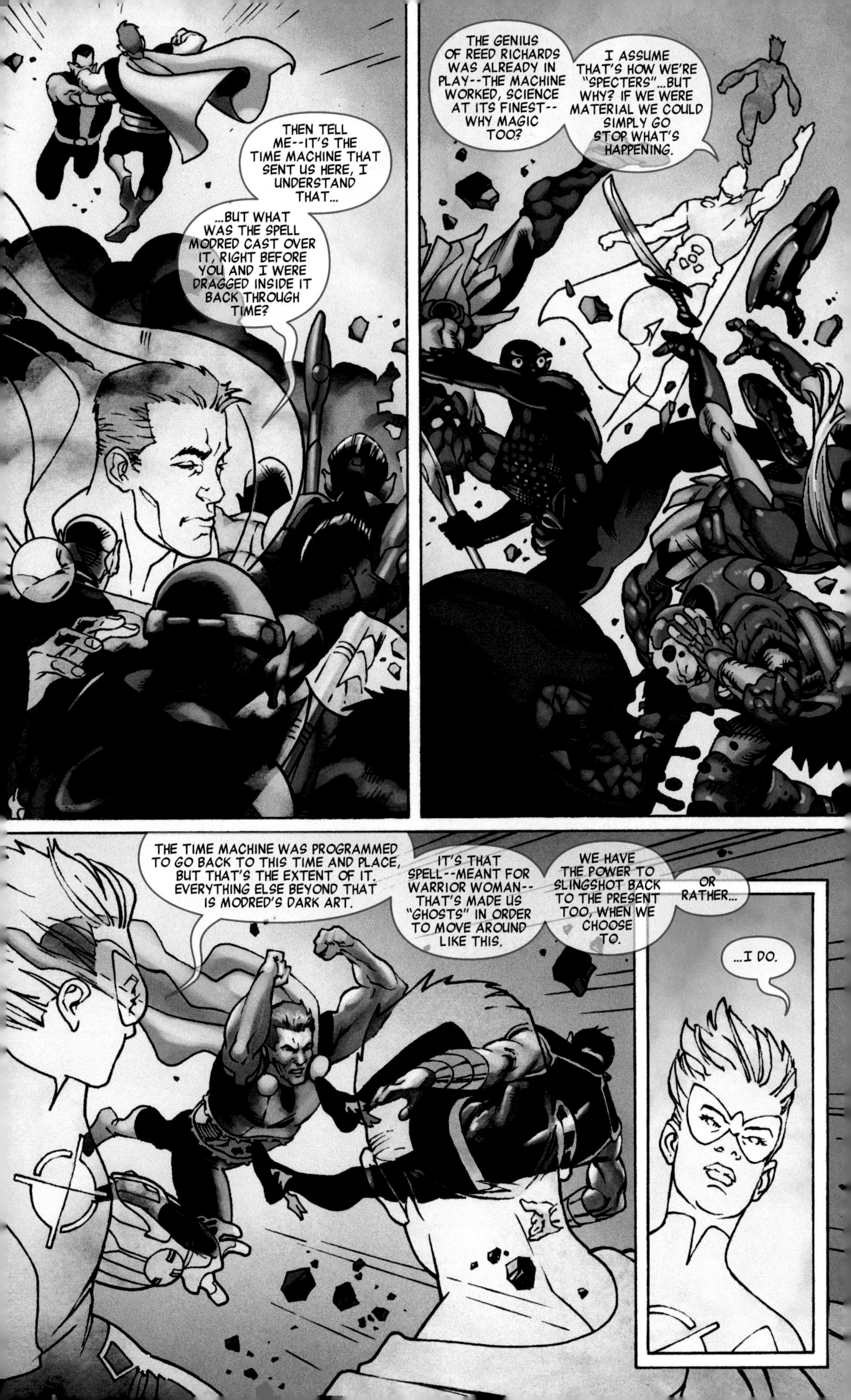
THEN TELL ME--IT'S THE TIME MACHINE THAT SENT US HERE, I UNDERSTAND THAT...
...BUT WHAT WAS THE SPELL MODRED CAST OVER IT, RIGHT BEFORE YOU AND I WERE DRAGGED INSIDE IT BACK THROUGH TIME?
THE GENIUS OF REED RICHARDS WAS ALREADY IN PLAY--THE MACHINE WORKED, SCIENCE AT ITS FINEST--WHY MAGIC TOO?
I ASSUME THAT'S HOW WE'RE "SPECTERS"...BUT WHY? IF WE WERE MATERIAL WE COULD SIMPLY GO STOP WHAT'S HAPPENING.
THE TIME MACHINE WAS PROGRAMMED TO GO BACK TO THIS TIME AND PLACE, BUT THAT'S THE EXTENT OF IT. EVERYTHING ELSE BEYOND THAT IS MODRED'S DARK ART.
IT'S THAT SPELL--MEANT FOR WARRIOR WOMAN--THAT'S MADE US "GHOSTS" IN ORDER TO MOVE AROUND LIKE THIS.
WE HAVE THE POWER TO SLINGSHOT BACK TO THE PRESENT TOO, WHEN WE CHOOSE TO.
OR RATHER...
...I DO.

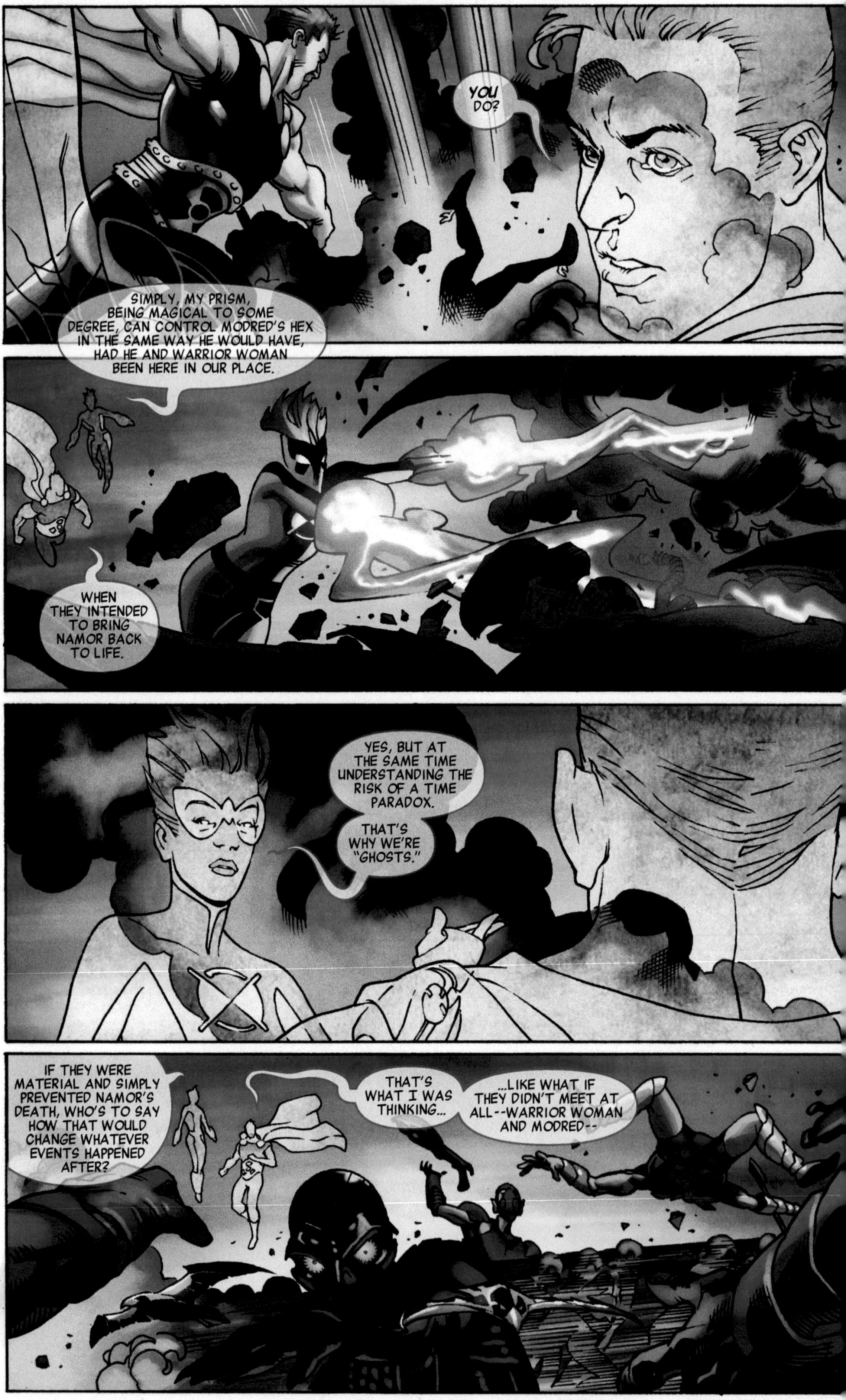
YOU DO?
SIMPLY, MY PRISM, BEING MAGICAL TO SOME DEGREE, CAN CONTROL MODRED'S HEX IN THE SAME WAY HE WOULD HAVE, HAD HE AND WARRIOR WOMAN BEEN HERE IN OUR PLACE.
WHEN THEY INTENDED TO BRING NAMOR BACK TO LIFE.
YES, BUT AT THE SAME TIME UNDERSTANDING THE RISK OF A TIME PARADOX.
THAT'S WHY WE'RE "GHOSTS."
IF THEY WERE MATERIAL AND SIMPLY PREVENTED NAMOR'S DEATH, WHO'S TO SAY HOW THAT WOULD CHANGE WHATEVER EVENTS HAPPENED AFTER?
THAT'S WHAT I WAS THINKING...
...LIKE WHAT IF THEY DIDN'T MEET AT ALL--WARRIOR WOMAN AND MODRED--

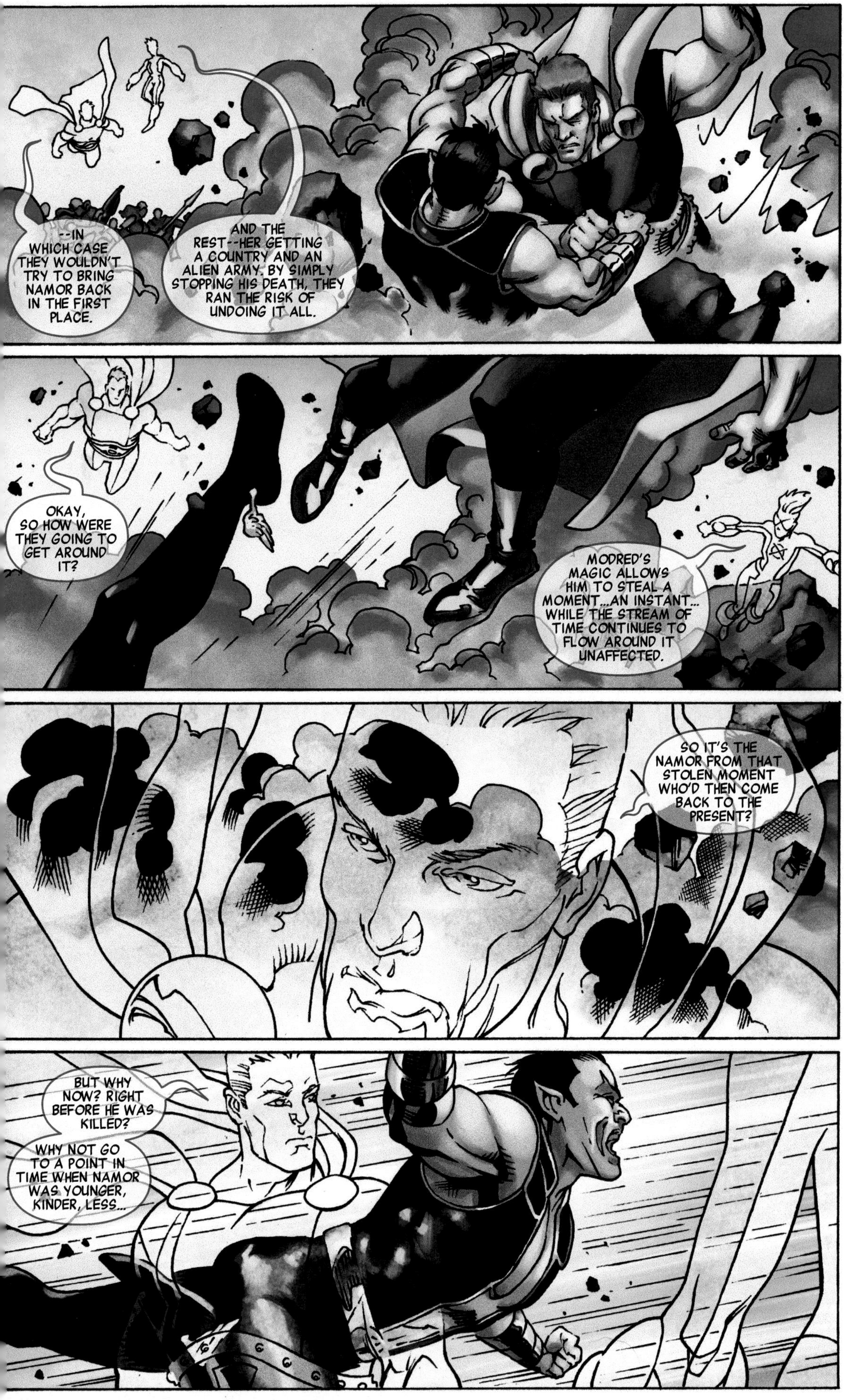
--IN WHICH CASE THEY WOULDN'T TRY TO BRING NAMOR BACK IN THE FIRST PLACE.
AND THE REST--HER GETTING A COUNTRY AND AN ALIEN ARMY. BY SIMPLY STOPPING HIS DEATH, THEY RAN THE RISK OF UNDOING IT ALL.
OKAY, SO HOW WERE THEY GOING TO GET AROUND IT?
MODRED'S MAGIC ALLOWS HIM TO STEAL A MOMENT...AN INSTANT... WHILE THE STREAM OF TIME CONTINUES TO FLOW AROUND IT UNAFFECTED.
SO IT'S THE NAMOR FROM THAT STOLEN MOMENT WHO'D THEN COME BACK TO THE PRESENT?
BUT WHY NOW? RIGHT BEFORE HE WAS KILLED?
WHY NOT GO TO A POINT IN TIME WHEN NAMOR WAS YOUNGER, KINDER, LESS...

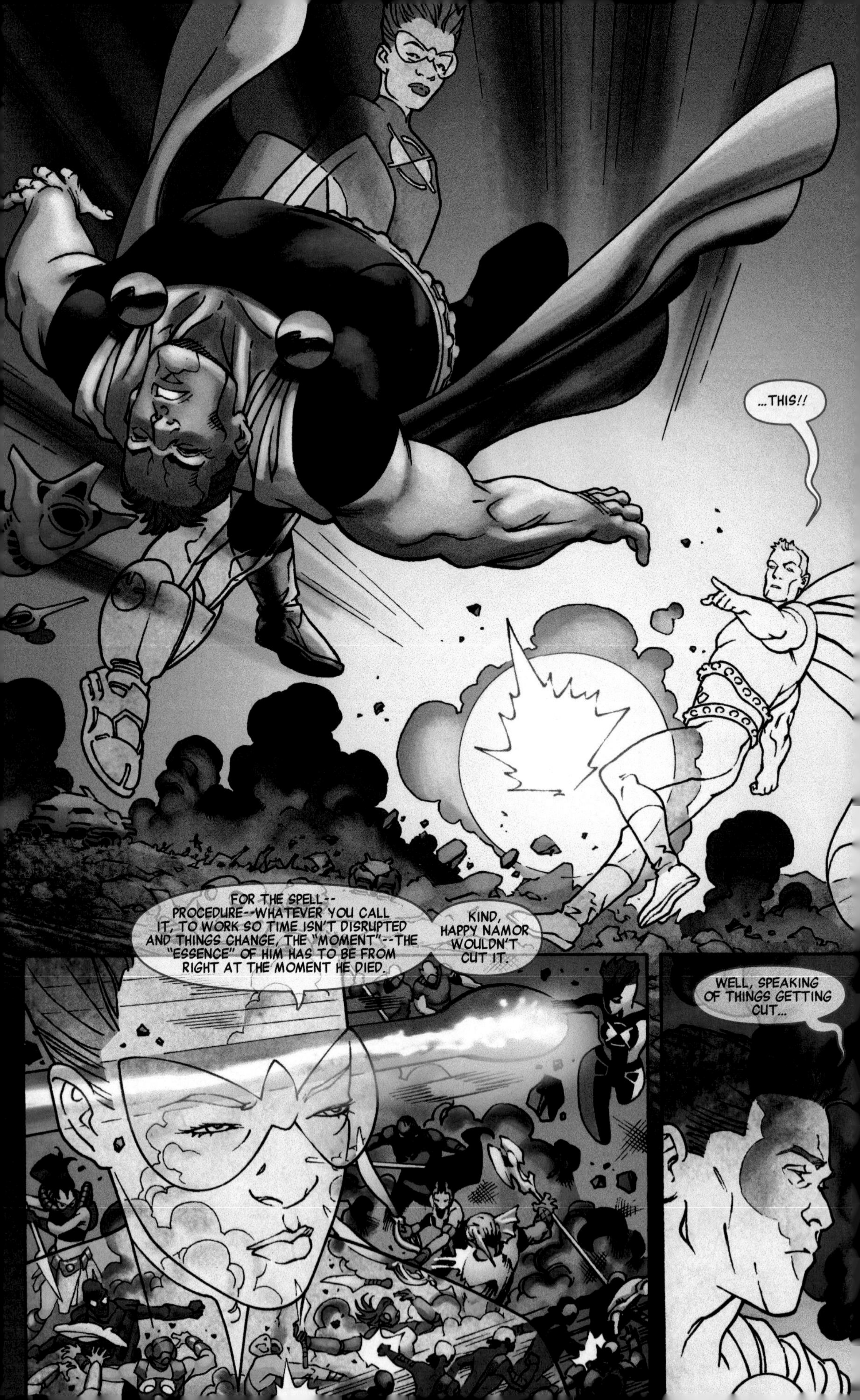
...THIS!!
FOR THE SPELL-- PROCEDURE--WHATEVER YOU CALL IT, TO WORK SO TIME ISN'T DISRUPTED AND THINGS CHANGE, THE "MOMENT"--THE "ESSENCE" OF HIM HAS TO BE FROM RIGHT AT THE MOMENT HE DIED.
KIND, HAPPY NAMOR WOULDN'T CUT IT.
WELL, SPEAKING OF THINGS GETTING CUT...

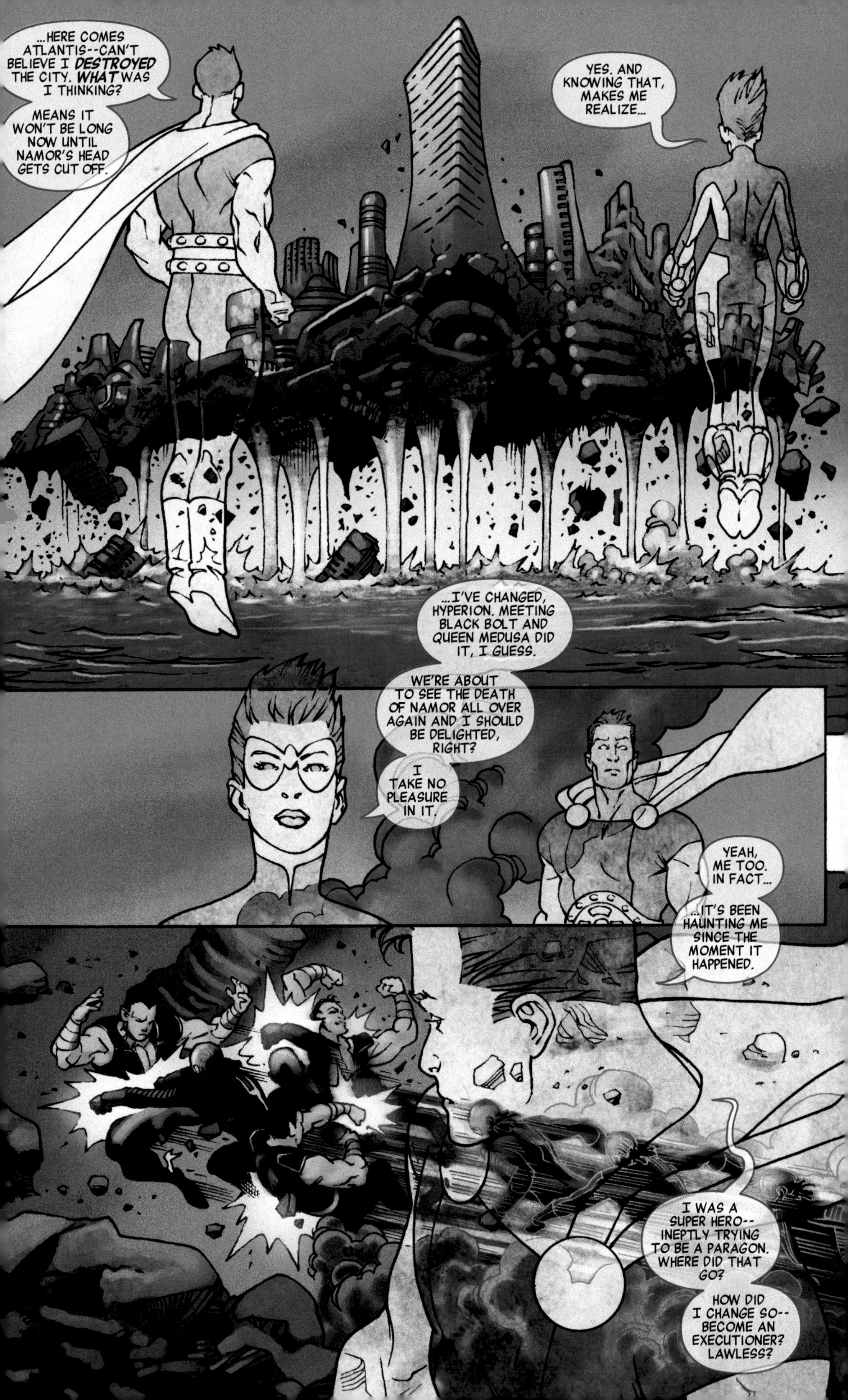

...HERE COMES ATLANTIS--CAN'T BELIEVE I DESTROYED THE CITY. WHAT WAS I THINKING?
MEANS IT WON'T BE LONG NOW UNTIL NAMOR'S HEAD GETS CUT OFF.
YES. AND KNOWING THAT, MAKES ME REALIZE...
...I'VE CHANGED, HYPERION. MEETING BLACK BOLT AND QUEEN MEDUSA DID IT, I GUESS.
WE'RE ABOUT TO SEE THE DEATH OF NAMOR ALL OVER AGAIN AND I SHOULD BE DELIGHTED, RIGHT?
I TAKE NO PLEASURE IN IT.
YEAH, ME TOO. IN FACT...
...IT'S BEEN HAUNTING ME SINCE THE MOMENT IT HAPPENED.
I WAS A SUPER HERO--INEPTLY TRYING TO BE A PARAGON. WHERE DID THAT GO?
HOW DID I CHANGE SO--BECOME AN EXECUTIONER? LAWLESS?

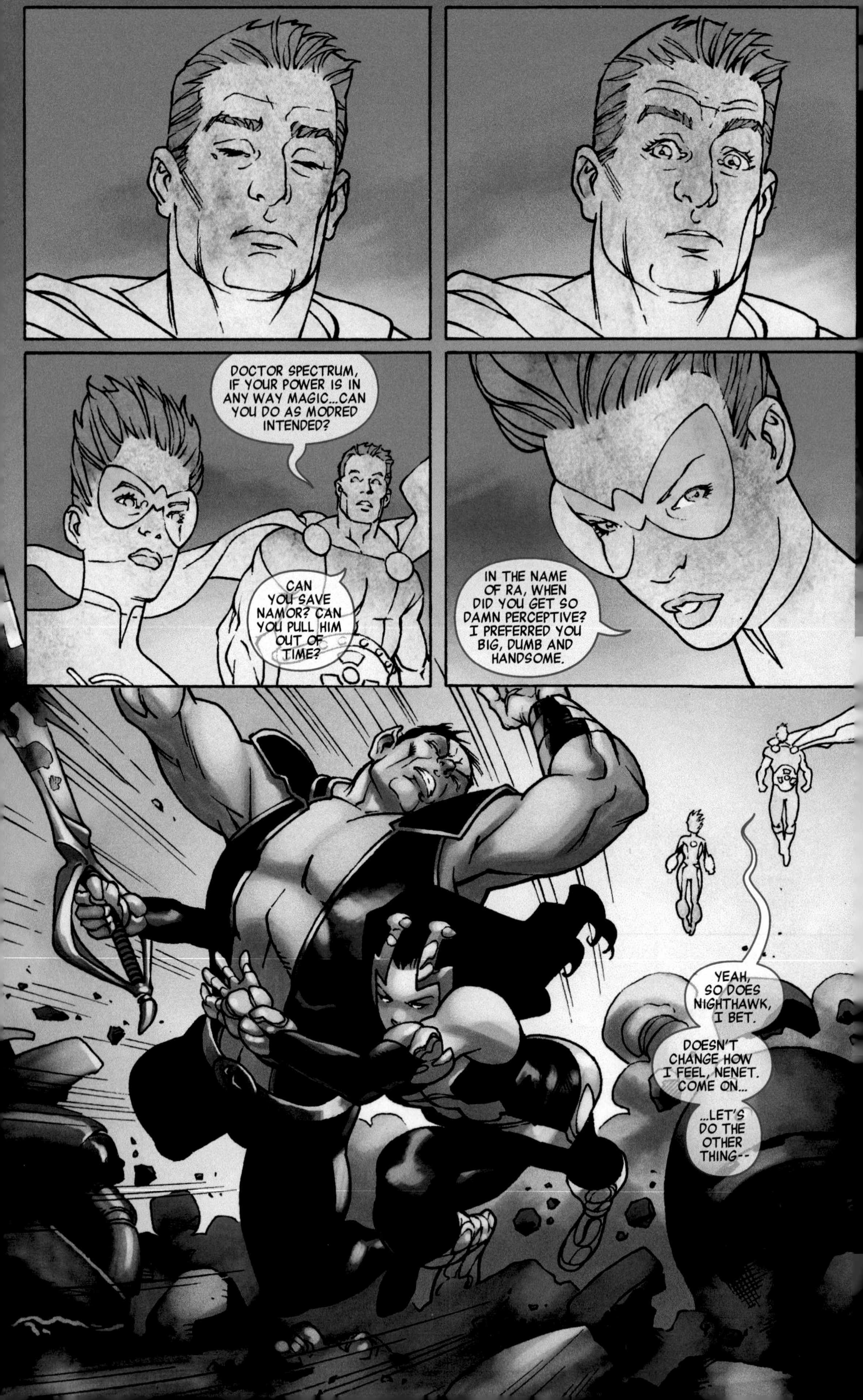
DOCTOR SPECTRUM, IF YOUR POWER IS IN ANY WAY MAGIC...CAN YOU DO AS MODRED INTENDED?
CAN YOU SAVE NAMOR? CAN YOU PULL HIM OUT OF TIME?
IN THE NAME OF RA, WHEN DID YOU GET SO DAMN PERCEPTIVE? I PREFERRED YOU BIG, DUMB AND HANDSOME.
YEAH, SO DOES NIGHTHAWK, I BET.
DOESN'T CHANGE HOW I FEEL, NENET. COME ON...
...LET'S DO THE OTHER THING--

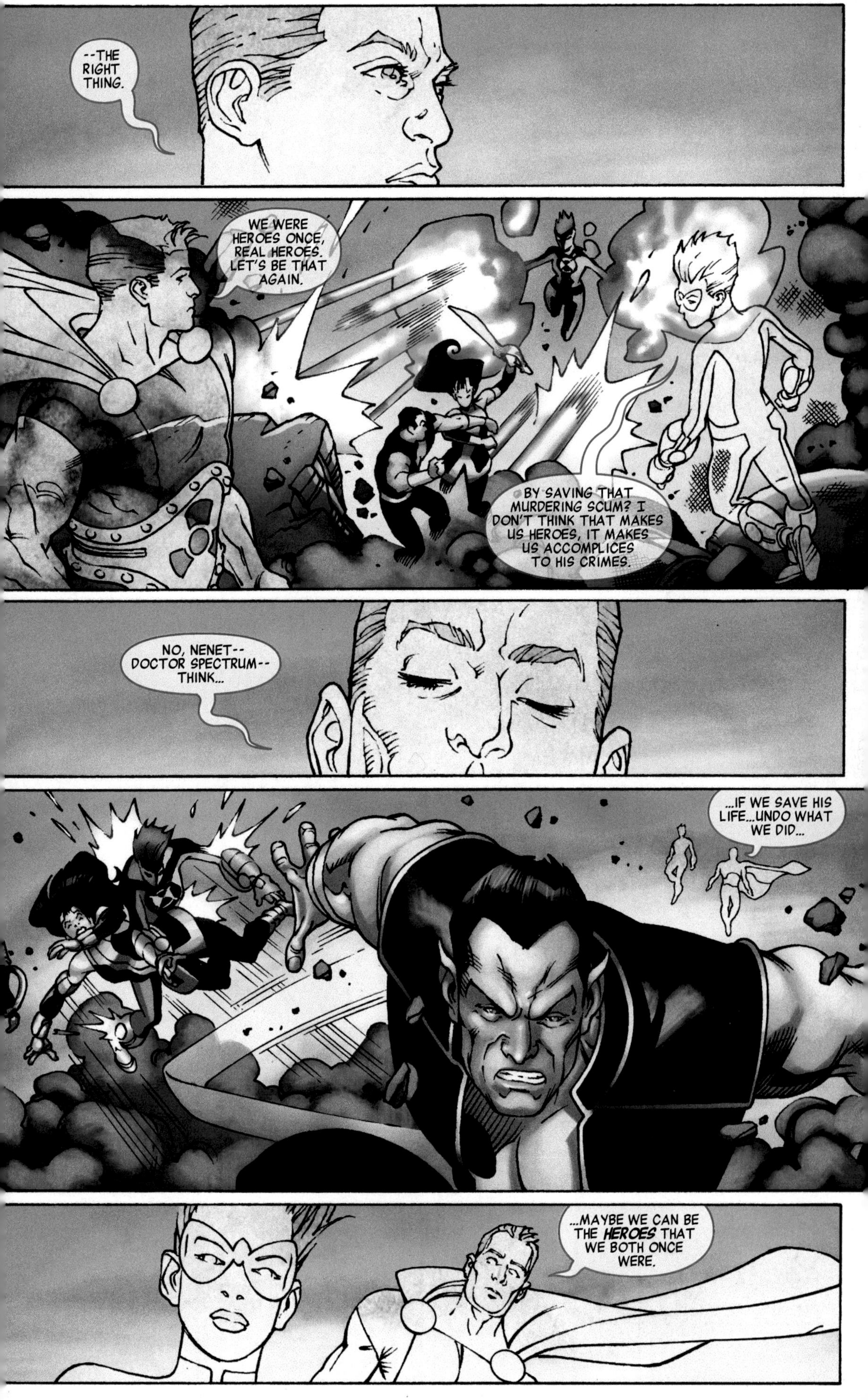
--THE RIGHT THING.
WE WERE HEROES ONCE, REAL HEROES. LET'S BE THAT AGAIN.
BY SAVING THAT MURDERING SCUM? I DON'T THINK THAT MAKES US HEROES, IT MAKES US ACCOMPLICES TO HIS CRIMES.
NO, NENET--DOCTOR SPECTRUM--THINK...
...IF WE SAVE HIS LIFE...UNDO WHAT WE DID...
...MAYBE WE CAN BE THE HEROES THAT WE BOTH ONCE WERE.

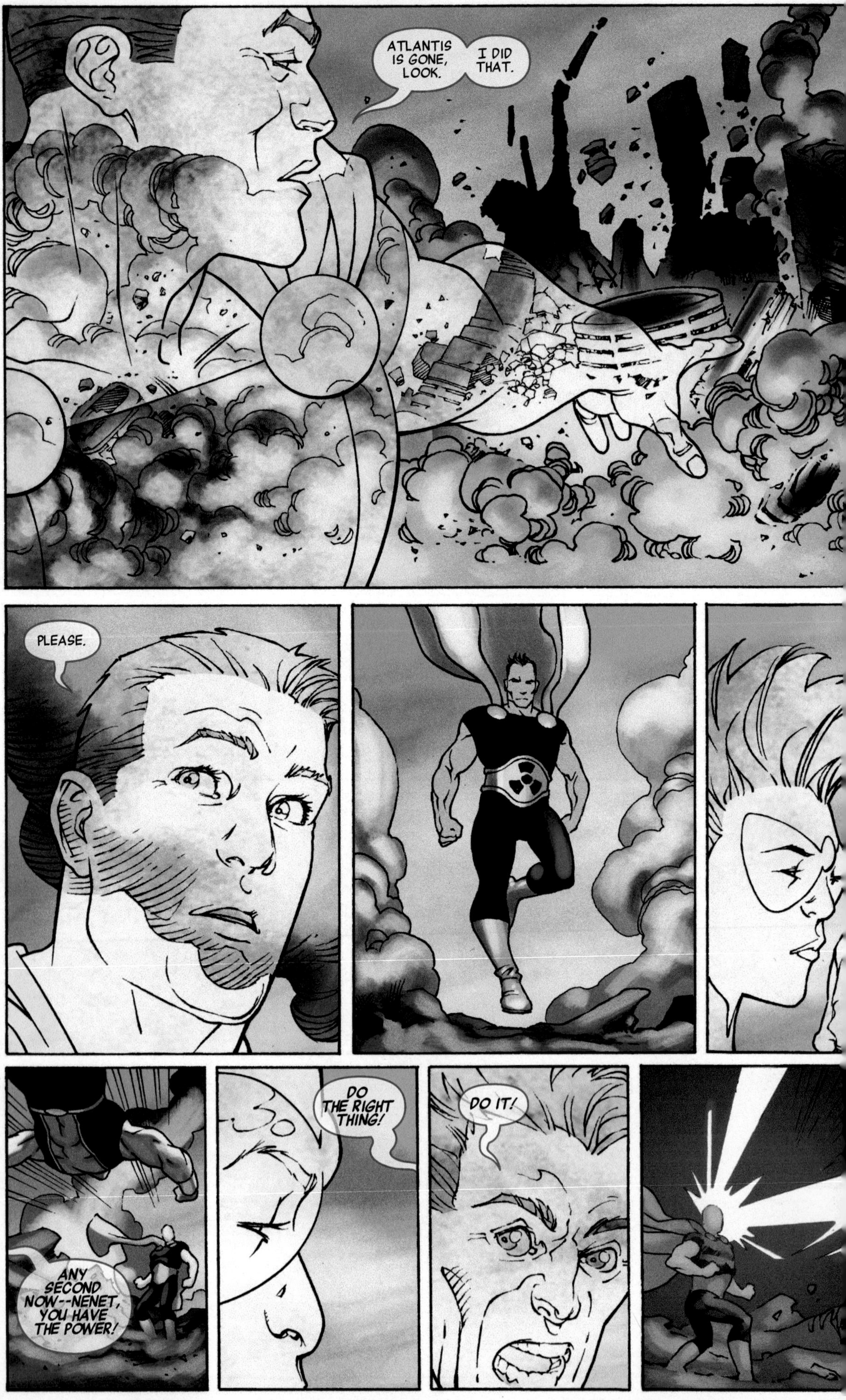
ATLANTIS IS GONE, LOOK.
I DID THAT.
PLEASE.
DO THE RIGHT THING!
DO IT!
ANY SECOND NOW--NENET, YOU HAVE THE POWER!

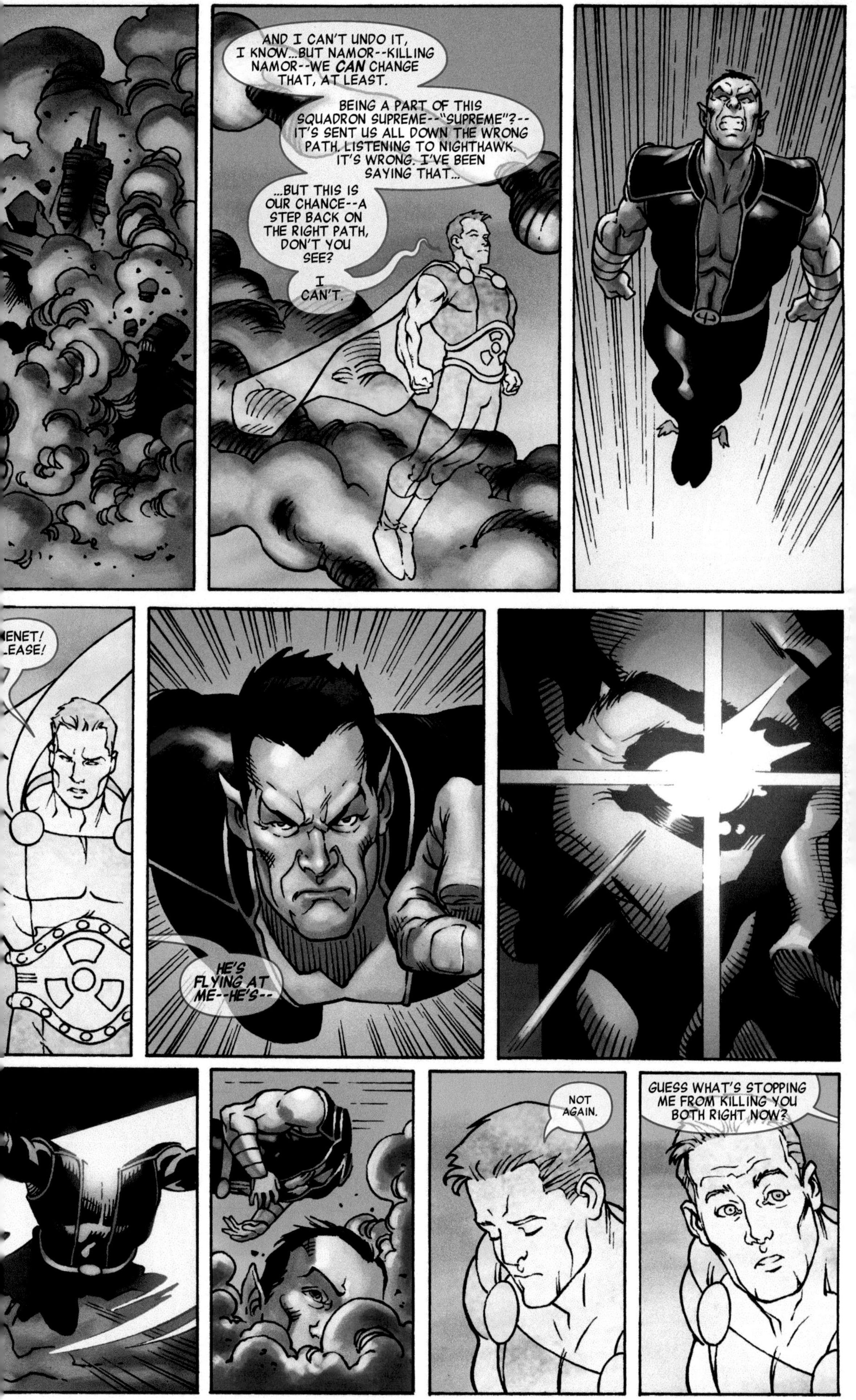
AND I CAN'T UNDO IT, I KNOW...BUT NAMOR--KILLING NAMOR--WE CAN CHANGE THAT, AT LEAST.
BEING A PART OF THIS SQUADRON SUPREME--"SUPREME"?--IT'S SENT US ALL DOWN THE WRONG PATH. LISTENING TO NIGHTHAWK. IT'S WRONG. I'VE BEEN SAYING THAT...
...BUT THIS IS OUR CHANCE--A STEP BACK ON THE RIGHT PATH, DON'T YOU SEE?
I CAN'T.
HE'S FLYING AT ME--HE'S--
NOT AGAIN.
GUESS WHAT'S STOPPING ME FROM KILLING YOU BOTH RIGHT NOW?

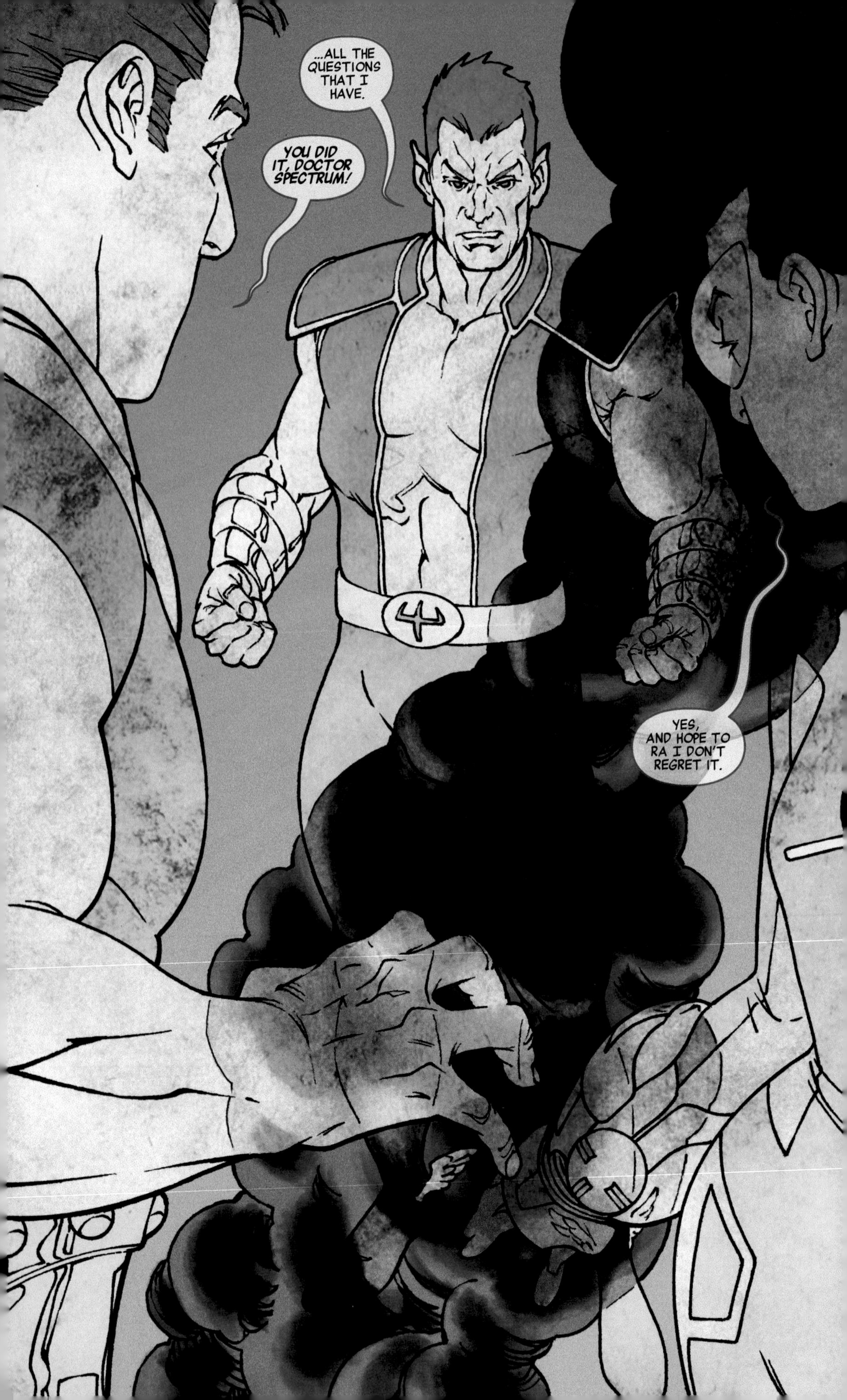
...ALL THE QUESTIONS THAT I HAVE.
YOU DID IT, DOCTOR SPECTRUM!
YES, AND HOPE TO RA I DON'T REGRET IT.

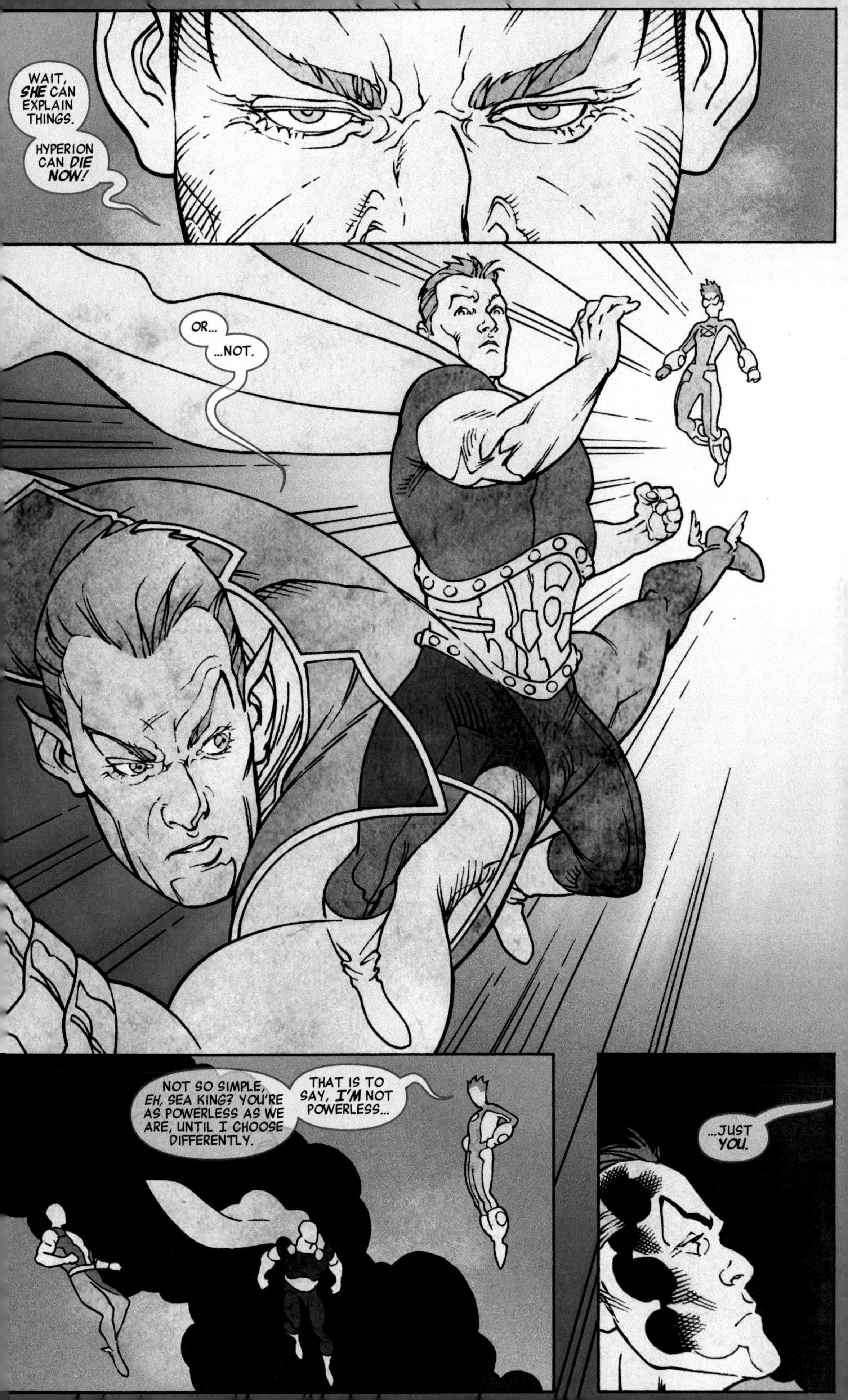
WAIT, SHE CAN EXPLAIN THINGS.
HYPERION CAN DIE NOW!
OR...
...NOT.
NOT SO SIMPLE, EH, SEA KING? YOU'RE AS POWERLESS AS WE ARE, UNTIL I CHOOSE DIFFERENTLY.
THAT IS TO SAY, I'M NOT POWERLESS...
...JUST YOU.

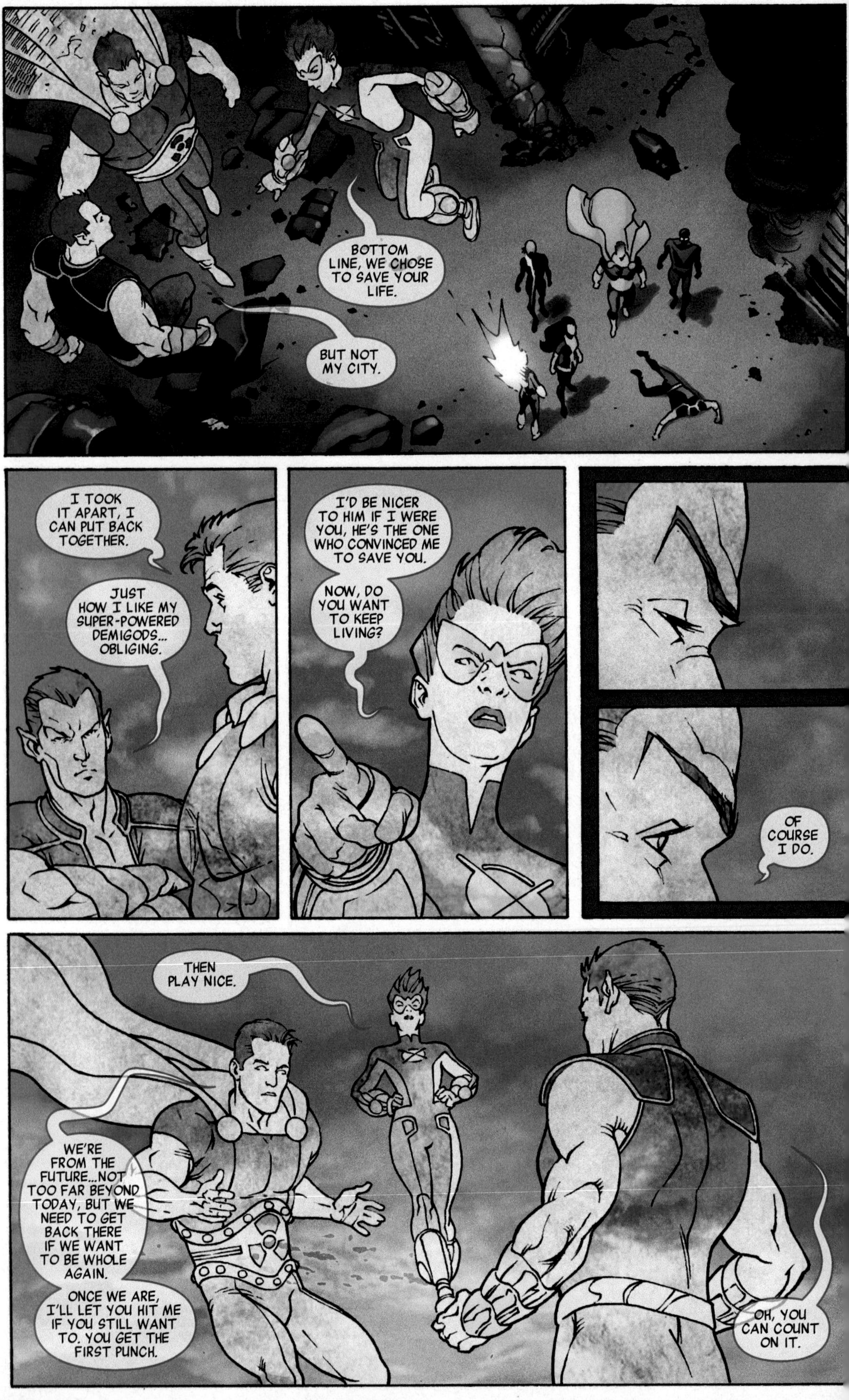
BOTTOM LINE, WE CHOSE TO SAVE YOUR LIFE.
BUT NOT MY CITY.
I TOOK IT APART, I CAN PUT BACK TOGETHER.
JUST HOW I LIKE MY SUPER-POWERED DEMIGODS... OBLIGING.
I'D BE NICER TO HIM IF I WERE YOU, HE'S THE ONE WHO CONVINCED ME TO SAVE YOU.
NOW, DO YOU WANT TO KEEP LIVING?
OF COURSE I DO.
THEN PLAY NICE.
WE'RE FROM THE FUTURE...NOT TOO FAR BEYOND TODAY, BUT WE NEED TO GET BACK THERE IF WE WANT TO BE WHOLE AGAIN.
ONCE WE ARE, I'LL LET YOU HIT ME IF YOU STILL WANT TO. YOU GET THE FIRST PUNCH.
OH, YOU CAN COUNT ON IT.

YOUNG LADY, THAT'S YOU IN THE PAST--MY PRESENT--DOWN THERE, RIGHT?

ERR. WHY?

DID YOU JUST KICK MY SEVERED HEAD?

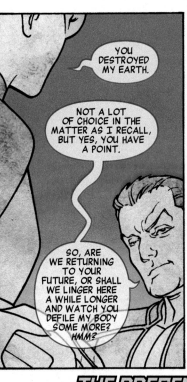

YOU DESTROYED MY EARTH.

NOT A LOT OF CHOICE IN THE MATTER AS I RECALL, BUT YES, YOU HAVE A POINT.

SO, ARE WE RETURNING TO YOUR FUTURE, OR SHALL WE LINGER HERE A WHILE LONGER AND WATCH YOU DEFILE MY BODY SOME MORE? HMM?

LET'S GO, DOCTOR SPECTRUM... YOU'RE SURE YOU KNOW HOW TO GET US BACK?

I THINK SO.

THOUGH, SET ONLY KNOWS WHAT AWAITS US WHEN WE GET THERE.

YEAH...

THE PRESENT.

"...WE HAVE TWO TEAMMATES CAPTURED, WARRIOR WOMAN'S GOD KNOWS WHERE. SAME FOR POWER PRINCESS..."

"AND THEN THERE'S *NIGHTHAWK*--

"--HOPEFULLY ALREADY TRYING TO *FREE* THE TEAM..."

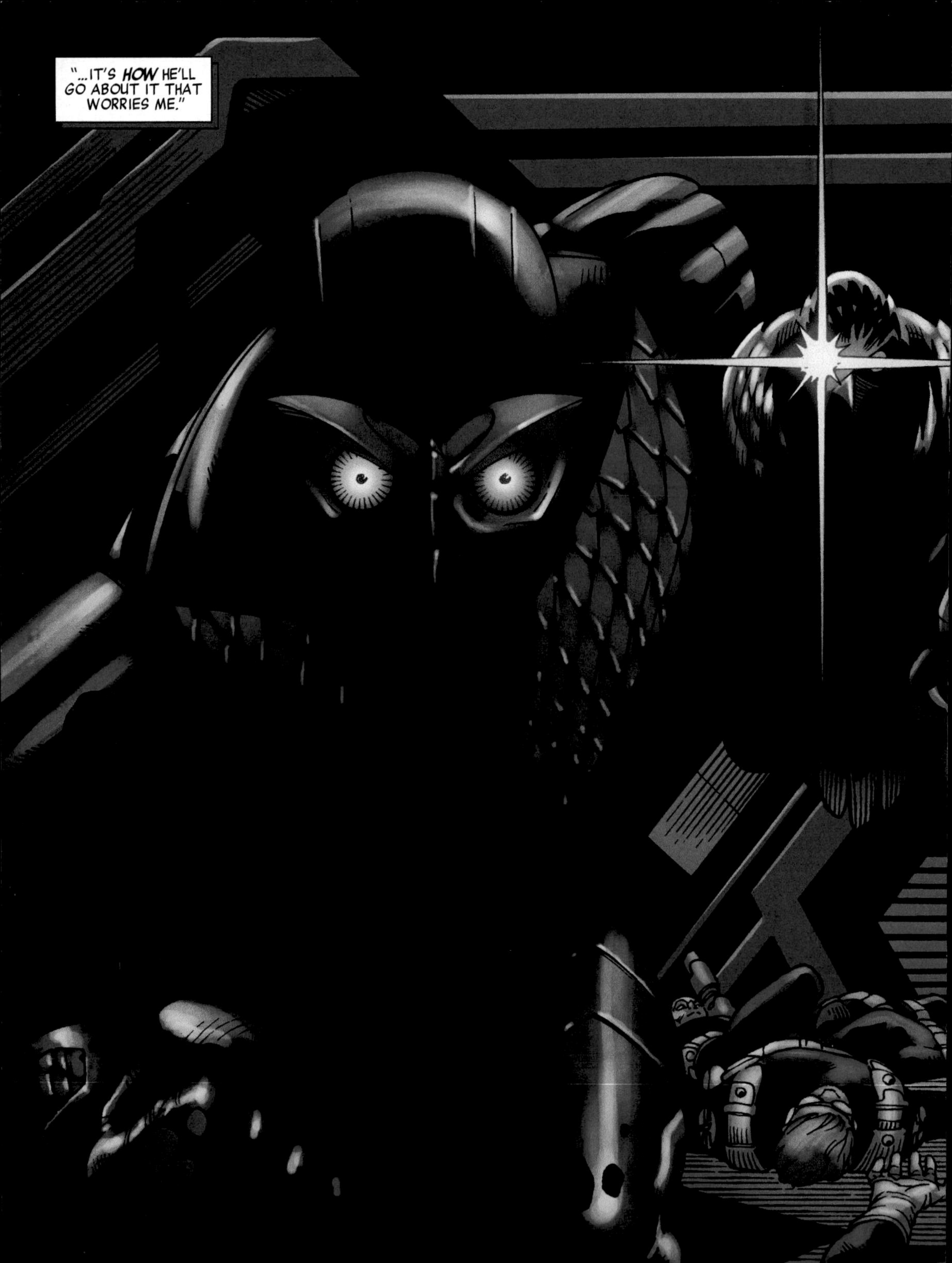
"...IT'S HOW HE'LL GO ABOUT IT THAT WORRIES ME."

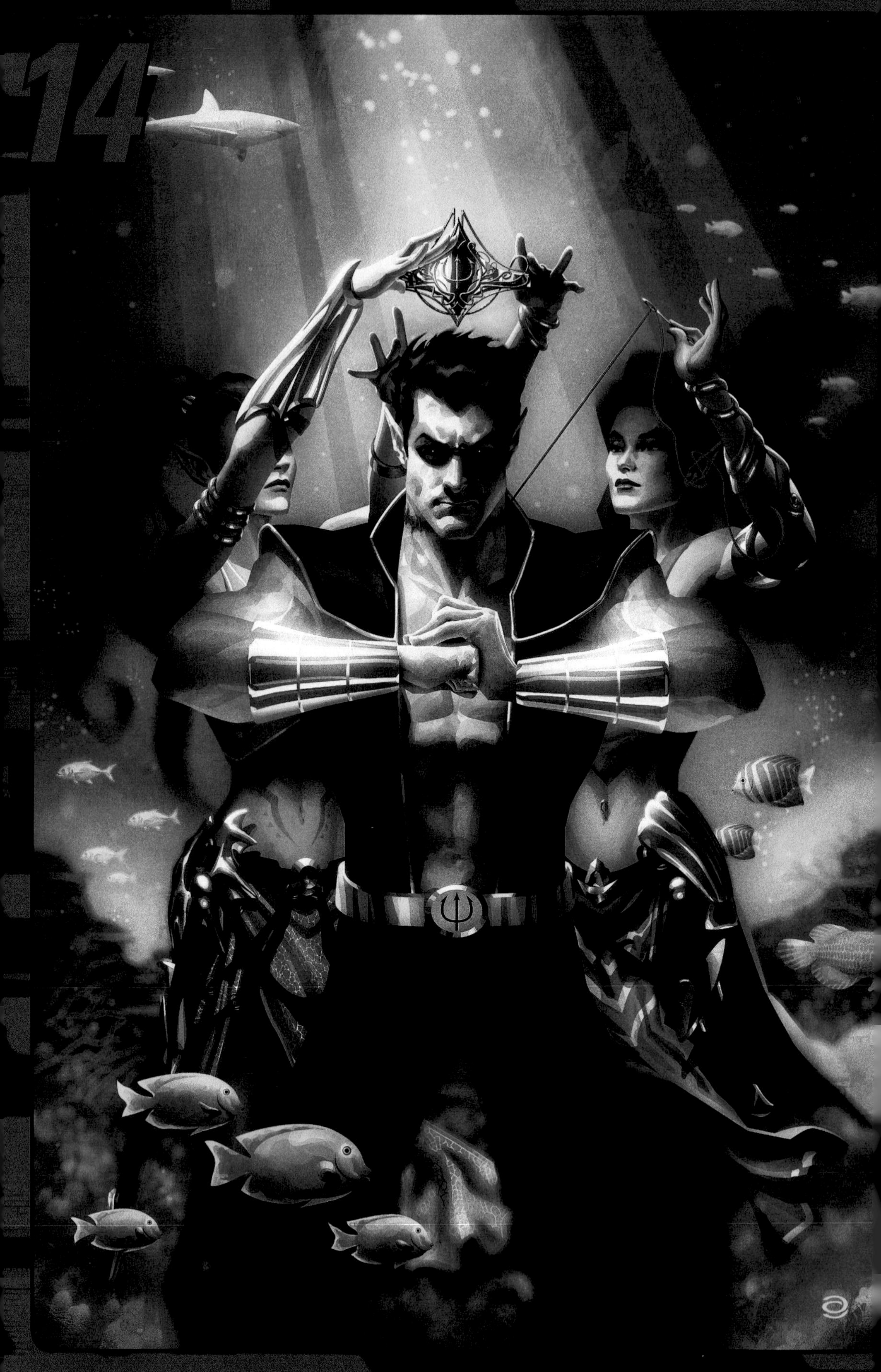
14

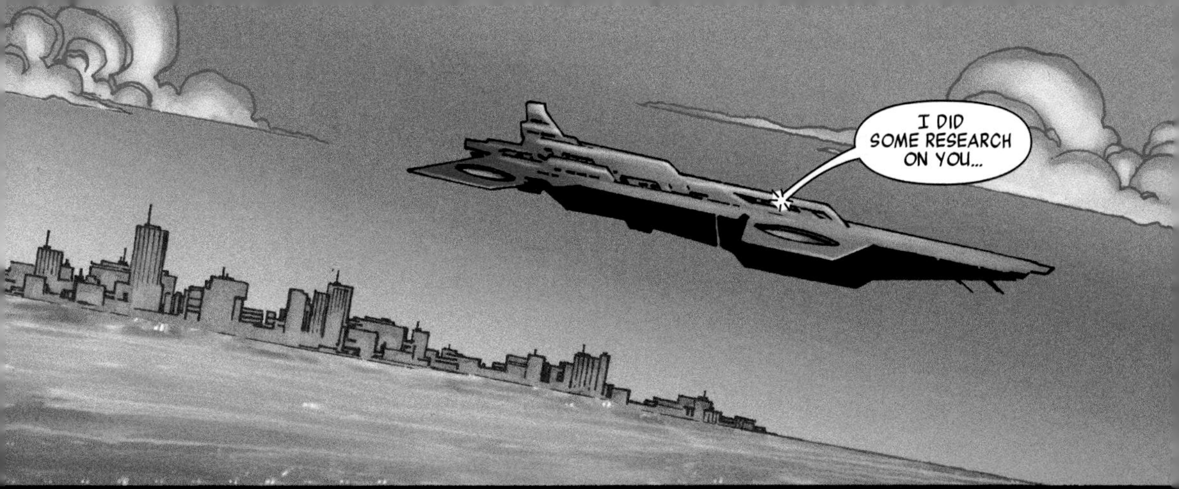
I DID SOME RESEARCH ON YOU...

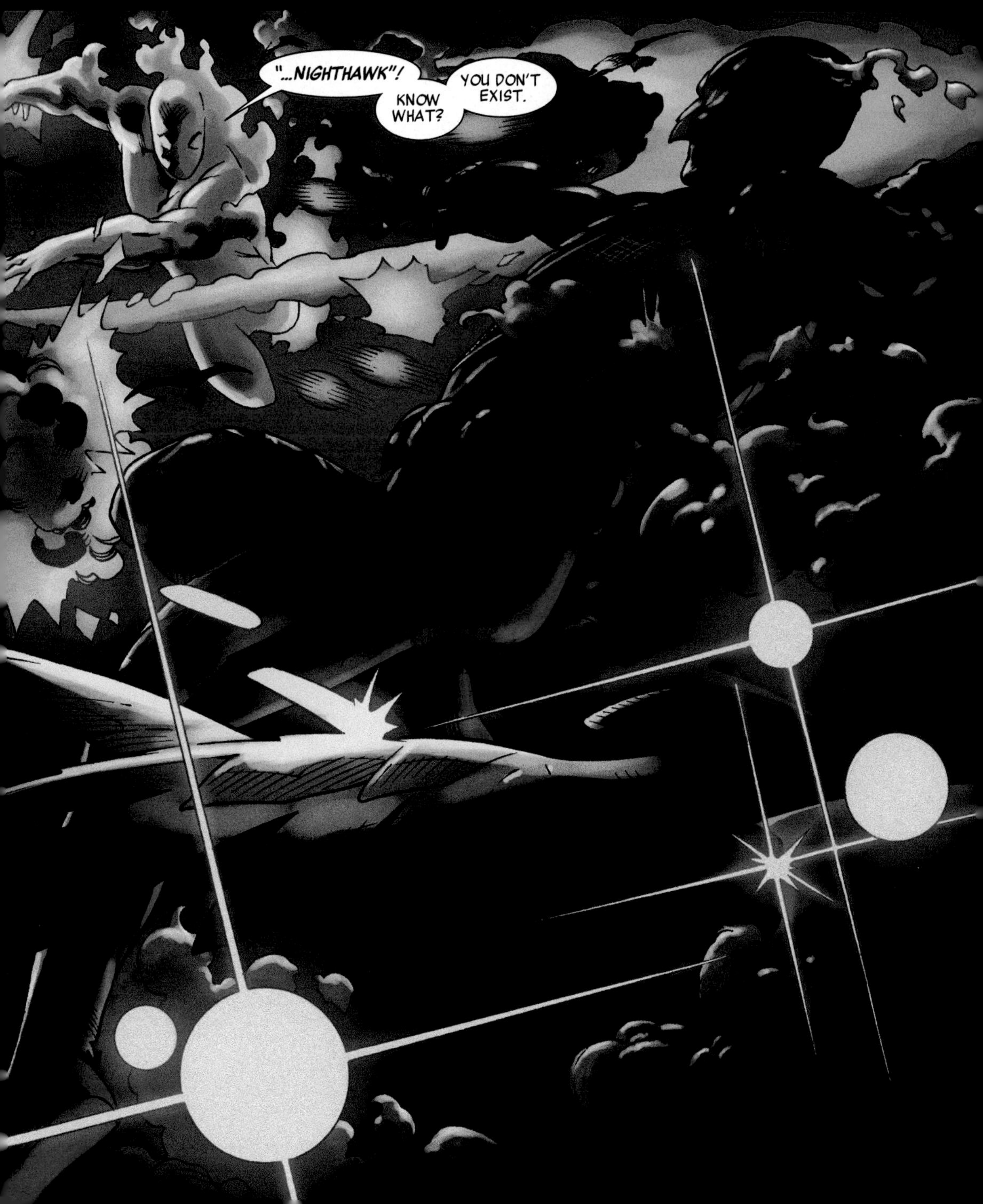
"...NIGHTHAWK"!
KNOW WHAT?
YOU DON'T EXIST.

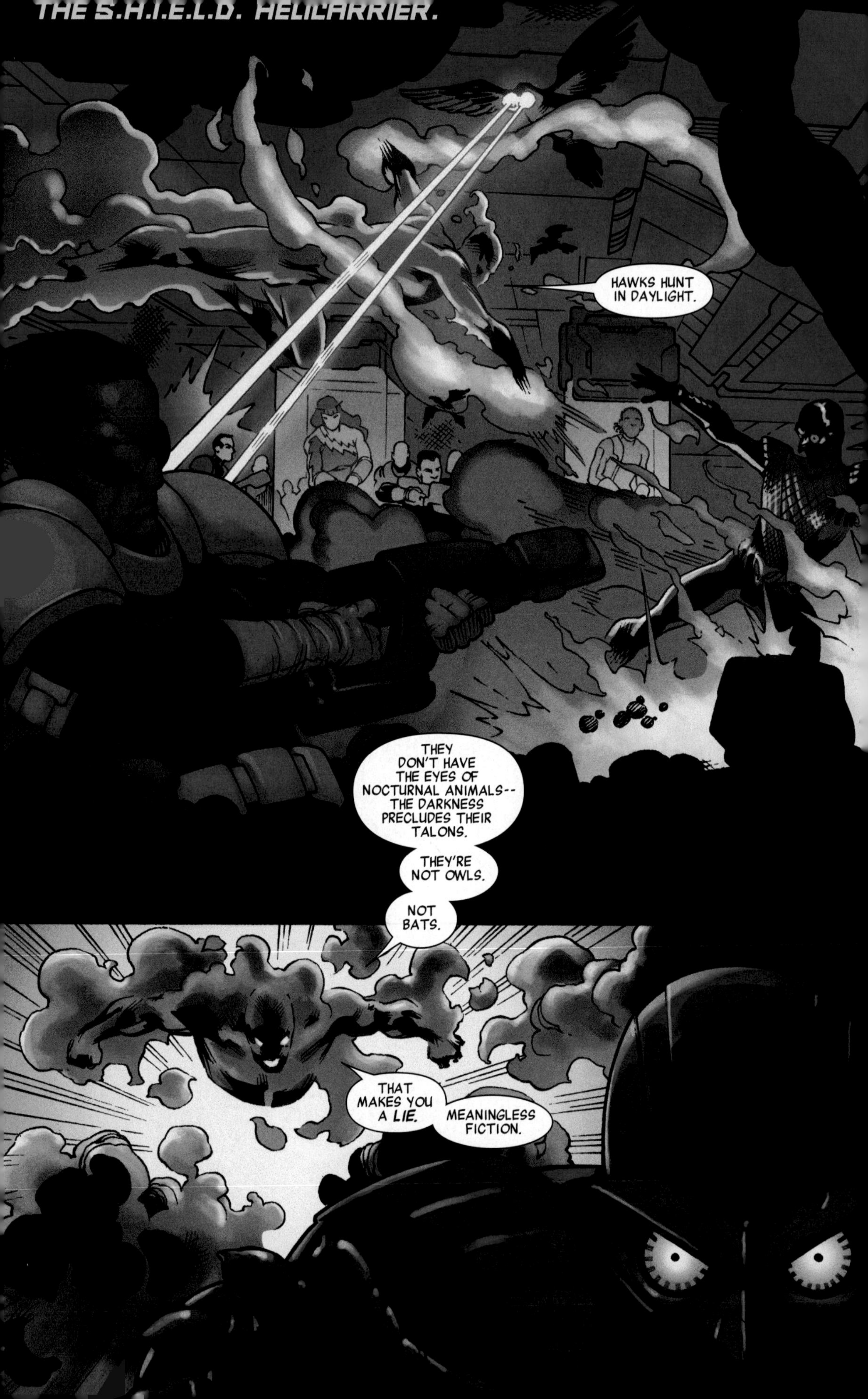
THE S.H.I.E.L.D. HELICARRIER.
HAWKS HUNT IN DAYLIGHT.
THEY DON'T HAVE THE EYES OF NOCTURNAL ANIMALS-- THE DARKNESS PRECLUDES THEIR TALONS.
THEY'RE NOT OWLS.
NOT BATS.
THAT MAKES YOU A *LIE.*
MEANINGLESS FICTION.

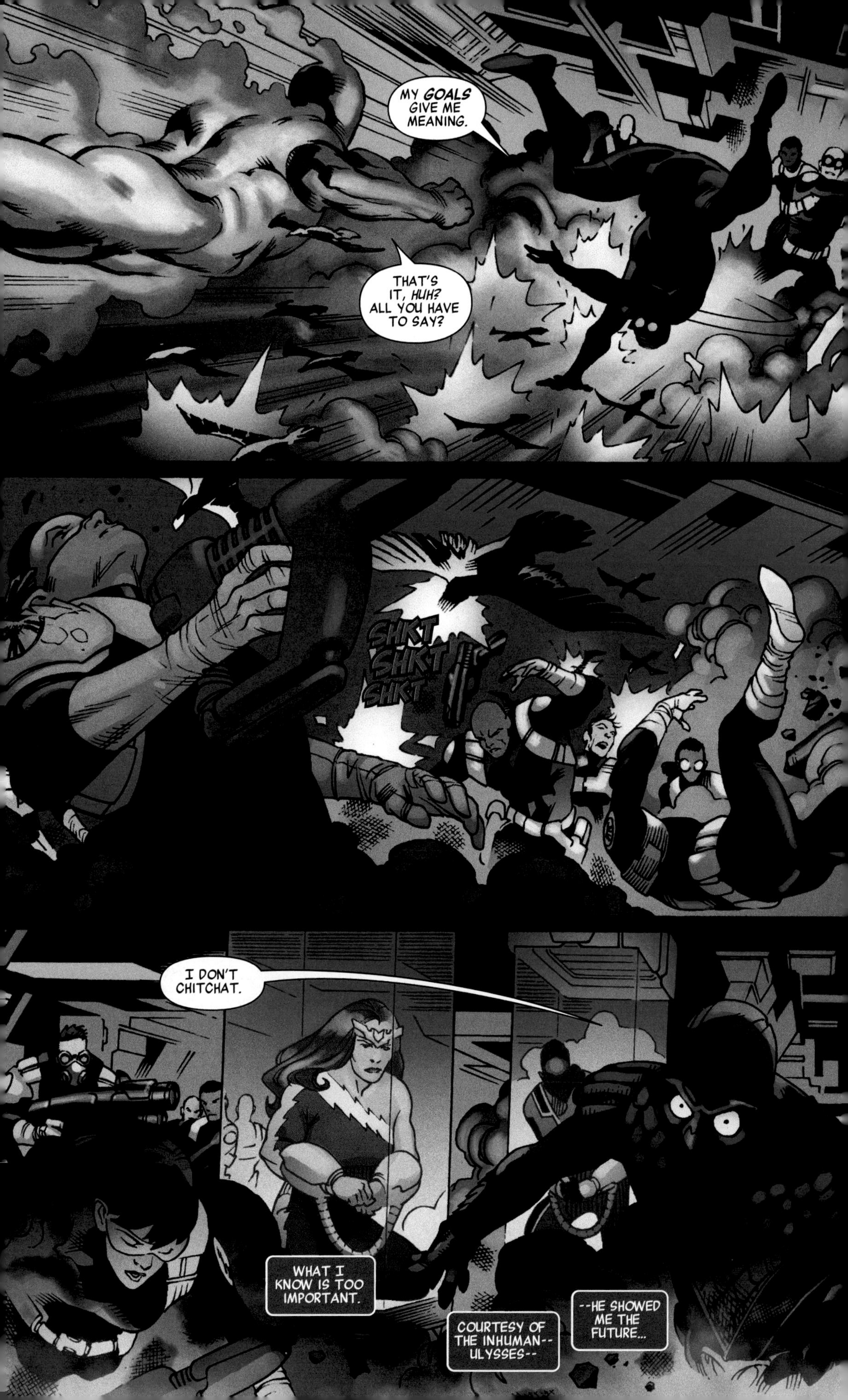
MY GOALS GIVE ME MEANING.
THAT'S IT, HUH? ALL YOU HAVE TO SAY?
SHKT SHKT SHKT
I DON'T CHITCHAT.
WHAT I KNOW IS TOO IMPORTANT.
COURTESY OF THE INHUMAN-- ULYSSES--
--HE SHOWED ME THE FUTURE...

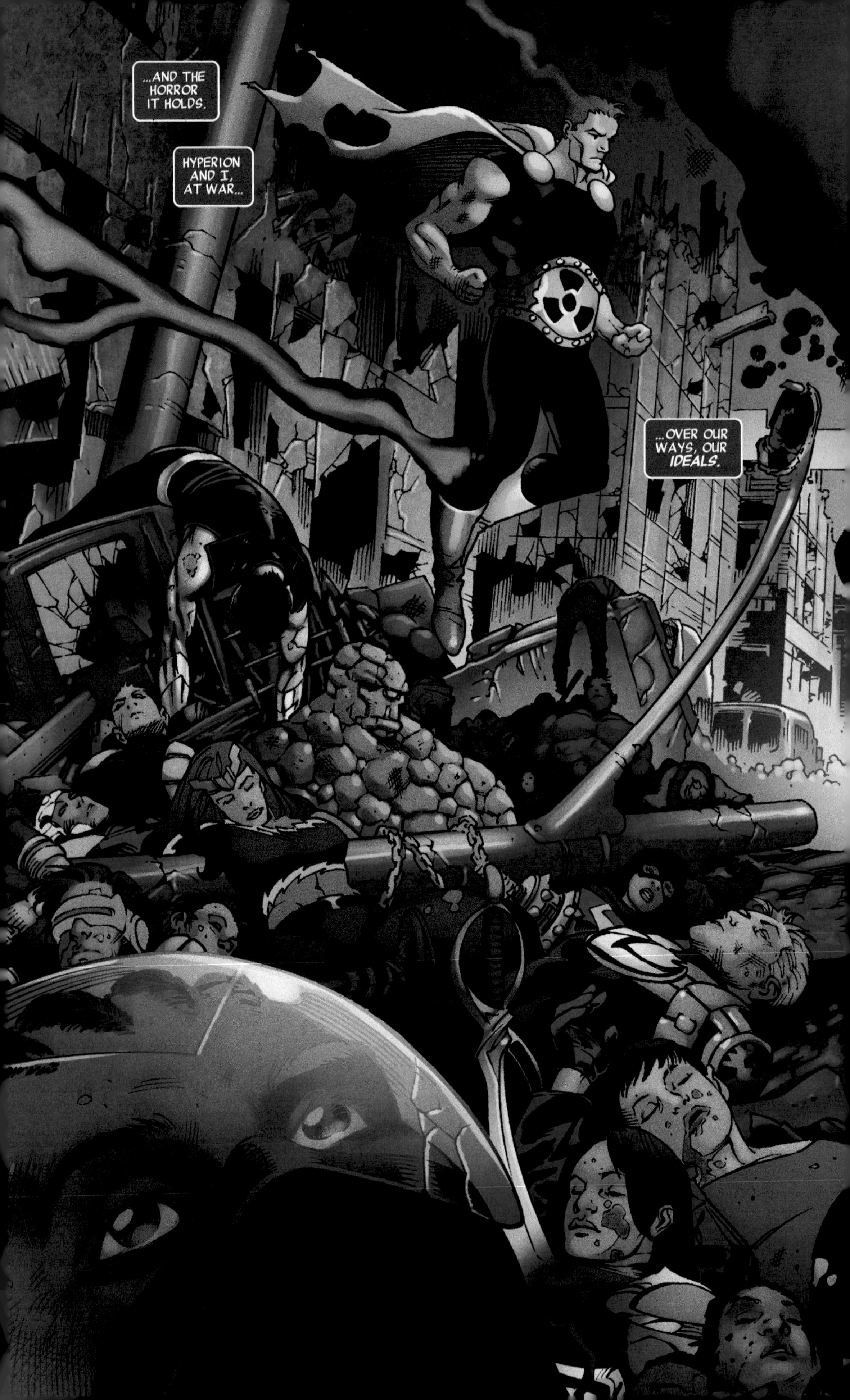
...AND THE HORROR IT HOLDS.
HYPERION AND I, AT WAR...
...OVER OUR WAYS, OUR *IDEALS*.

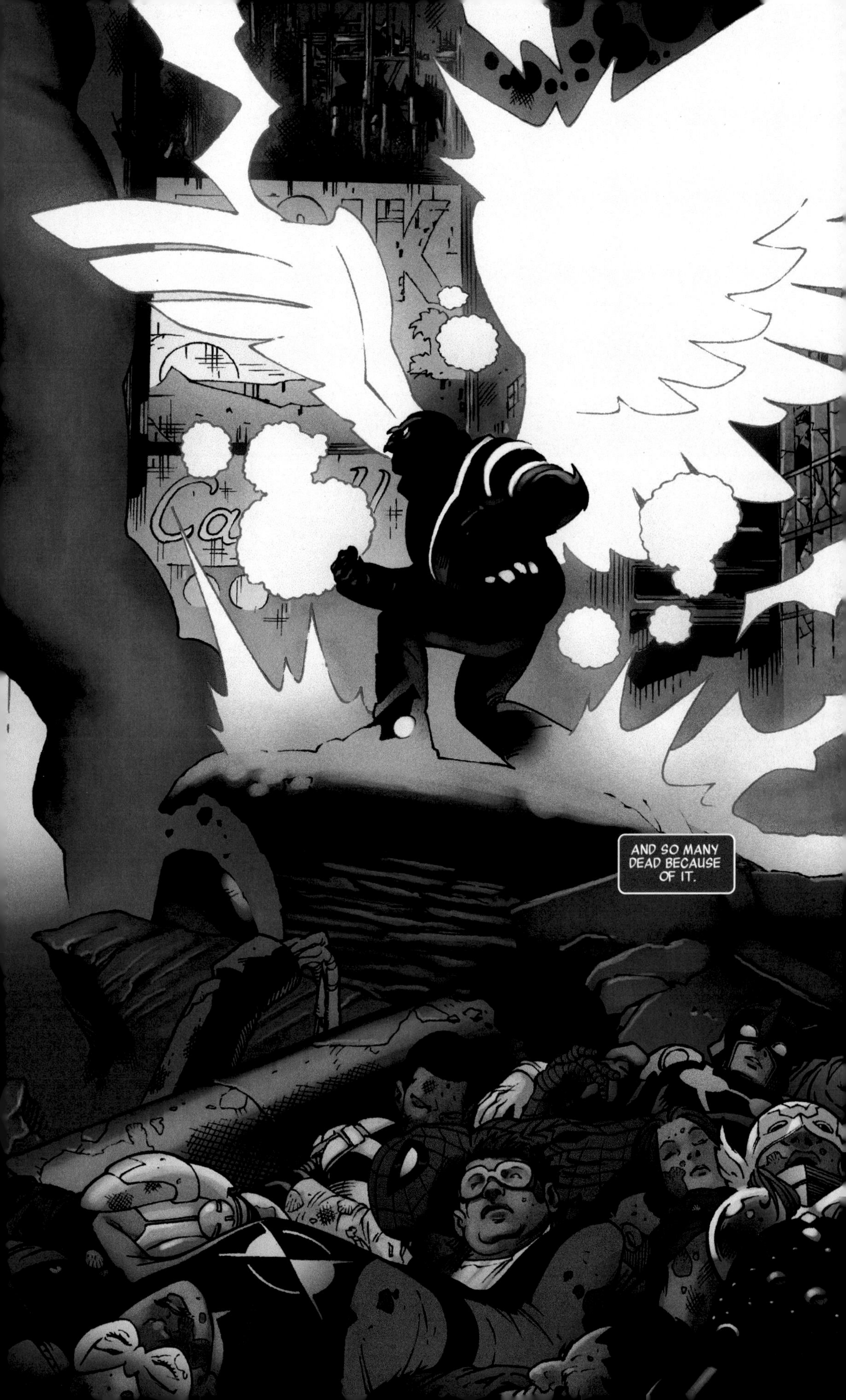
AND SO MANY DEAD BECAUSE OF IT.

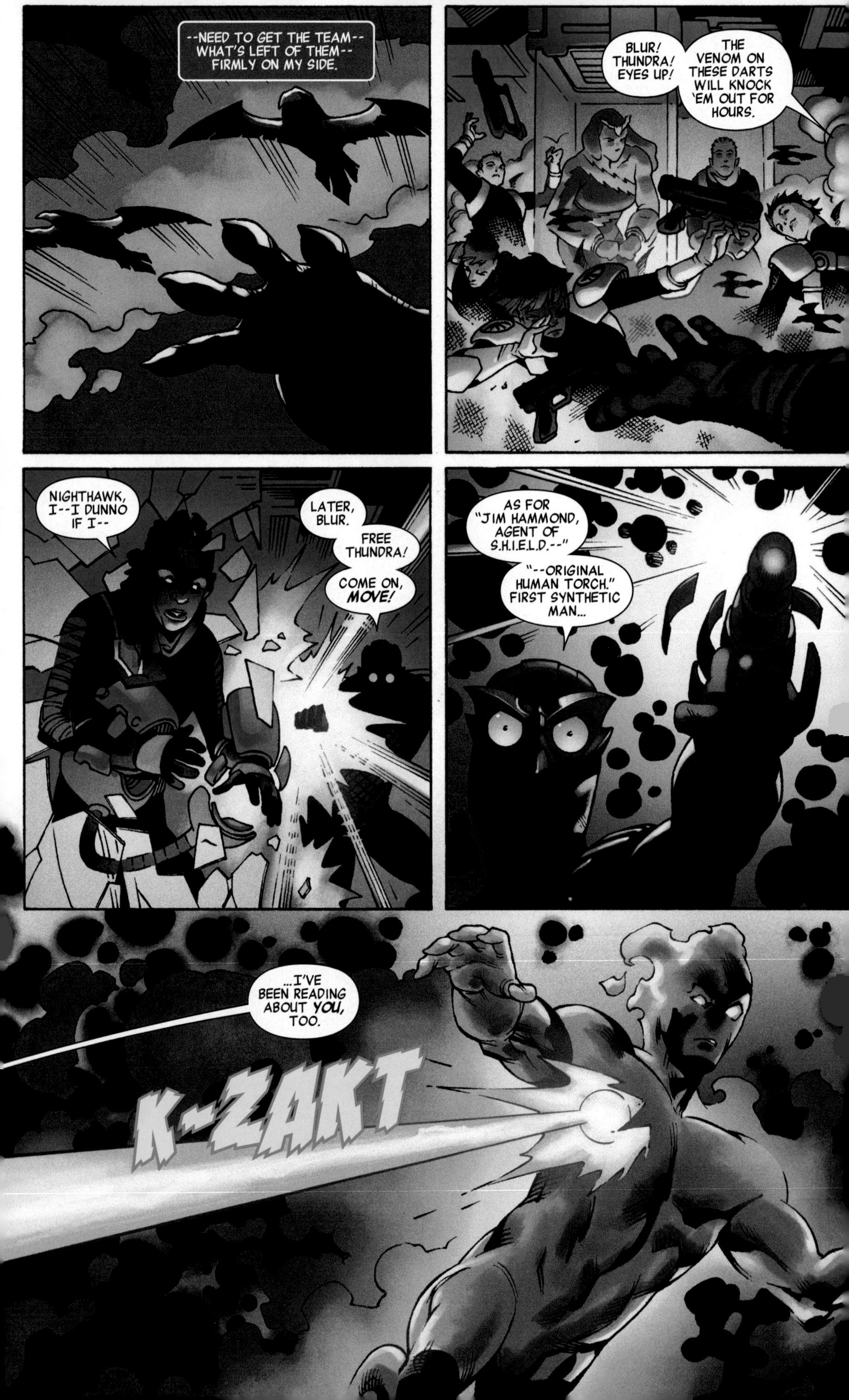
--NEED TO GET THE TEAM--
WHAT'S LEFT OF THEM--
FIRMLY ON MY SIDE.
BLUR! THUNDRA! EYES UP!
THE VENOM ON THESE DARTS WILL KNOCK 'EM OUT FOR HOURS.
NIGHTHAWK, I--I DUNNO IF I--
LATER, BLUR.
FREE THUNDRA!
COME ON, MOVE!
AS FOR "JIM HAMMOND, AGENT OF S.H.I.E.L.D.--"
"--ORIGINAL HUMAN TORCH." FIRST SYNTHETIC MAN...
...I'VE BEEN READING ABOUT YOU, TOO.
K-ZAKT

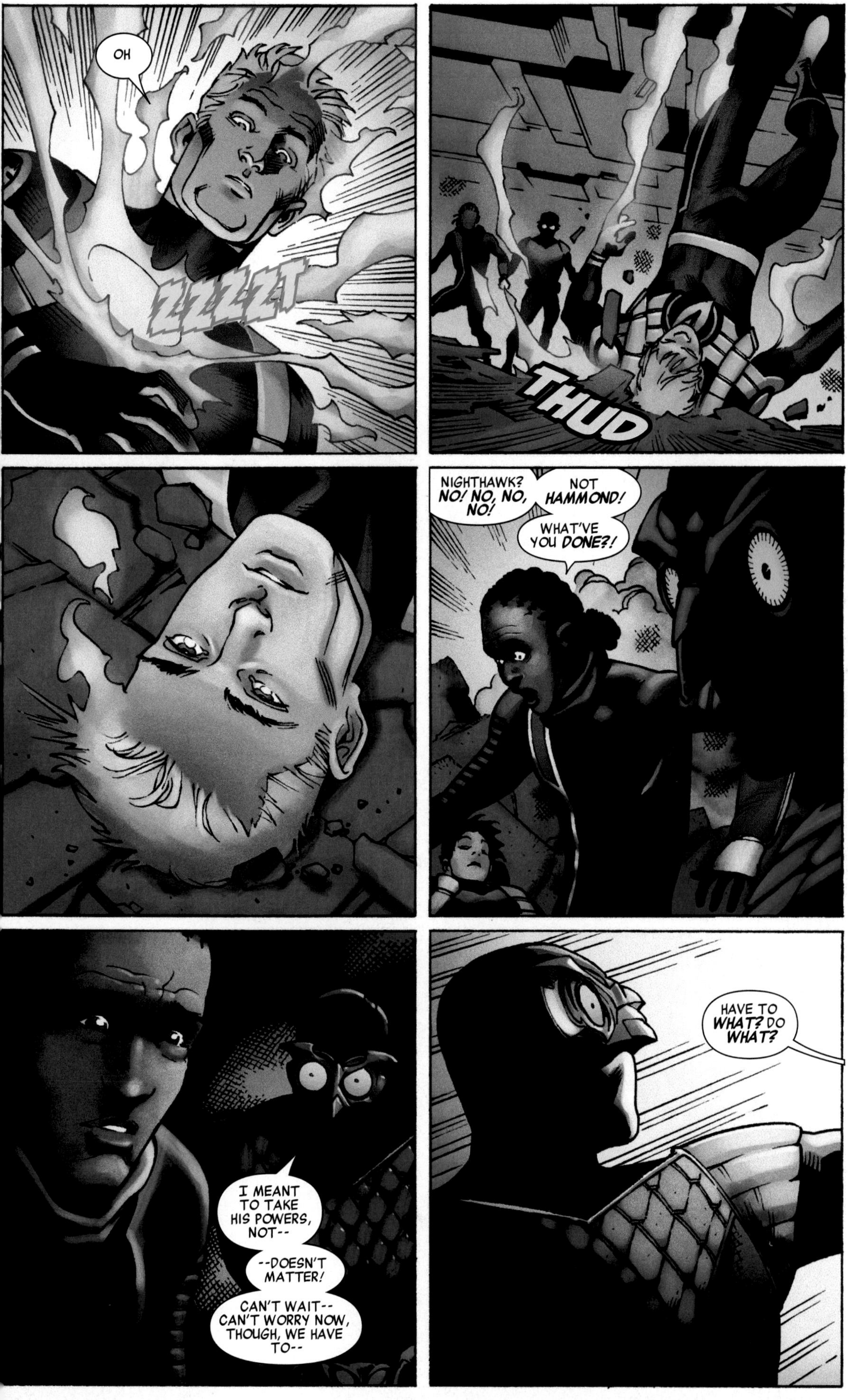
OH
ZZZZT
THUD
NIGHTHAWK? NO! NO, NO, NO!
NOT HAMMOND!
WHAT'VE YOU DONE?!
I MEANT TO TAKE HIS POWERS, NOT--
--DOESN'T MATTER!
CAN'T WAIT-- CAN'T WORRY NOW, THOUGH, WE HAVE TO--
HAVE TO WHAT? DO WHAT?

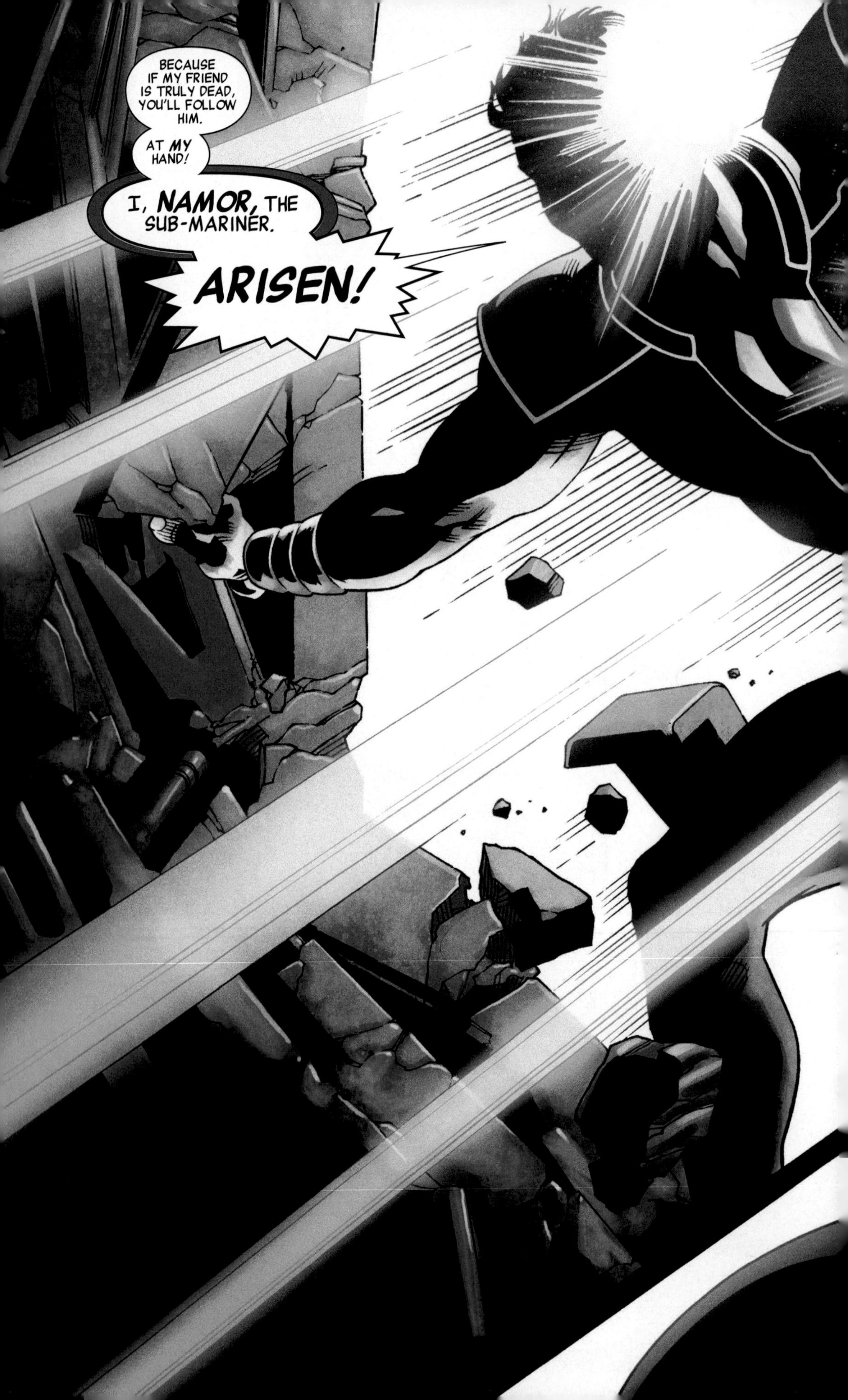
BECAUSE IF MY FRIEND IS TRULY DEAD, YOU'LL FOLLOW HIM.
AT MY HAND!
I, NAMOR, THE SUB-MARINER.
ARISEN!

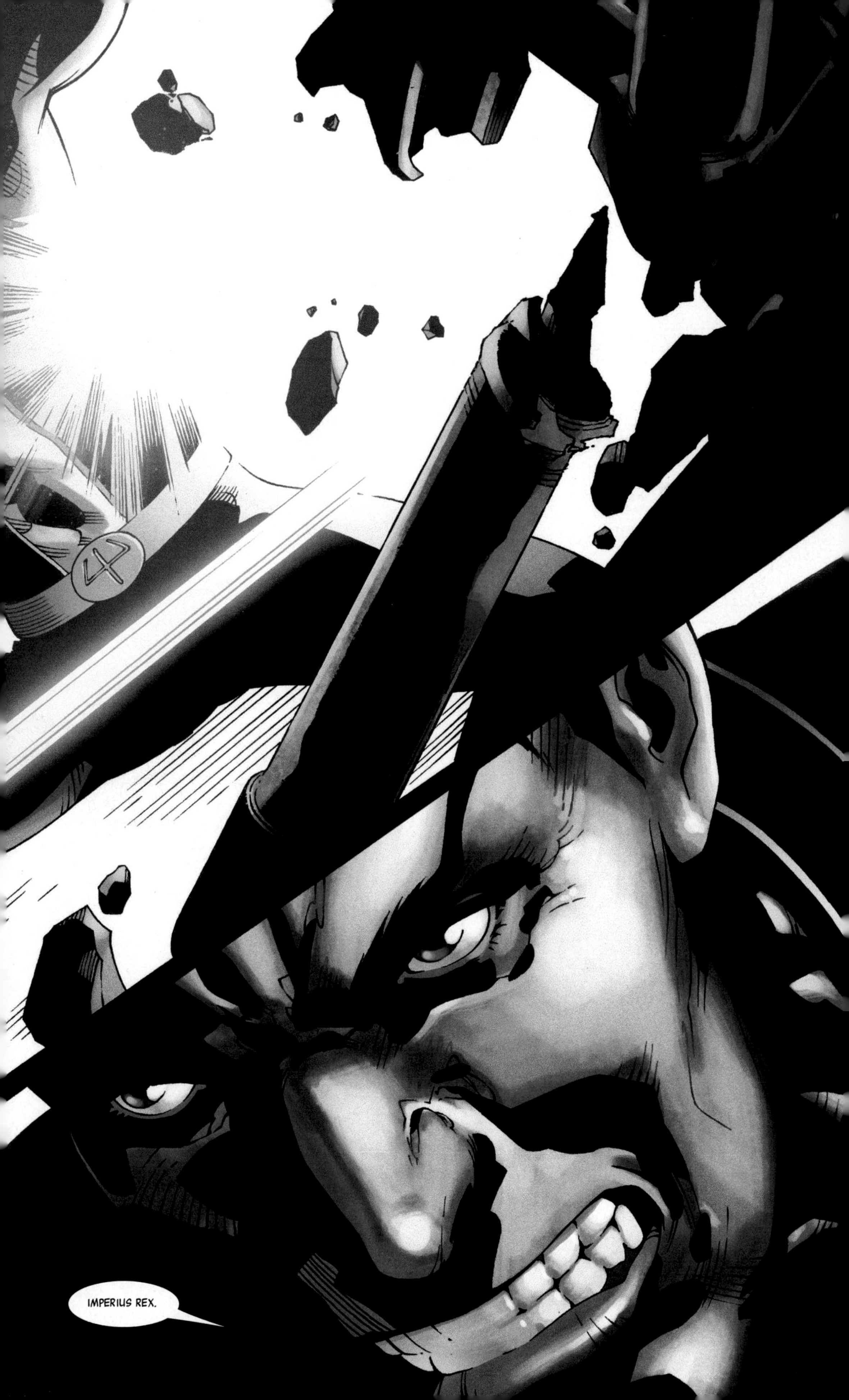
IMPERIUS REX.

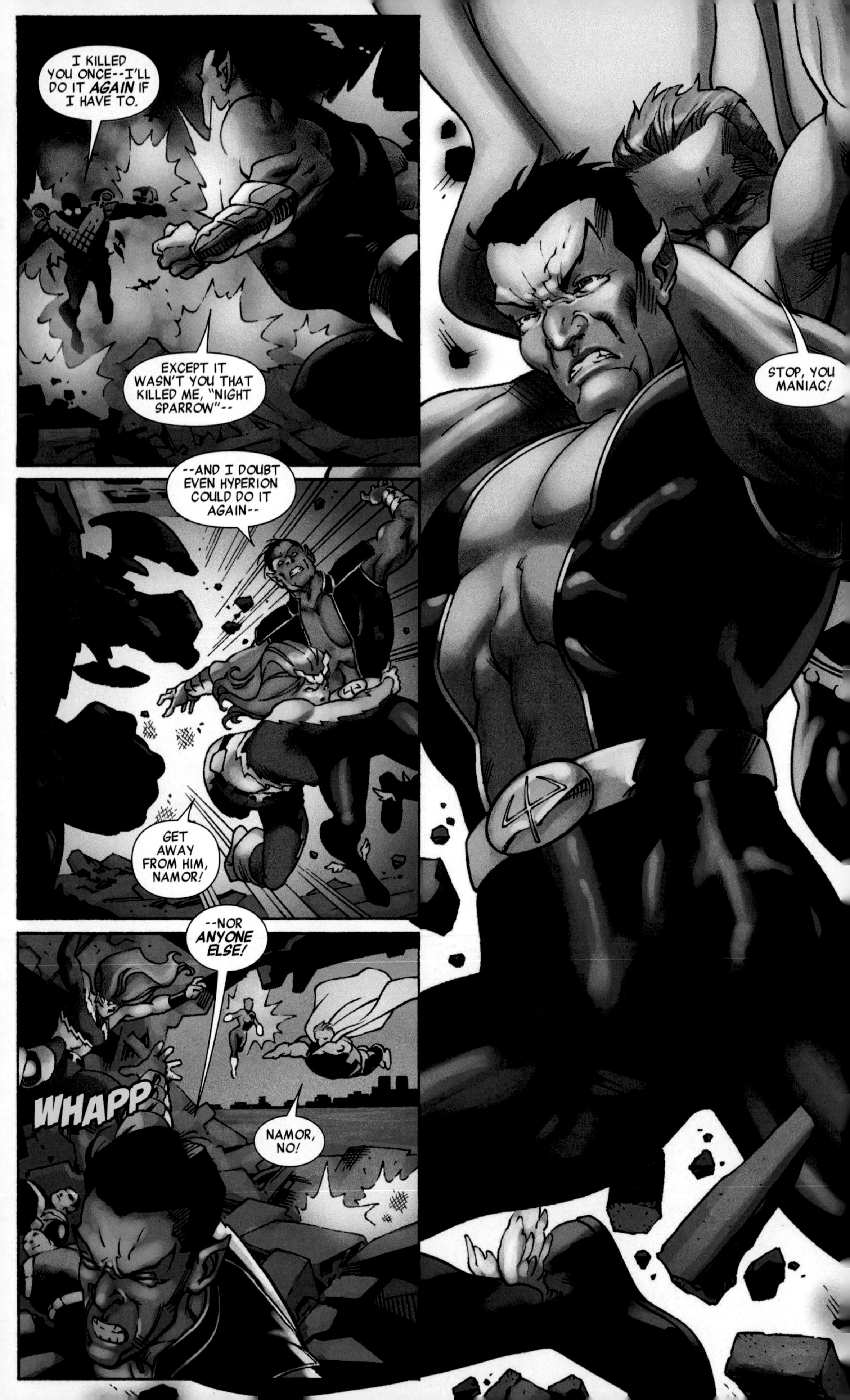
I KILLED YOU ONCE--I'LL DO IT AGAIN IF I HAVE TO.
EXCEPT IT WASN'T YOU THAT KILLED ME, "NIGHT SPARROW"--
--AND I DOUBT EVEN HYPERION COULD DO IT AGAIN--
GET AWAY FROM HIM, NAMOR!
--NOR ANYONE ELSE!
WHAPP
NAMOR, NO!
STOP, YOU MANIAC!

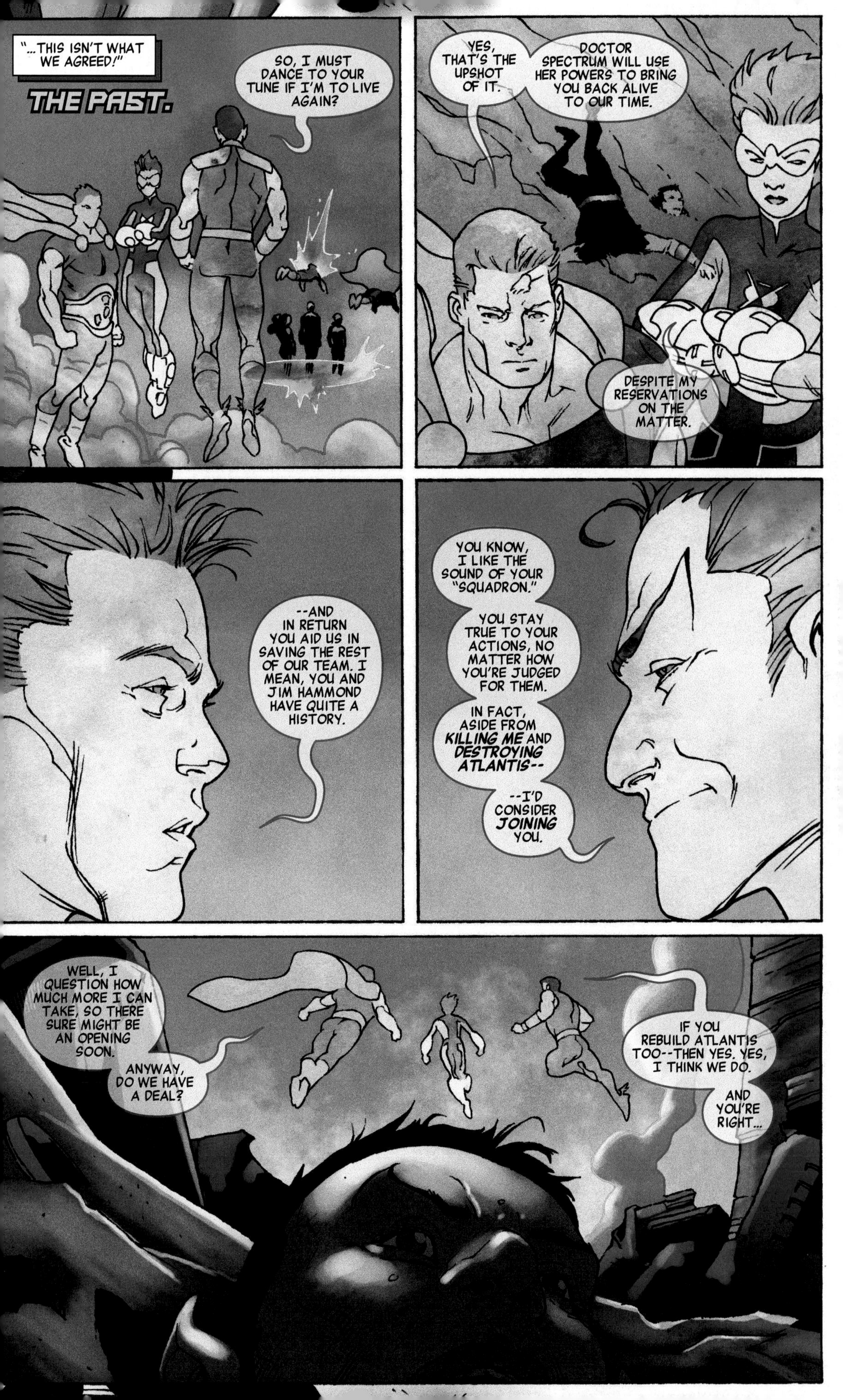
"...THIS ISN'T WHAT WE AGREED!"
THE PAST.
SO, I MUST DANCE TO YOUR TUNE IF I'M TO LIVE AGAIN?
YES, THAT'S THE UPSHOT OF IT.
DOCTOR SPECTRUM WILL USE HER POWERS TO BRING YOU BACK ALIVE TO OUR TIME.
DESPITE MY RESERVATIONS ON THE MATTER.
--AND IN RETURN YOU AID US IN SAVING THE REST OF OUR TEAM. I MEAN, YOU AND JIM HAMMOND HAVE QUITE A HISTORY.
YOU KNOW, I LIKE THE SOUND OF YOUR "SQUADRON."
YOU STAY TRUE TO YOUR ACTIONS, NO MATTER HOW YOU'RE JUDGED FOR THEM.
IN FACT, ASIDE FROM KILLING ME AND DESTROYING ATLANTIS--
--I'D CONSIDER JOINING YOU.
WELL, I QUESTION HOW MUCH MORE I CAN TAKE, SO THERE SURE MIGHT BE AN OPENING SOON.
ANYWAY, DO WE HAVE A DEAL?
IF YOU REBUILD ATLANTIS TOO--THEN YES. YES, I THINK WE DO.
AND YOU'RE RIGHT...

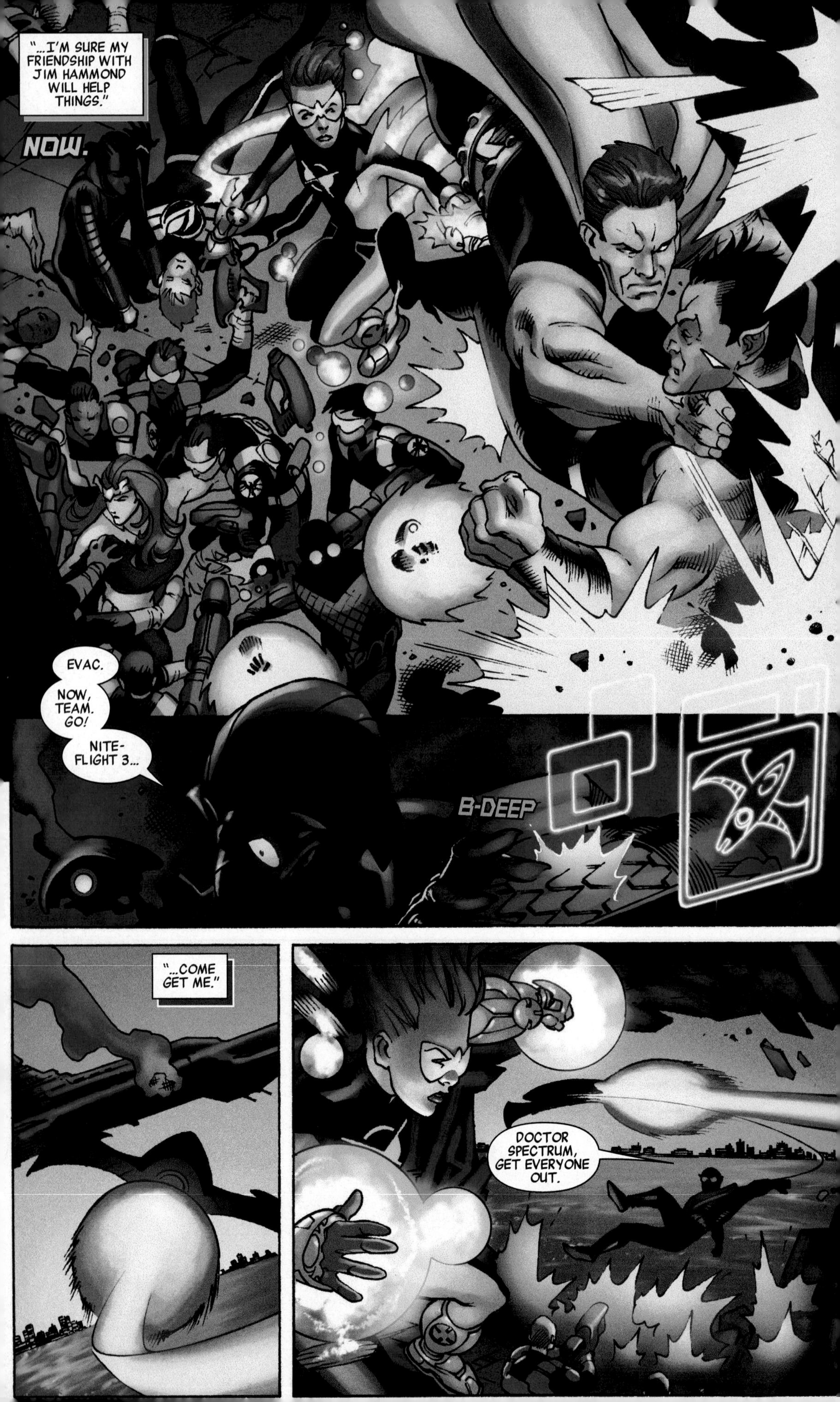
"...I'M SURE MY FRIENDSHIP WITH JIM HAMMOND WILL HELP THINGS."
NOW.
EVAC.
NOW, TEAM. GO!
NITE-FLIGHT 3...
B-DEEP
"...COME GET ME."
DOCTOR SPECTRUM, GET EVERYONE OUT.

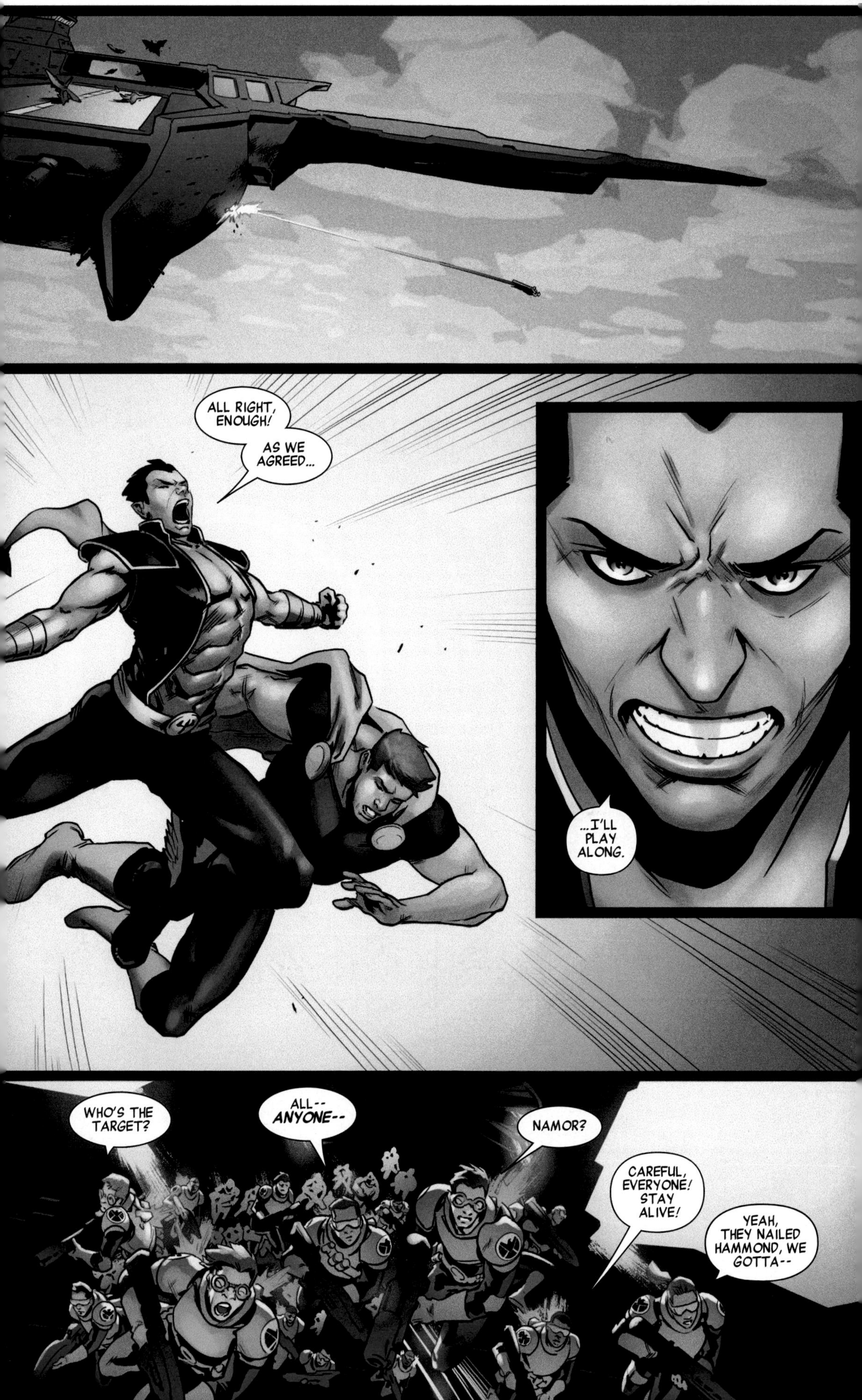
ALL RIGHT, ENOUGH!
AS WE AGREED...
...I'LL PLAY ALONG.
WHO'S THE TARGET?
ALL-- ANYONE--
NAMOR?
CAREFUL, EVERYONE! STAY ALIVE!
YEAH, THEY NAILED HAMMOND, WE GOTTA--

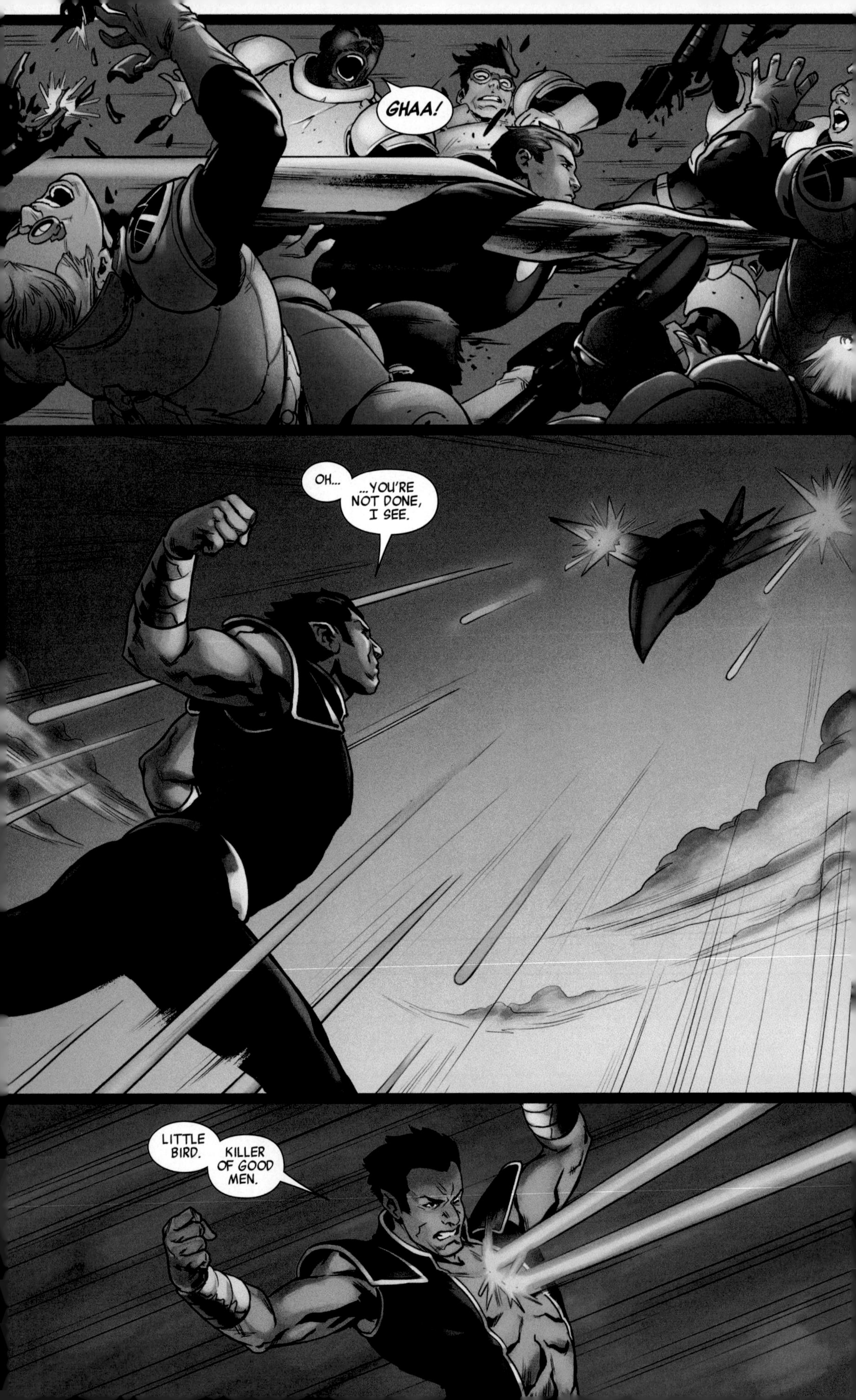
GHAA!
OH...
...YOU'RE NOT DONE, I SEE.
LITTLE BIRD.
KILLER OF GOOD MEN.

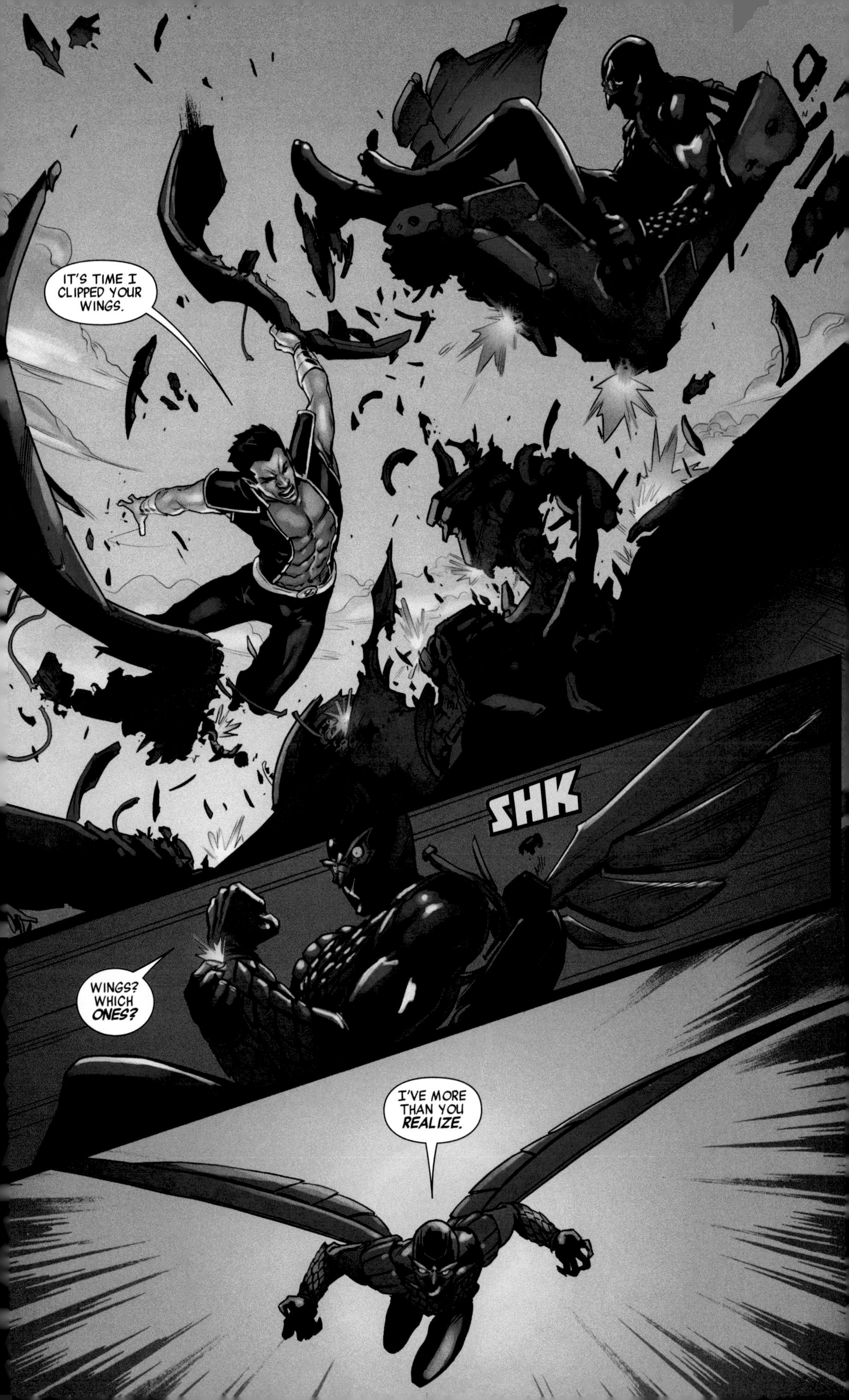
IT'S TIME I CLIPPED YOUR WINGS.
SHK
WINGS? WHICH *ONES?*
I'VE MORE THAN YOU *REALIZE.*

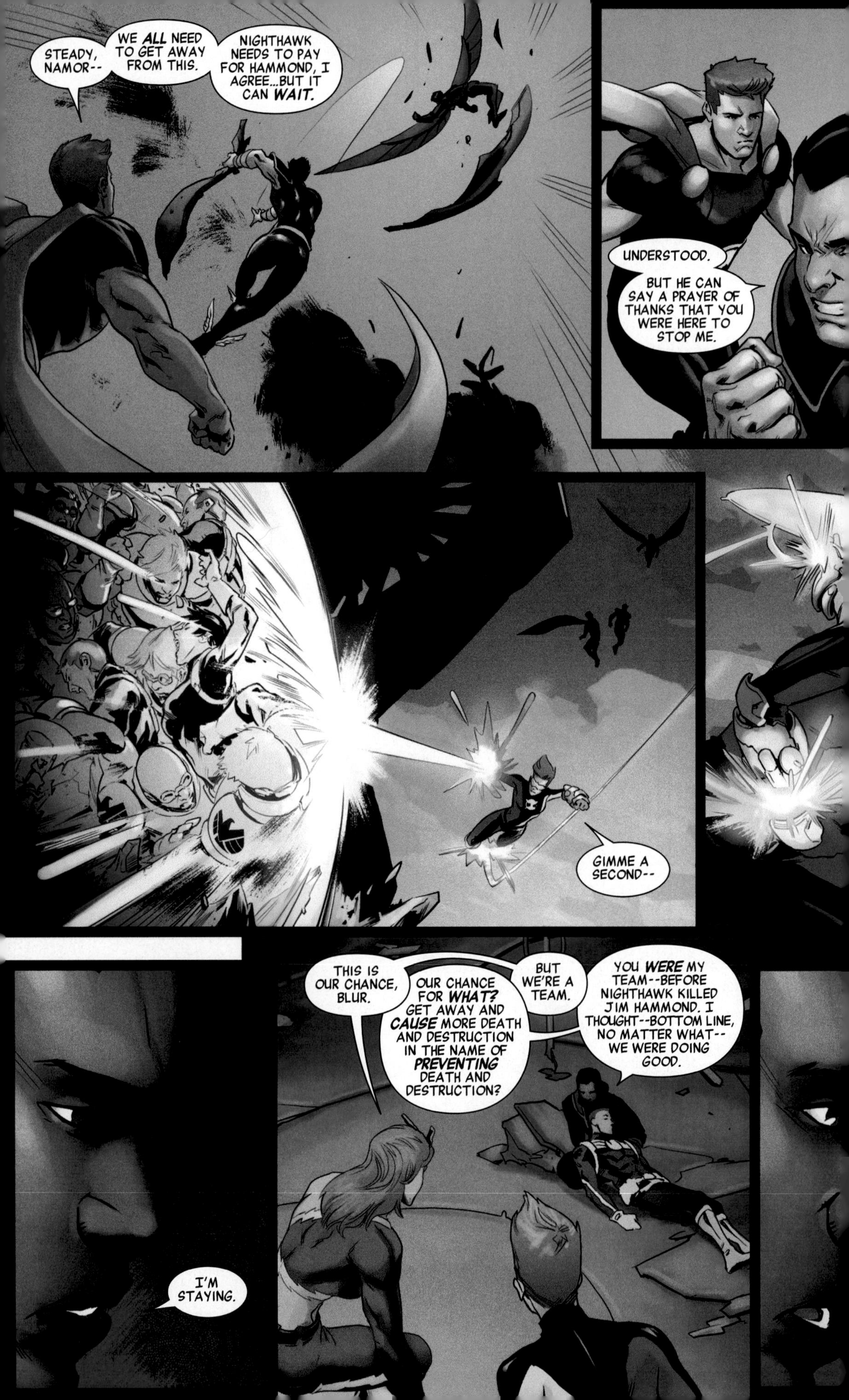
STEADY, NAMOR--
WE ALL NEED TO GET AWAY FROM THIS.
NIGHTHAWK NEEDS TO PAY FOR HAMMOND, I AGREE...BUT IT CAN WAIT.
UNDERSTOOD.
BUT HE CAN SAY A PRAYER OF THANKS THAT YOU WERE HERE TO STOP ME.
GIMME A SECOND--
I'M STAYING.
THIS IS OUR CHANCE, BLUR.
OUR CHANCE FOR WHAT? GET AWAY AND CAUSE MORE DEATH AND DESTRUCTION IN THE NAME OF PREVENTING DEATH AND DESTRUCTION?
BUT WE'RE A TEAM.
YOU WERE MY TEAM--BEFORE NIGHTHAWK KILLED JIM HAMMOND. I THOUGHT--BOTTOM LINE, NO MATTER WHAT--WE WERE DOING GOOD.

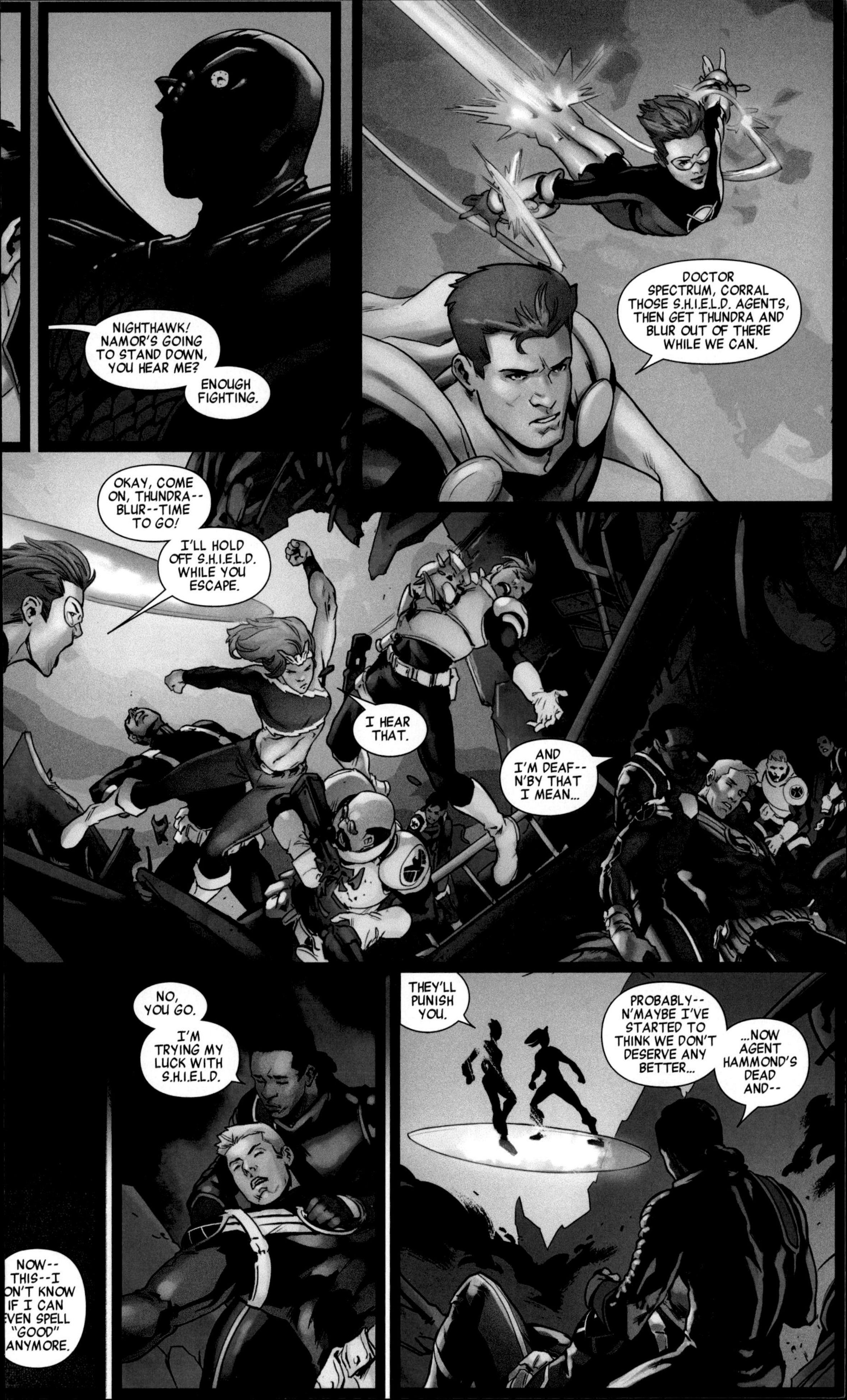
NIGHTHAWK! NAMOR'S GOING TO STAND DOWN, YOU HEAR ME?
ENOUGH FIGHTING.
DOCTOR SPECTRUM, CORRAL THOSE S.H.I.E.L.D. AGENTS, THEN GET THUNDRA AND BLUR OUT OF THERE WHILE WE CAN.
OKAY, COME ON, THUNDRA-- BLUR--TIME TO GO!
I'LL HOLD OFF S.H.I.E.L.D. WHILE YOU ESCAPE.
I HEAR THAT.
AND I'M DEAF-- N'BY THAT I MEAN...
NO, YOU GO.
I'M TRYING MY LUCK WITH S.H.I.E.L.D.
THEY'LL PUNISH YOU.
PROBABLY-- N'MAYBE I'VE STARTED TO THINK WE DON'T DESERVE ANY BETTER...
...NOW AGENT HAMMOND'S DEAD AND--
NOW-- THIS--I ON'T KNOW IF I CAN EVEN SPELL "GOOD" ANYMORE.

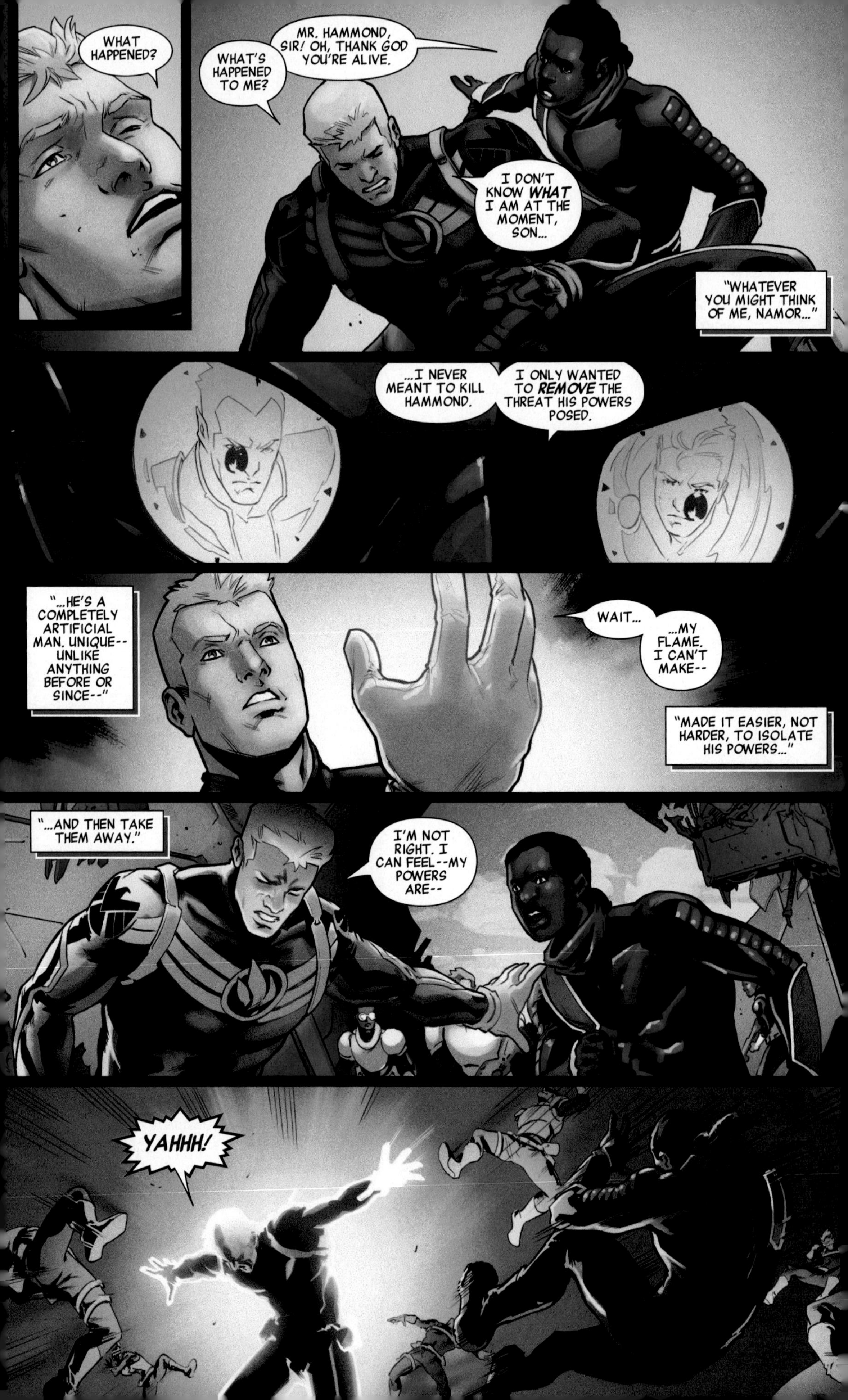
WHAT HAPPENED?
WHAT'S HAPPENED TO ME?
MR. HAMMOND, SIR! OH, THANK GOD YOU'RE ALIVE.
I DON'T KNOW WHAT I AM AT THE MOMENT, SON...
"WHATEVER YOU MIGHT THINK OF ME, NAMOR..."
...I NEVER MEANT TO KILL HAMMOND.
I ONLY WANTED TO REMOVE THE THREAT HIS POWERS POSED.
"...HE'S A COMPLETELY ARTIFICIAL MAN. UNIQUE--UNLIKE ANYTHING BEFORE OR SINCE--"
WAIT...
...MY FLAME. I CAN'T MAKE--
"MADE IT EASIER, NOT HARDER, TO ISOLATE HIS POWERS..."
"...AND THEN TAKE THEM AWAY."
I'M NOT RIGHT. I CAN FEEL--MY POWERS ARE--
YAHHH!

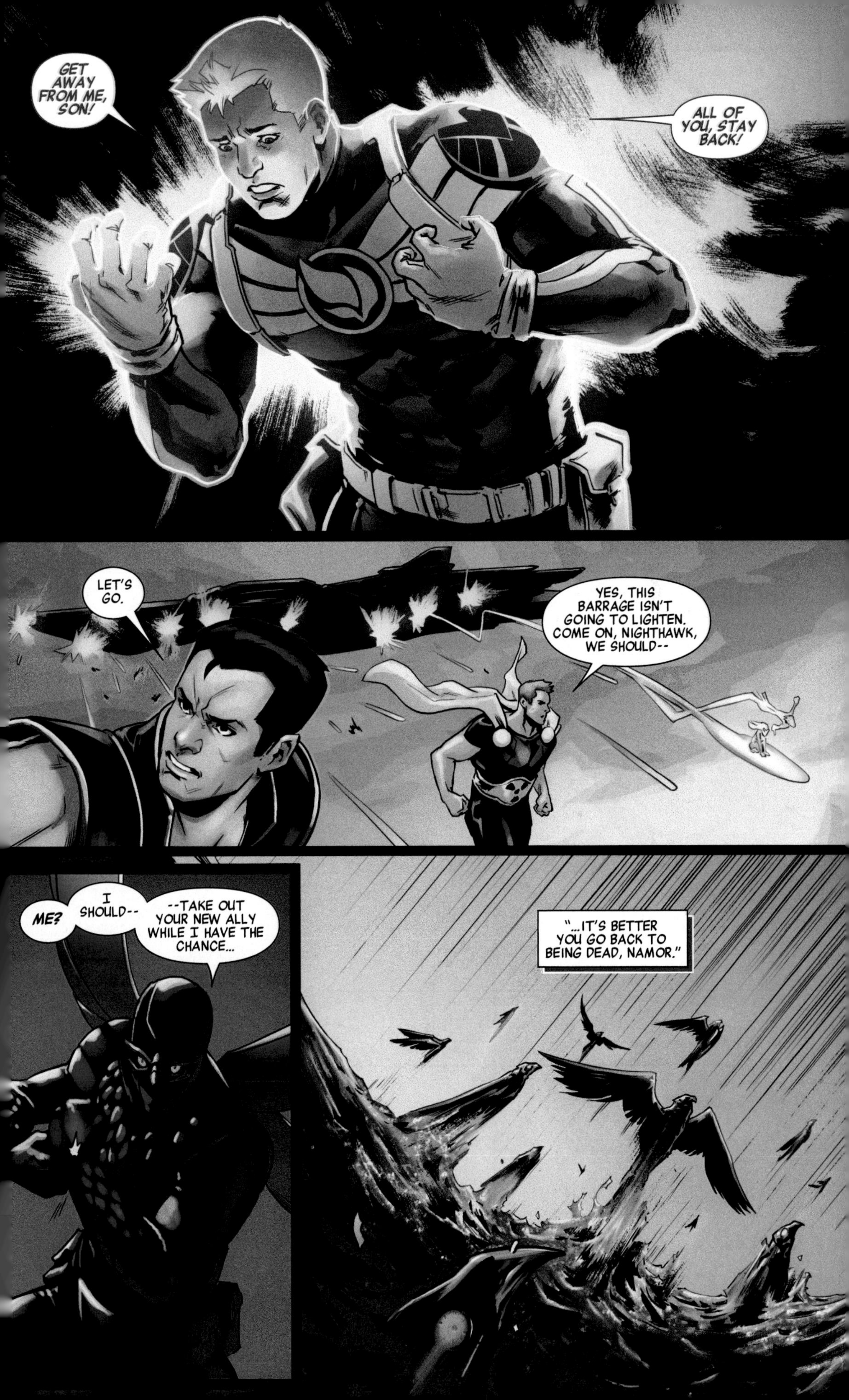
GET AWAY FROM ME, SON!
ALL OF YOU, STAY BACK!
LET'S GO.
YES, THIS BARRAGE ISN'T GOING TO LIGHTEN. COME ON, NIGHTHAWK, WE SHOULD--
ME?
I SHOULD--
--TAKE OUT YOUR NEW ALLY WHILE I HAVE THE CHANCE...
"...IT'S BETTER YOU GO BACK TO BEING DEAD, NAMOR."

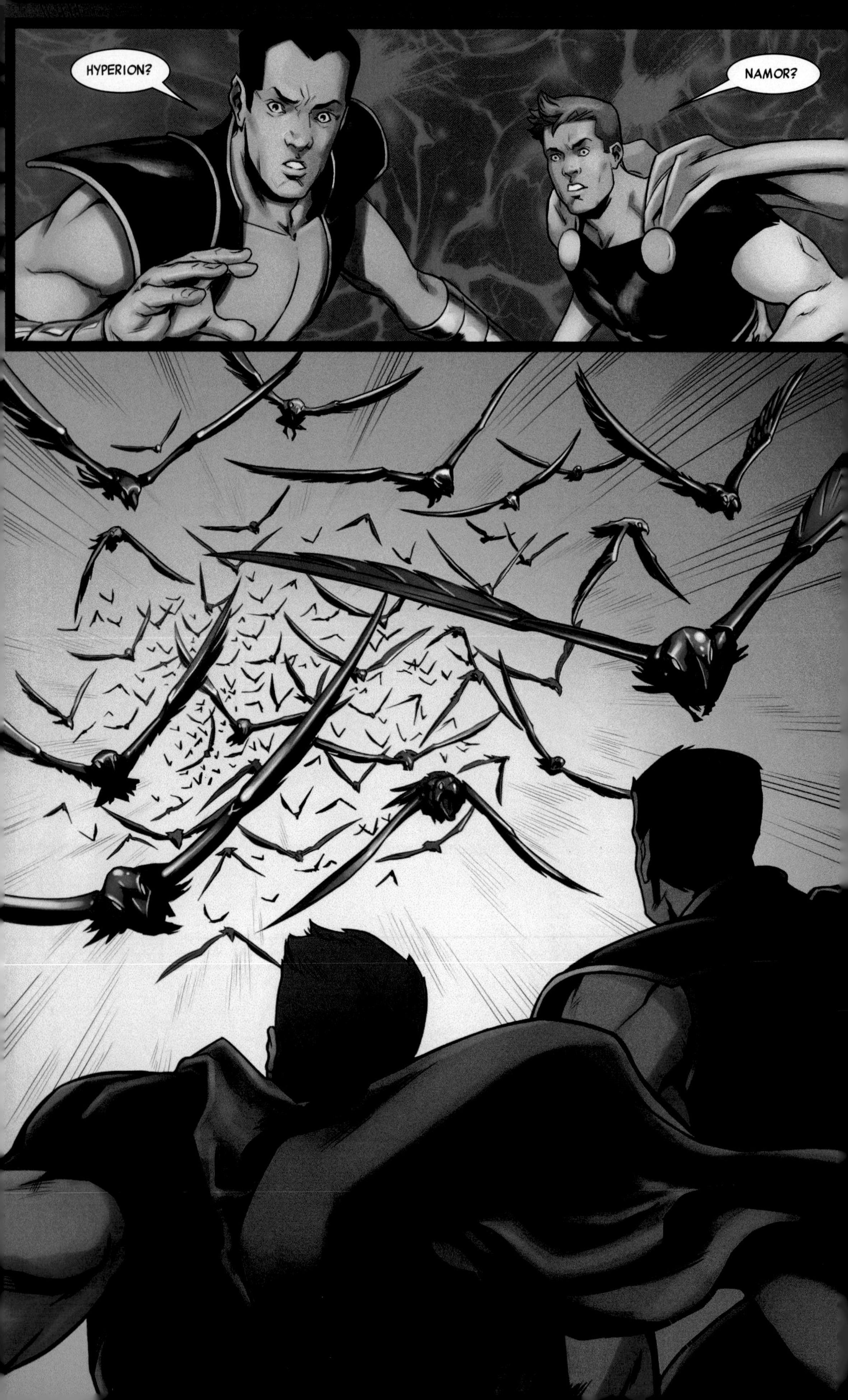
HYPERION?
NAMOR?

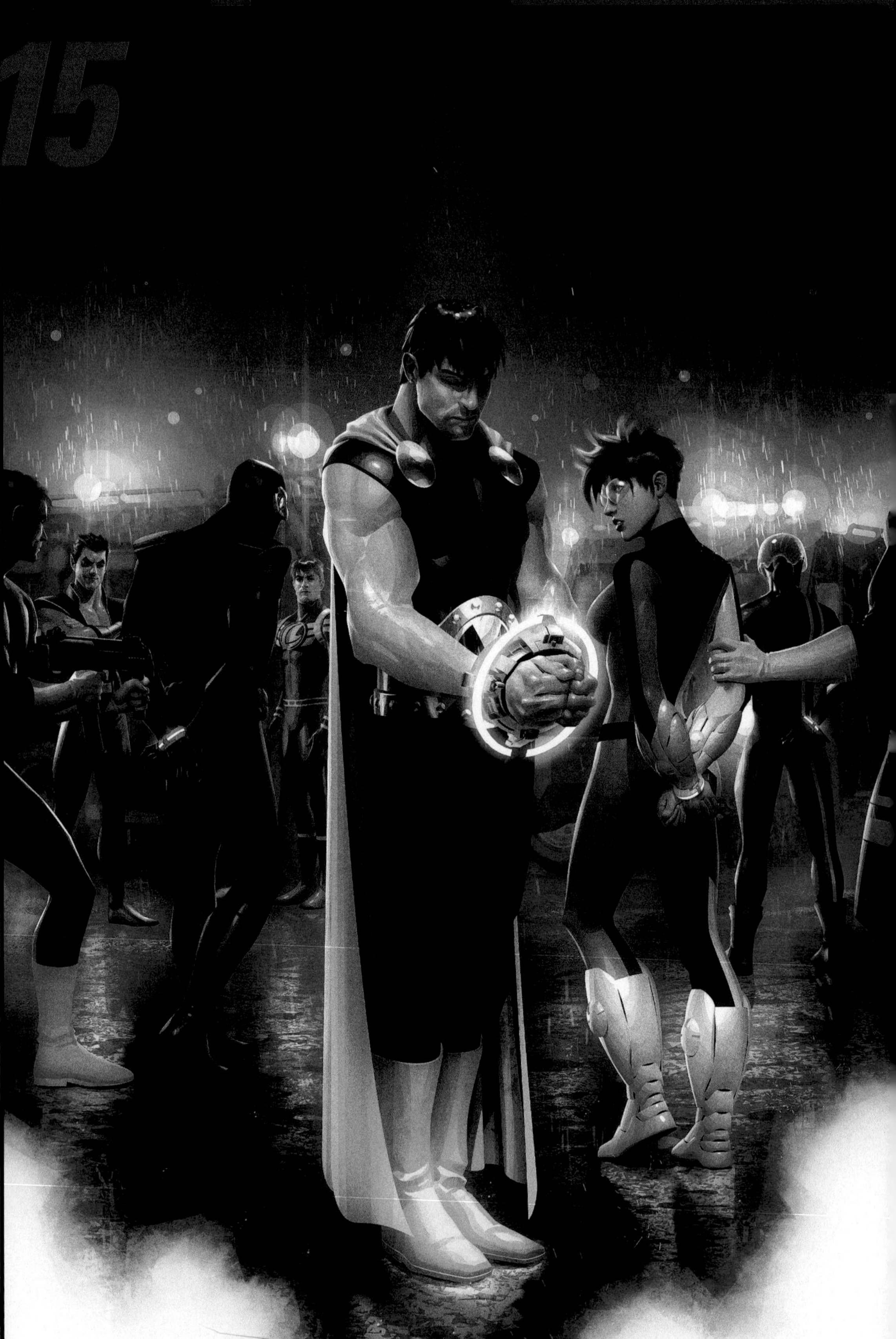
15

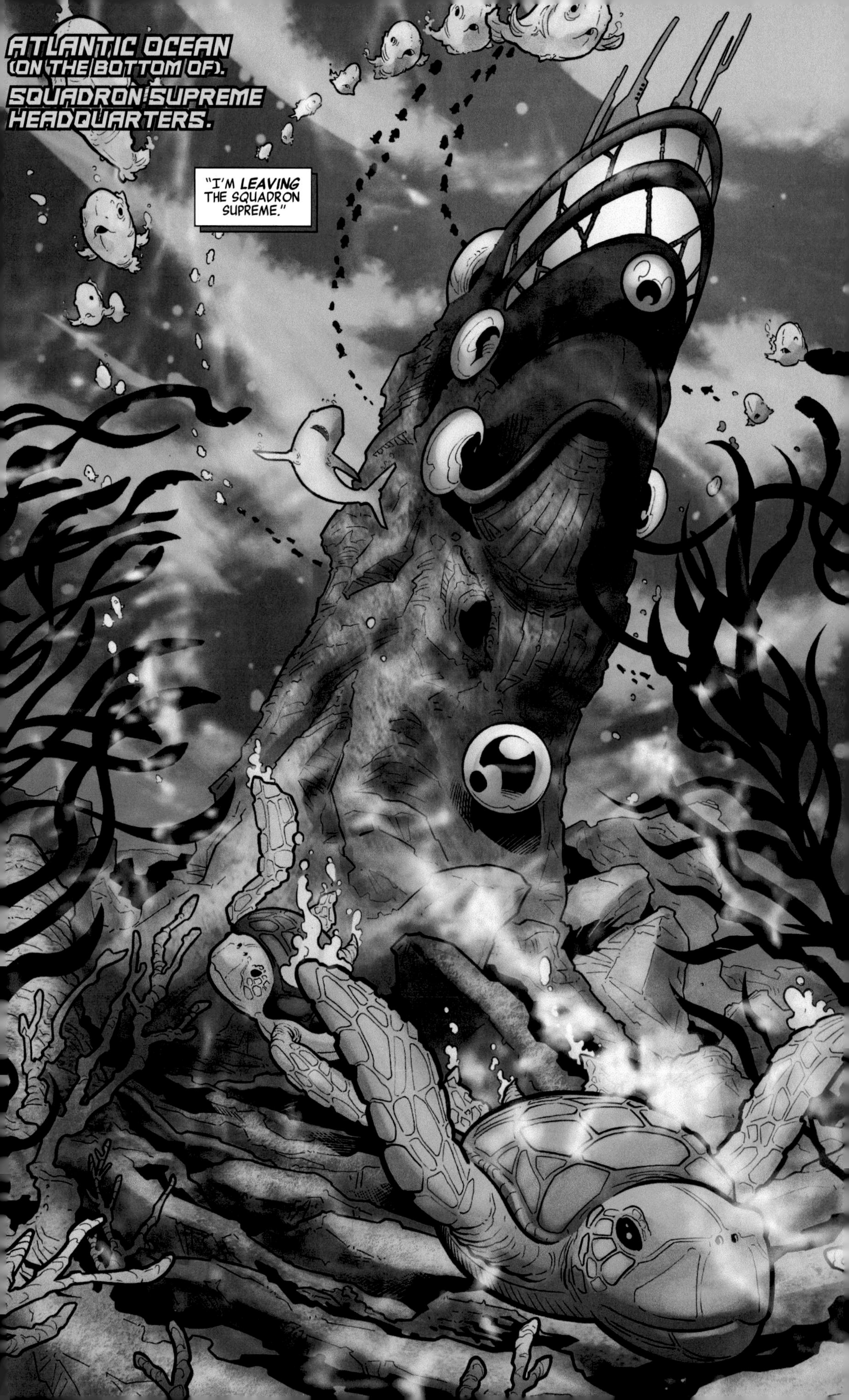
ATLANTIC OCEAN
(ON THE BOTTOM OF).
SQUADRON SUPREME
HEADQUARTERS.
"I'M *LEAVING* THE SQUADRON SUPREME."

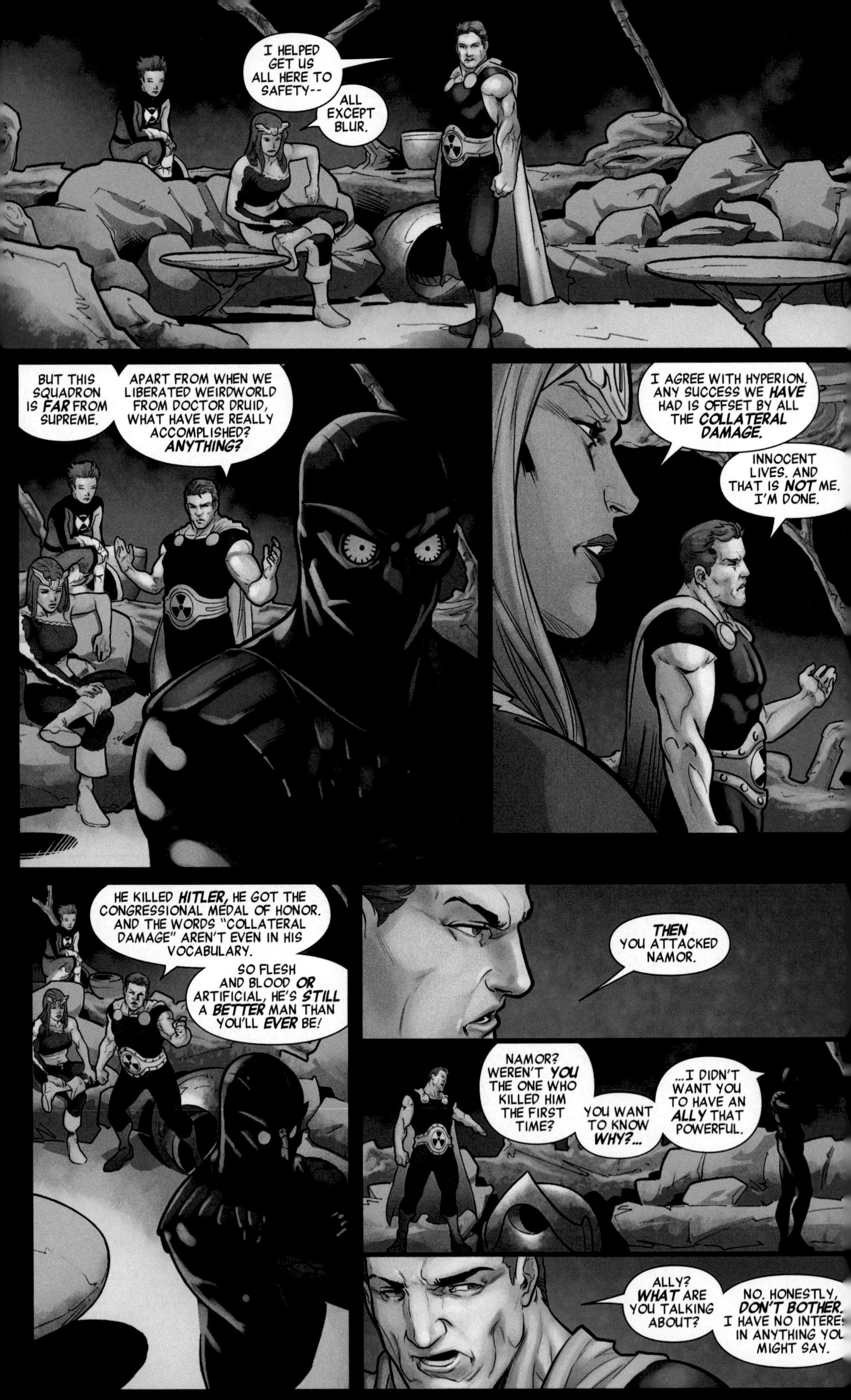
I HELPED GET US ALL HERE TO SAFETY--
ALL EXCEPT BLUR.
BUT THIS SQUADRON IS **FAR** FROM SUPREME.
APART FROM WHEN WE LIBERATED WEIRDWORLD FROM DOCTOR DRUID, WHAT HAVE WE REALLY ACCOMPLISHED? ***ANYTHING?***
I AGREE WITH HYPERION. ANY SUCCESS WE ***HAVE*** HAD IS OFFSET BY ALL THE ***COLLATERAL DAMAGE.***
INNOCENT LIVES. AND THAT IS ***NOT*** ME. I'M DONE.
HE KILLED ***HITLER,*** HE GOT THE CONGRESSIONAL MEDAL OF HONOR. AND THE WORDS "COLLATERAL DAMAGE" AREN'T EVEN IN HIS VOCABULARY.
SO FLESH AND BLOOD ***OR*** ARTIFICIAL, HE'S ***STILL*** A ***BETTER*** MAN THAN YOU'LL ***EVER*** BE!
THEN YOU ATTACKED NAMOR.
NAMOR? WEREN'T ***YOU*** THE ONE WHO KILLED HIM THE FIRST TIME?
YOU WANT TO KNOW ***WHY?...***
...I DIDN'T WANT YOU TO HAVE AN ***ALLY*** THAT POWERFUL.
ALLY? ***WHAT*** ARE YOU TALKING ABOUT?
NO. HONESTLY, ***DON'T BOTHER.*** I HAVE NO INTERE
IN ANYTHING YO
MIGHT SAY.

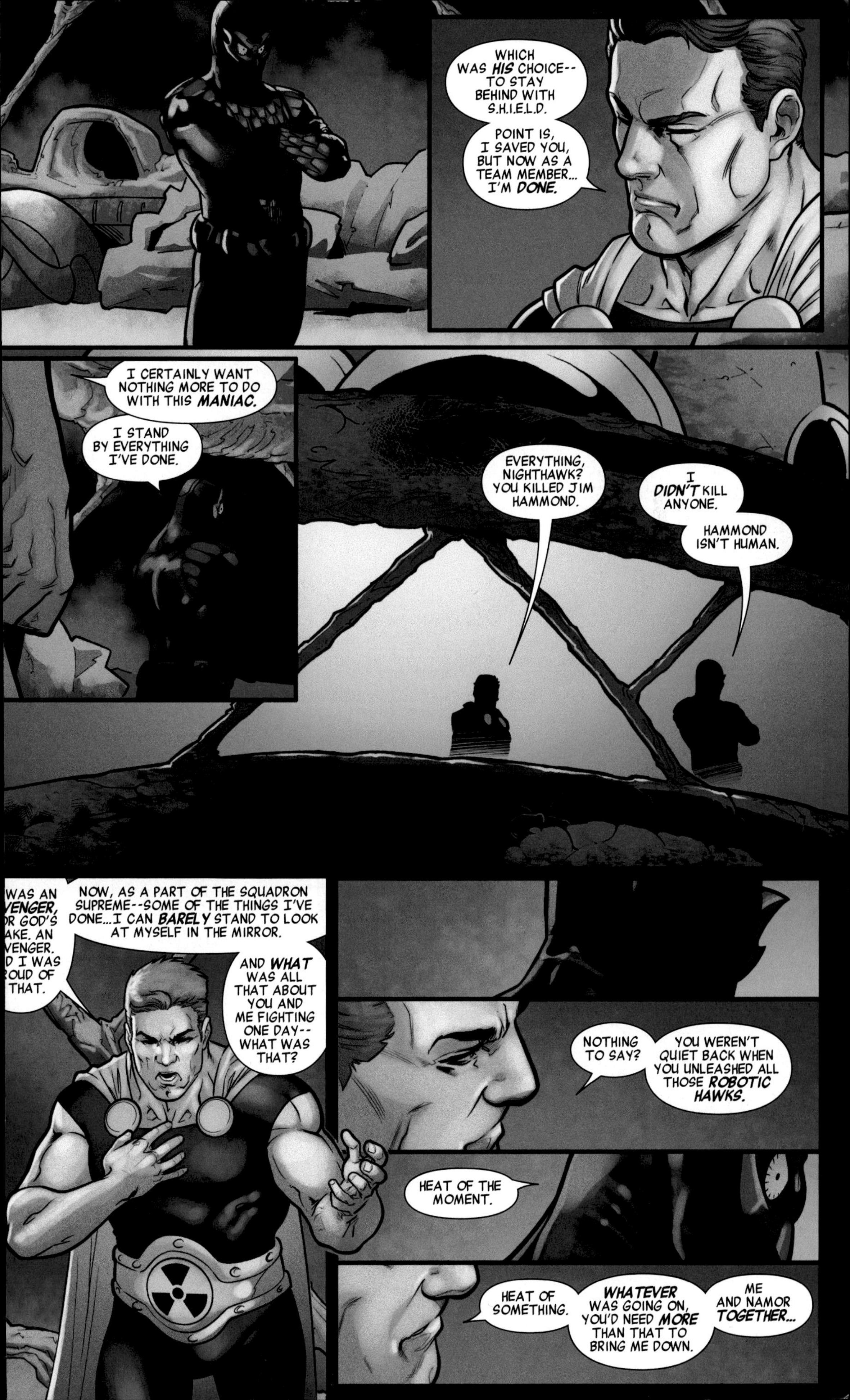

WHICH WAS HIS CHOICE-- TO STAY BEHIND WITH S.H.I.E.L.D.
POINT IS, I SAVED YOU, BUT NOW AS A TEAM MEMBER... I'M DONE.
I CERTAINLY WANT NOTHING MORE TO DO WITH THIS MANIAC.
I STAND BY EVERYTHING I'VE DONE.
EVERYTHING, NIGHTHAWK? YOU KILLED JIM HAMMOND.
I DIDN'T KILL ANYONE.
HAMMOND ISN'T HUMAN.
WAS AN VENGER, R GOD'S AKE. AN VENGER. D I WAS ROUD OF THAT.
NOW, AS A PART OF THE SQUADRON SUPREME--SOME OF THE THINGS I'VE DONE...I CAN BARELY STAND TO LOOK AT MYSELF IN THE MIRROR.
AND WHAT WAS ALL THAT ABOUT YOU AND ME FIGHTING ONE DAY-- WHAT WAS THAT?
NOTHING TO SAY?
YOU WEREN'T QUIET BACK WHEN YOU UNLEASHED ALL THOSE ROBOTIC HAWKS.
HEAT OF THE MOMENT.
HEAT OF SOMETHING.
WHATEVER WAS GOING ON, YOU'D NEED MORE THAN THAT TO BRING ME DOWN.
ME AND NAMOR TOGETHER...

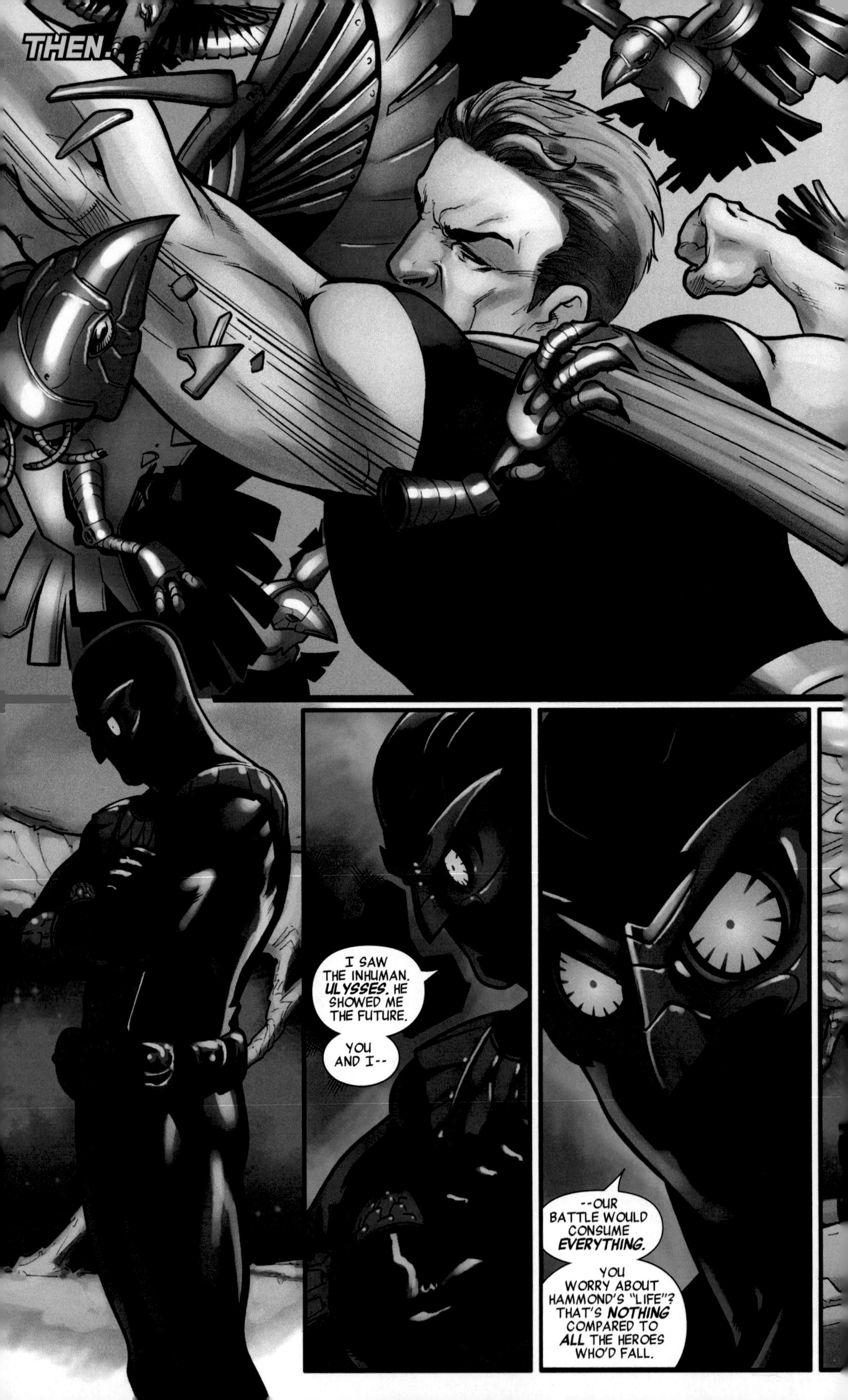
THEN...
I SAW THE INHUMAN. ULYSSES. HE SHOWED ME THE FUTURE.
YOU AND I--
--OUR BATTLE WOULD CONSUME EVERYTHING.
YOU WORRY ABOUT HAMMOND'S "LIFE"? THAT'S NOTHING COMPARED TO ALL THE HEROES WHO'D FALL.

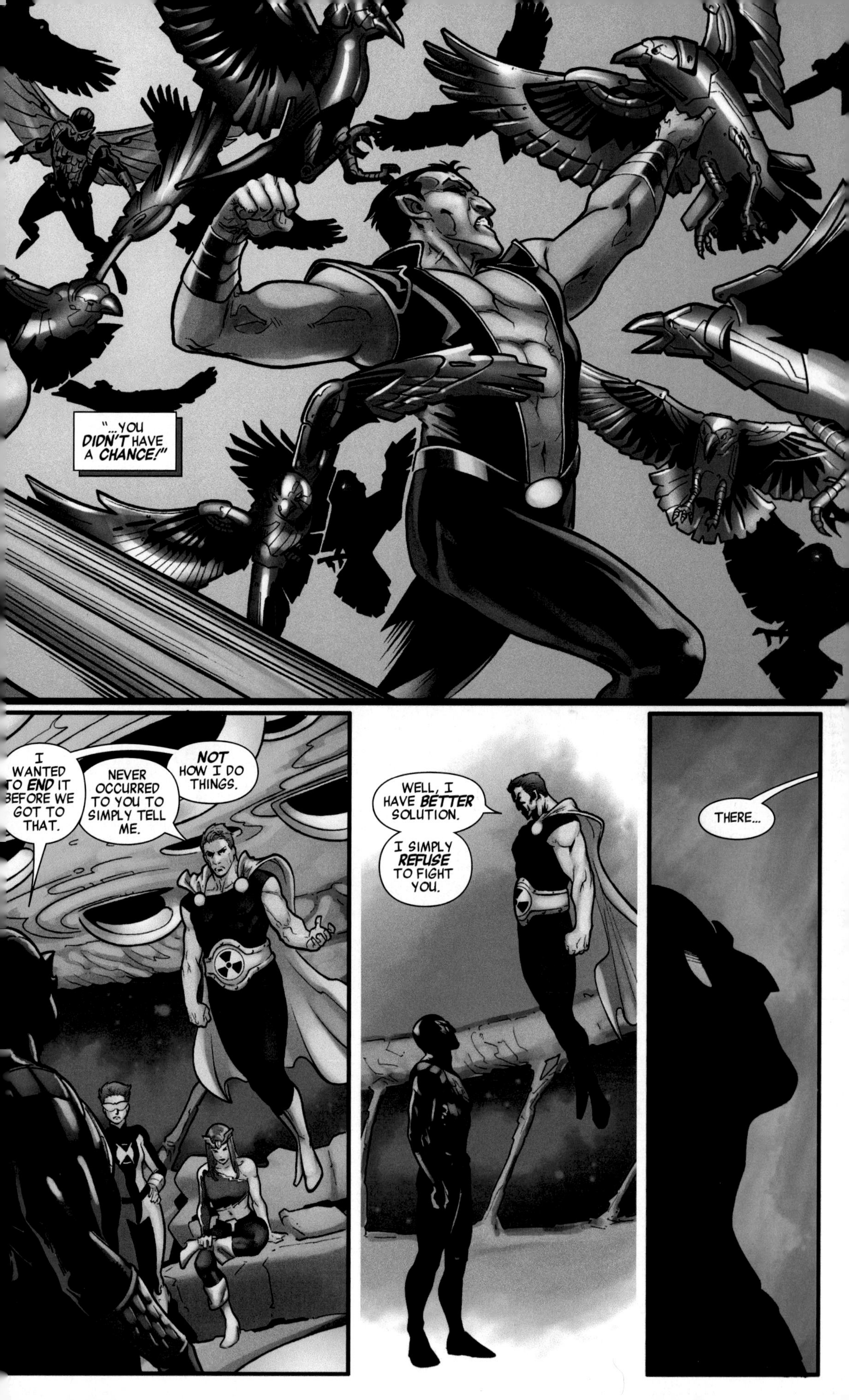
"...YOU DIDN'T HAVE A CHANCE!"
I WANTED TO END IT BEFORE WE GOT TO THAT.
NEVER OCCURRED TO YOU TO SIMPLY TELL ME.
NOT HOW I DO THINGS.
WELL, I HAVE BETTER SOLUTION.
I SIMPLY REFUSE TO FIGHT YOU.
THERE...

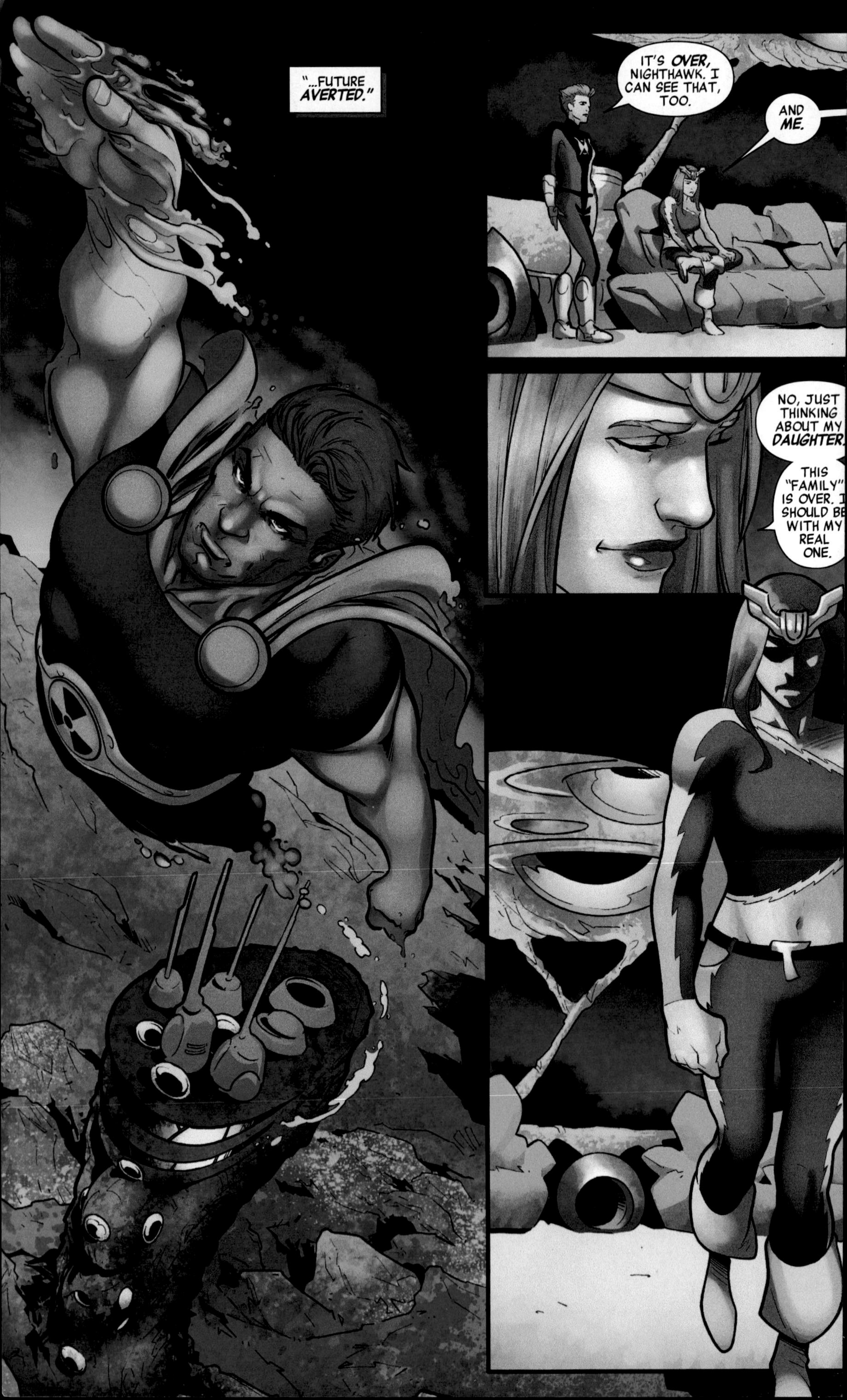
"...FUTURE AVERTED."
IT'S OVER, NIGHTHAWK. I CAN SEE THAT, TOO.
AND ME.
NO, JUST THINKING ABOUT MY DAUGHTER.
THIS "FAMILY" IS OVER. I SHOULD BE WITH MY REAL ONE.

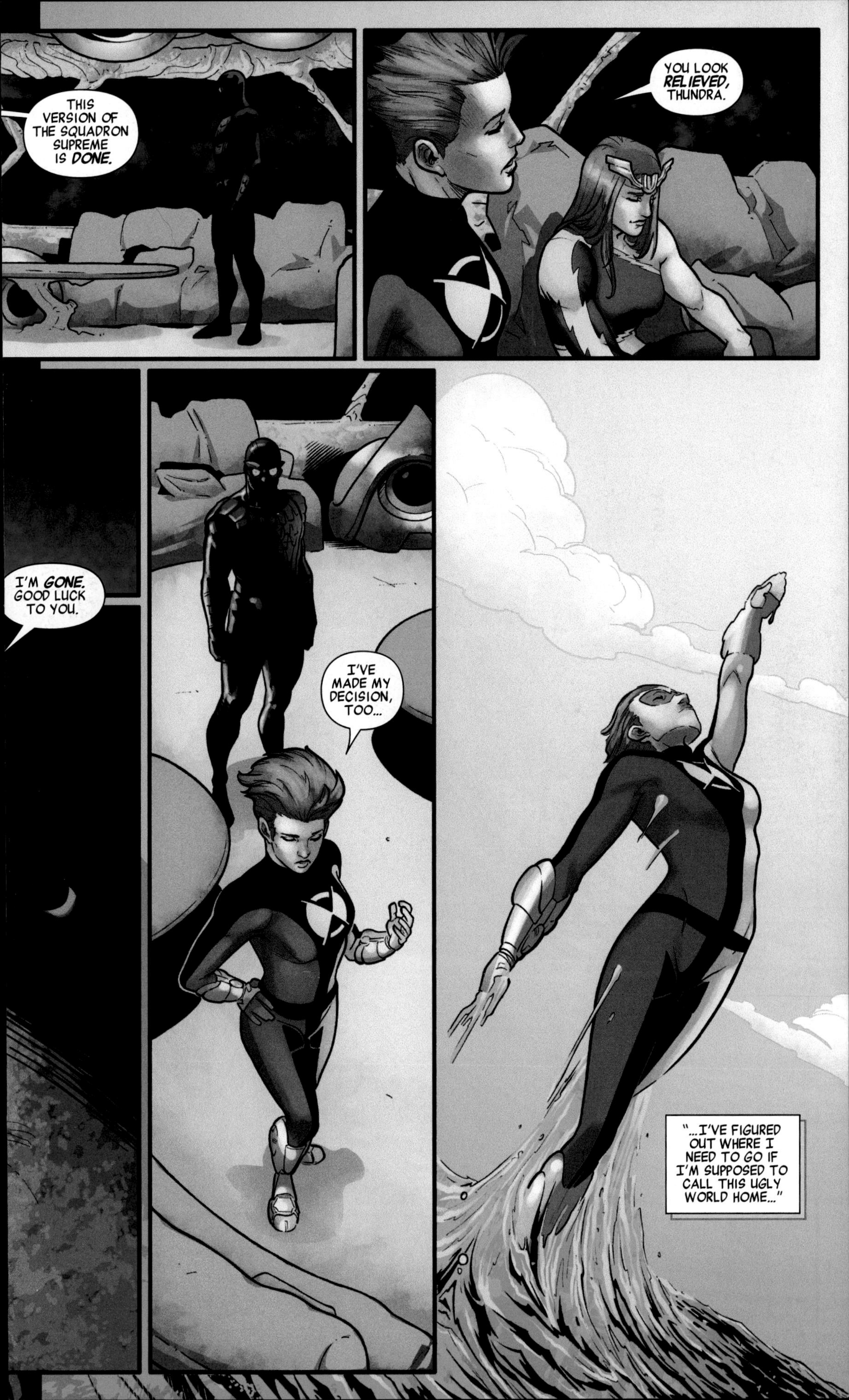
THIS VERSION OF THE SQUADRON SUPREME IS DONE.
YOU LOOK RELIEVED, THUNDRA.
I'M GONE. GOOD LUCK TO YOU.
I'VE MADE MY DECISION, TOO...
"...I'VE FIGURED OUT WHERE I NEED TO GO IF I'M SUPPOSED TO CALL THIS UGLY WORLD HOME..."

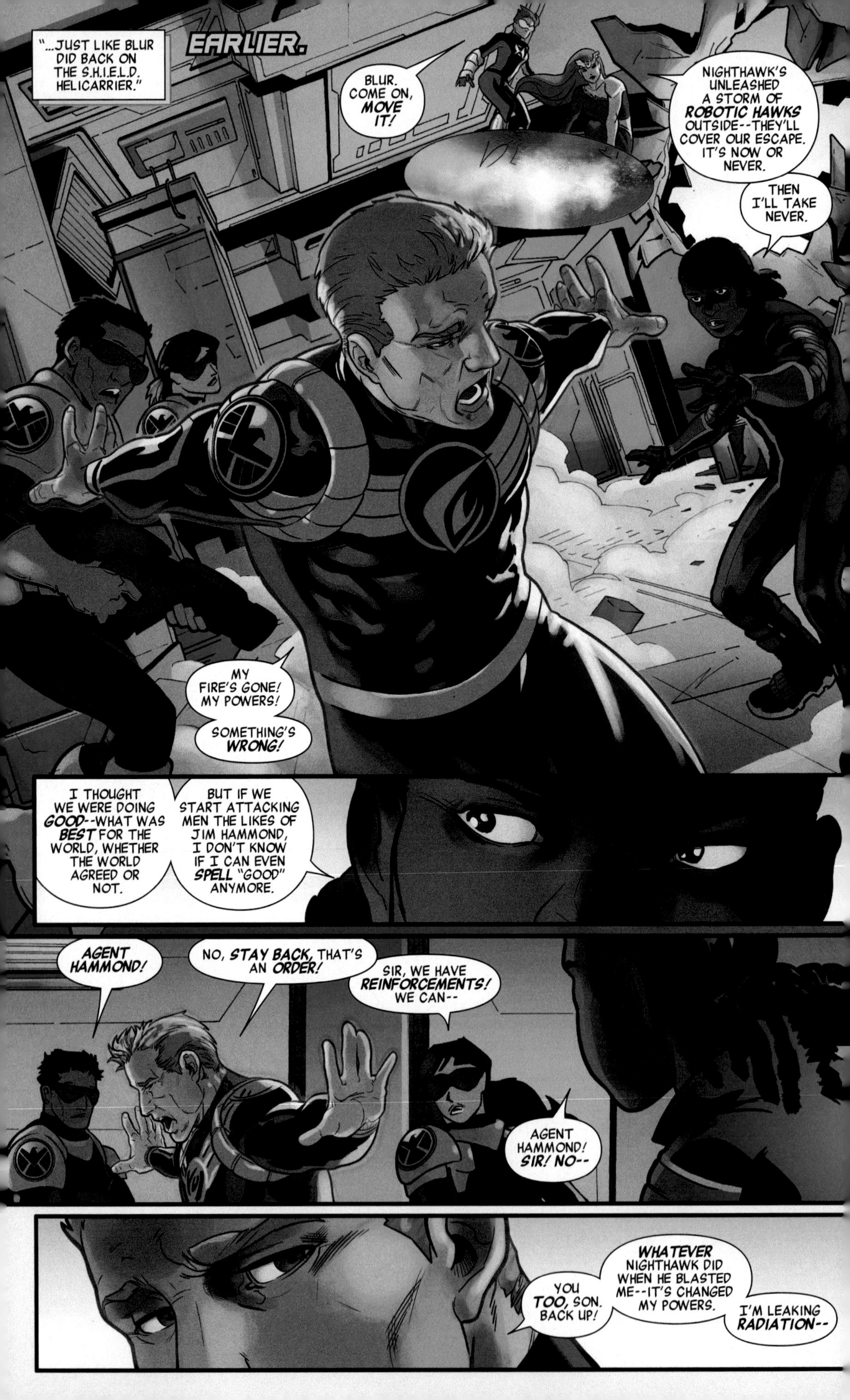
"...JUST LIKE BLUR DID BACK ON THE S.H.I.E.L.D. HELICARRIER."
EARLIER.
BLUR. COME ON, MOVE IT!
NIGHTHAWK'S UNLEASHED A STORM OF ROBOTIC HAWKS OUTSIDE--THEY'LL COVER OUR ESCAPE. IT'S NOW OR NEVER.
THEN I'LL TAKE NEVER.
MY FIRE'S GONE! MY POWERS!
SOMETHING'S WRONG!
I THOUGHT WE WERE DOING GOOD--WHAT WAS BEST FOR THE WORLD, WHETHER THE WORLD AGREED OR NOT.
BUT IF WE START ATTACKING MEN THE LIKES OF JIM HAMMOND, I DON'T KNOW IF I CAN EVEN SPELL "GOOD" ANYMORE.
AGENT HAMMOND!
NO, STAY BACK, THAT'S AN ORDER!
SIR, WE HAVE REINFORCEMENTS! WE CAN--
AGENT HAMMOND! SIR! NO--
YOU TOO, SON. BACK UP!
WHATEVER NIGHTHAWK DID WHEN HE BLASTED ME--IT'S CHANGED MY POWERS.
I'M LEAKING RADIATION--

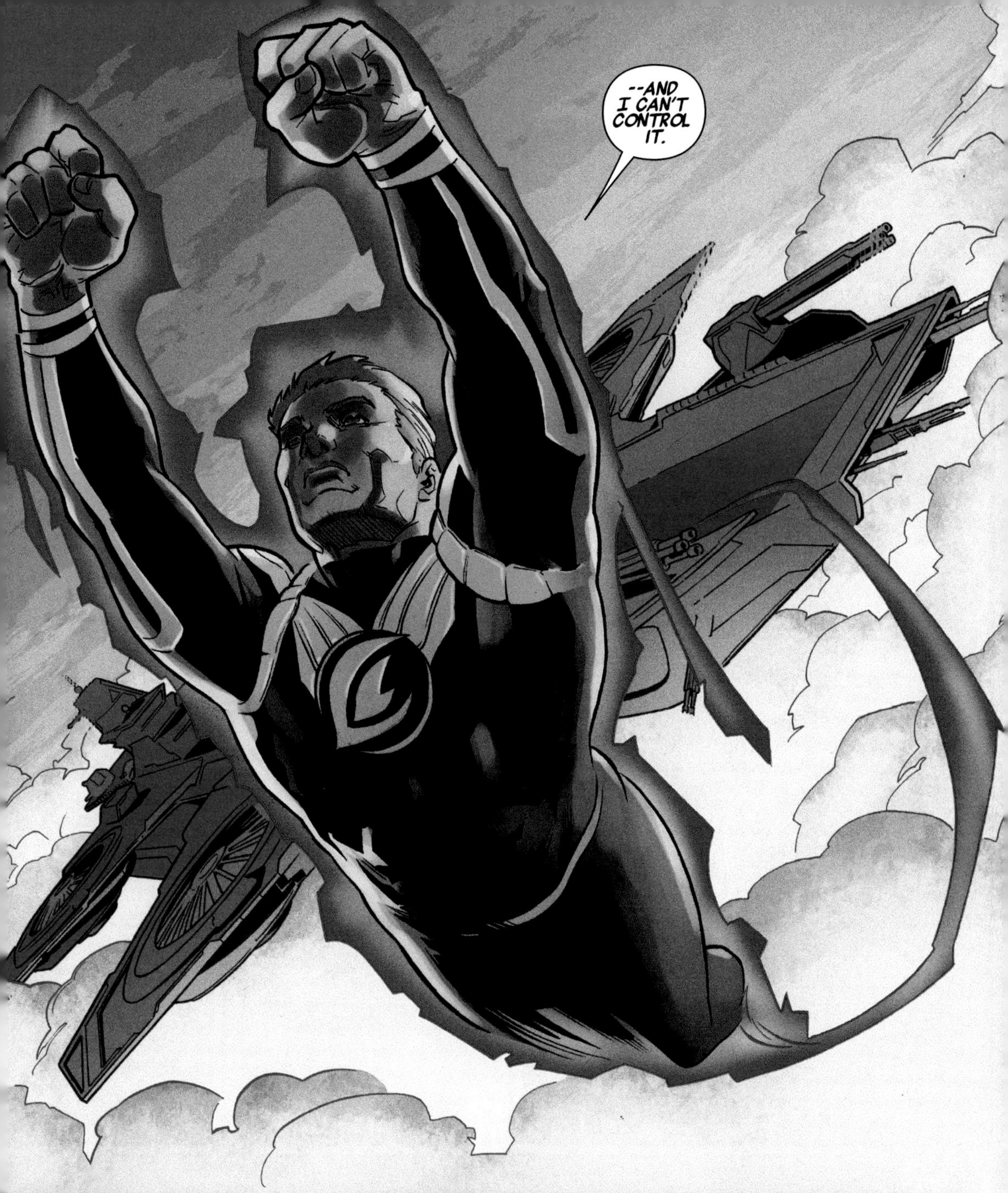
--AND I CAN'T CONTROL IT.

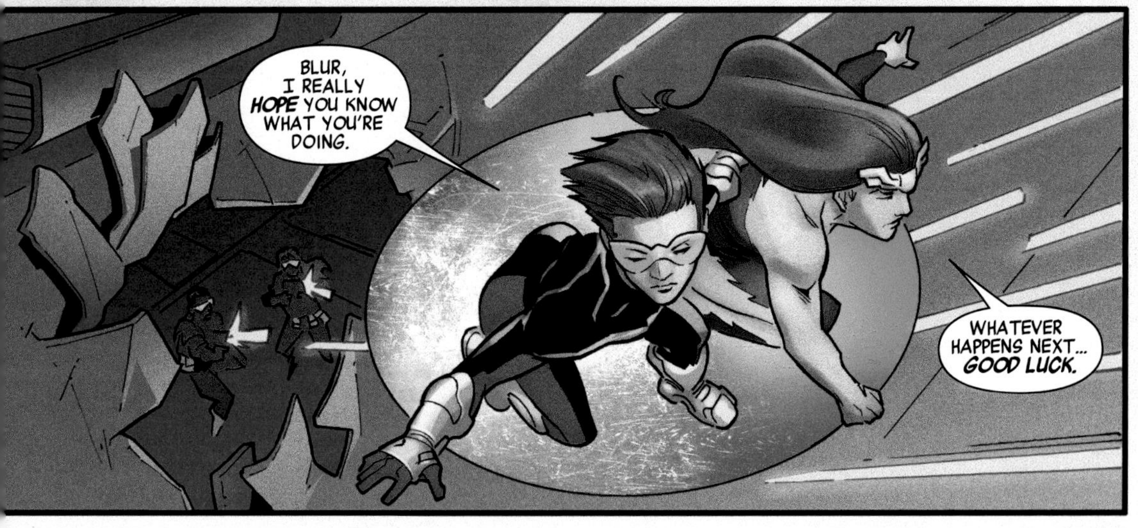
BLUR, I REALLY HOPE YOU KNOW WHAT YOU'RE DOING.
WHATEVER HAPPENS NEXT... GOOD LUCK.

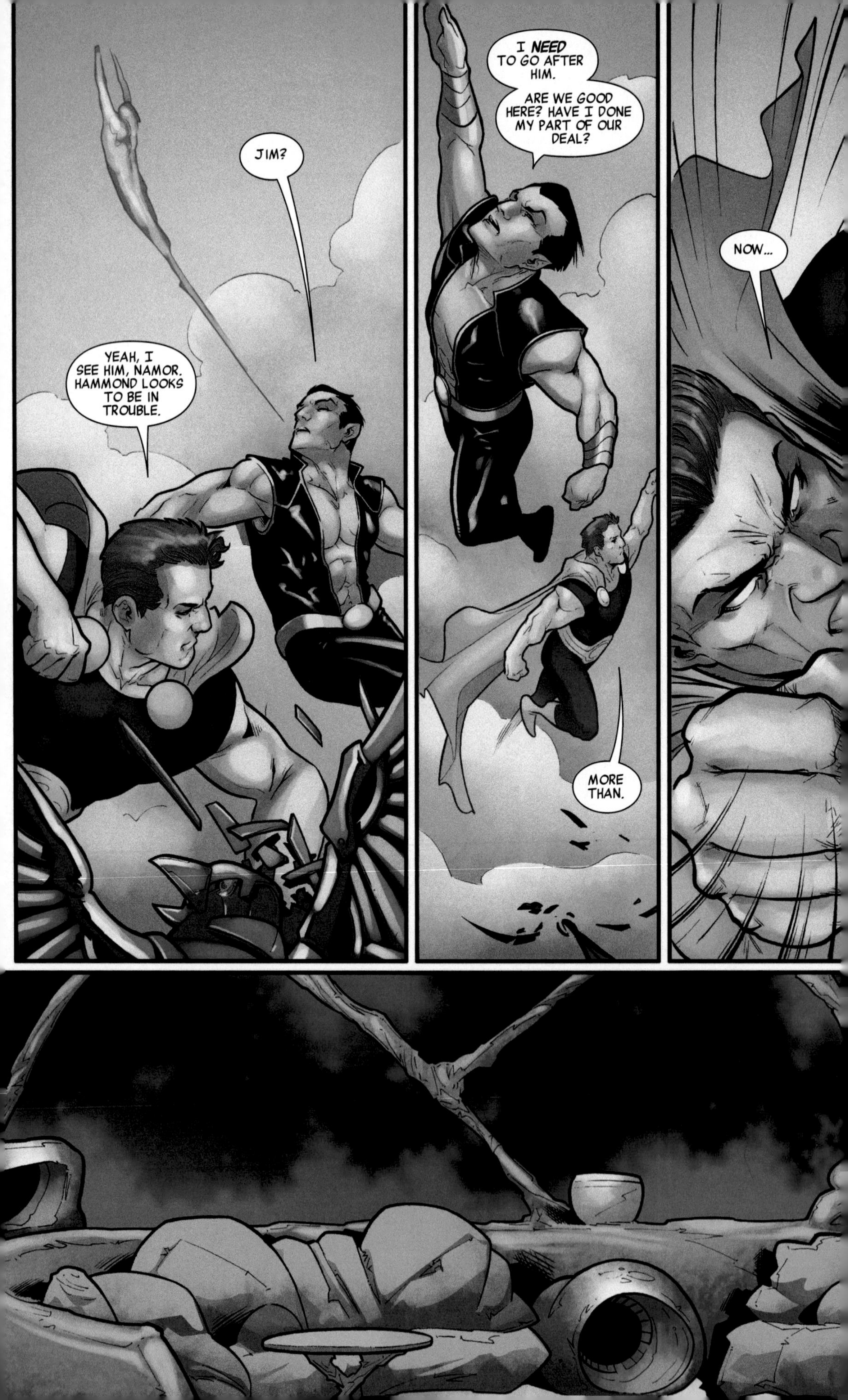
JIM?
YEAH, I SEE HIM, NAMOR. HAMMOND LOOKS TO BE IN TROUBLE.
I NEED TO GO AFTER HIM.
ARE WE GOOD HERE? HAVE I DONE MY PART OF OUR DEAL?
MORE THAN.
NOW...

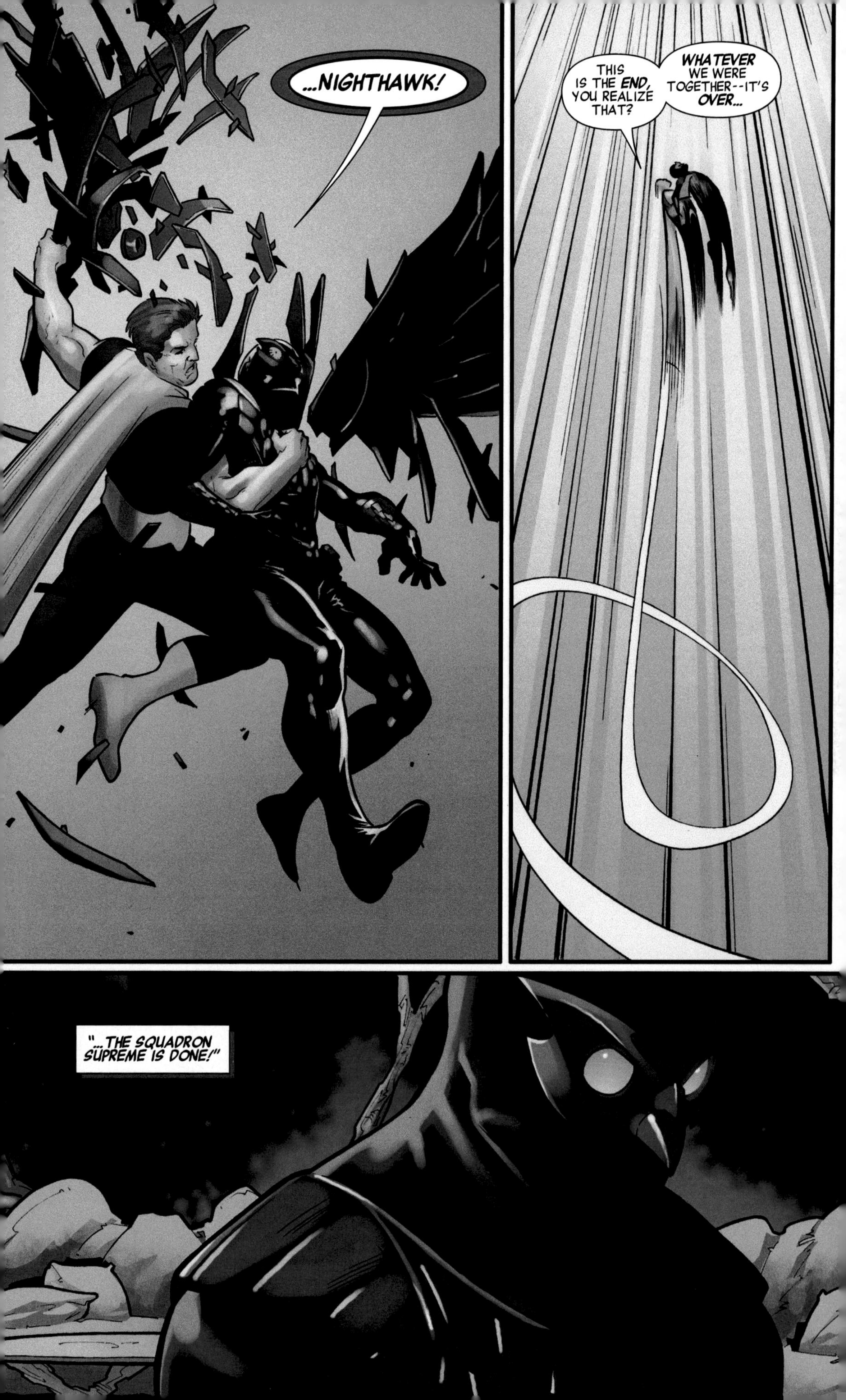

...NIGHTHAWK!
THIS IS THE END, YOU REALIZE THAT?
WHATEVER WE WERE TOGETHER--IT'S OVER...
"...THE SQUADRON SUPREME IS DONE!"

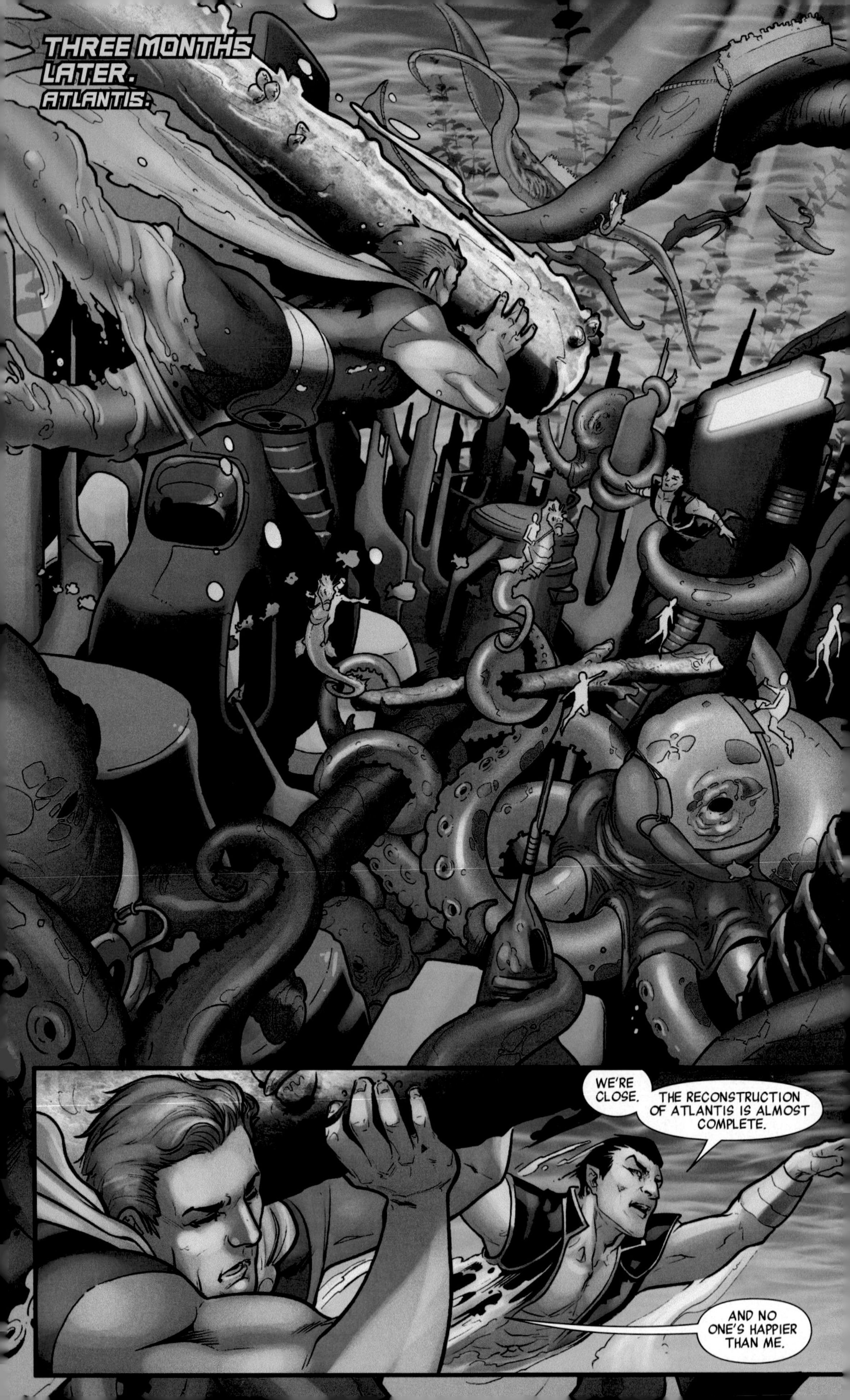
THREE MONTHS LATER. ATLANTIS.
WE'RE CLOSE.
THE RECONSTRUCTION OF ATLANTIS IS ALMOST COMPLETE.
AND NO ONE'S HAPPIER THAN ME.

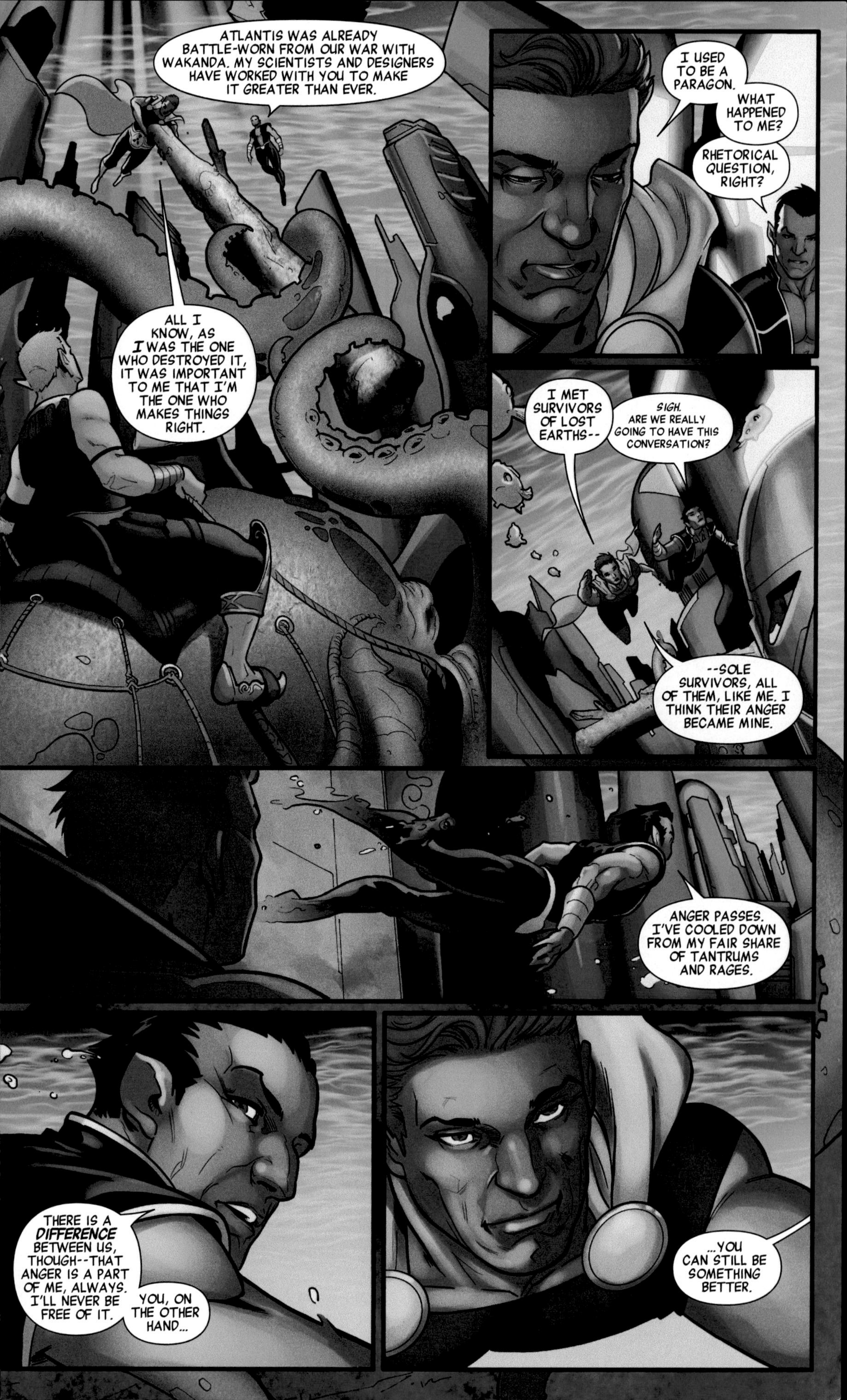
ATLANTIS WAS ALREADY BATTLE-WORN FROM OUR WAR WITH WAKANDA. MY SCIENTISTS AND DESIGNERS HAVE WORKED WITH YOU TO MAKE IT GREATER THAN EVER.
ALL I KNOW, AS I WAS THE ONE WHO DESTROYED IT, IT WAS IMPORTANT TO ME THAT I'M THE ONE WHO MAKES THINGS RIGHT.
I USED TO BE A PARAGON.
WHAT HAPPENED TO ME?
RHETORICAL QUESTION, RIGHT?
I MET SURVIVORS OF LOST EARTHS--
SIGH. ARE WE REALLY GOING TO HAVE THIS CONVERSATION?
--SOLE SURVIVORS, ALL OF THEM, LIKE ME. I THINK THEIR ANGER BECAME MINE.
ANGER PASSES. I'VE COOLED DOWN FROM MY FAIR SHARE OF TANTRUMS AND RAGES.
THERE IS A DIFFERENCE BETWEEN US, THOUGH--THAT ANGER IS A PART OF ME, ALWAYS. I'LL NEVER BE FREE OF IT.
YOU, ON THE OTHER HAND...
...YOU CAN STILL BE SOMETHING BETTER.

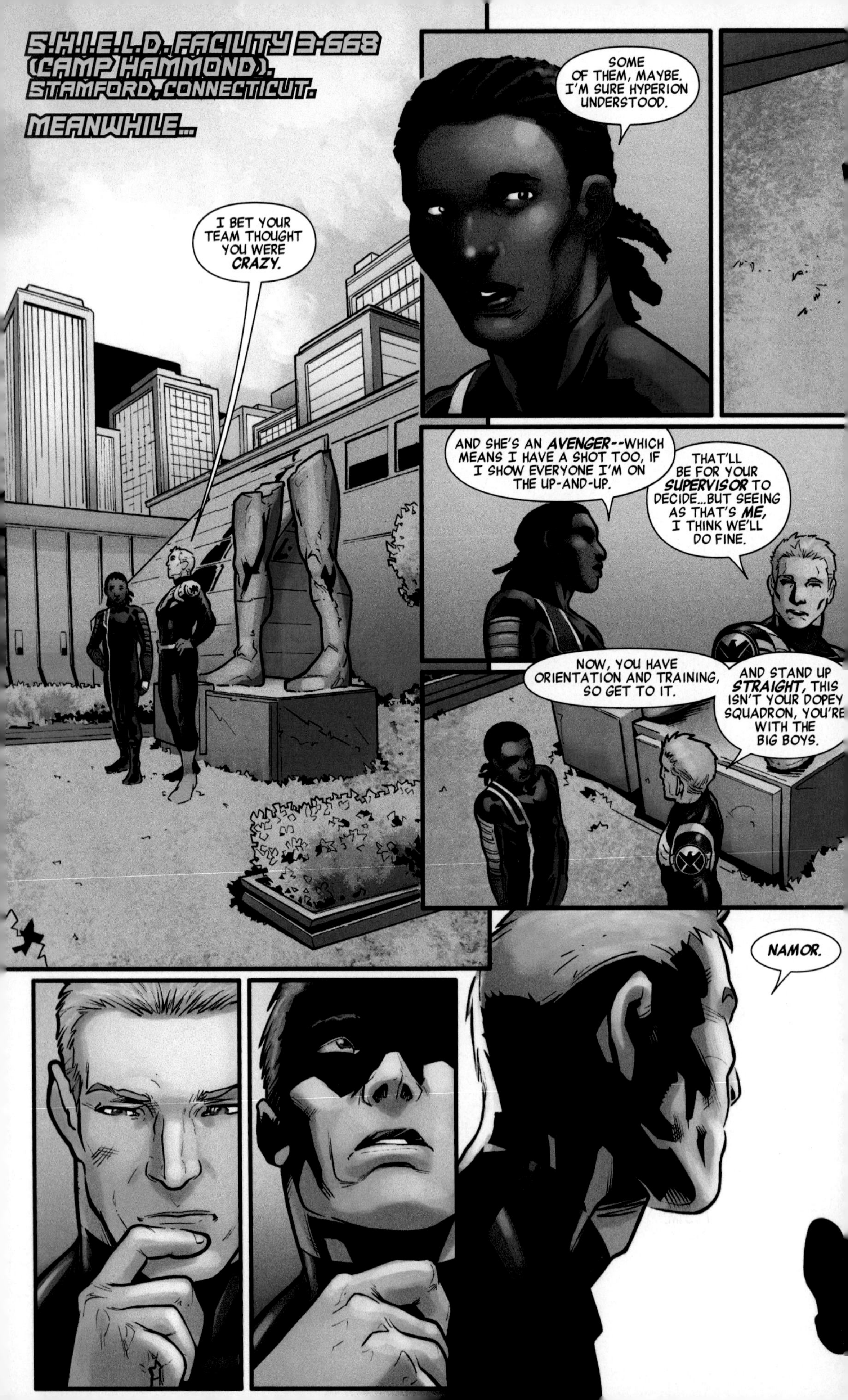
S.H.I.E.L.D. FACILITY 3-668 (CAMP HAMMOND). STAMFORD, CONNECTICUT.
MEANWHILE...
I BET YOUR TEAM THOUGHT YOU WERE CRAZY.
SOME OF THEM, MAYBE. I'M SURE HYPERION UNDERSTOOD.
AND SHE'S AN AVENGER--WHICH MEANS I HAVE A SHOT TOO, IF I SHOW EVERYONE I'M ON THE UP-AND-UP.
THAT'LL BE FOR YOUR SUPERVISOR TO DECIDE...BUT SEEING AS THAT'S ME, I THINK WE'LL DO FINE.
NOW, YOU HAVE ORIENTATION AND TRAINING, SO GET TO IT.
AND STAND UP STRAIGHT, THIS ISN'T YOUR DOPEY SQUADRON, YOU'RE WITH THE BIG BOYS.
NAMOR.

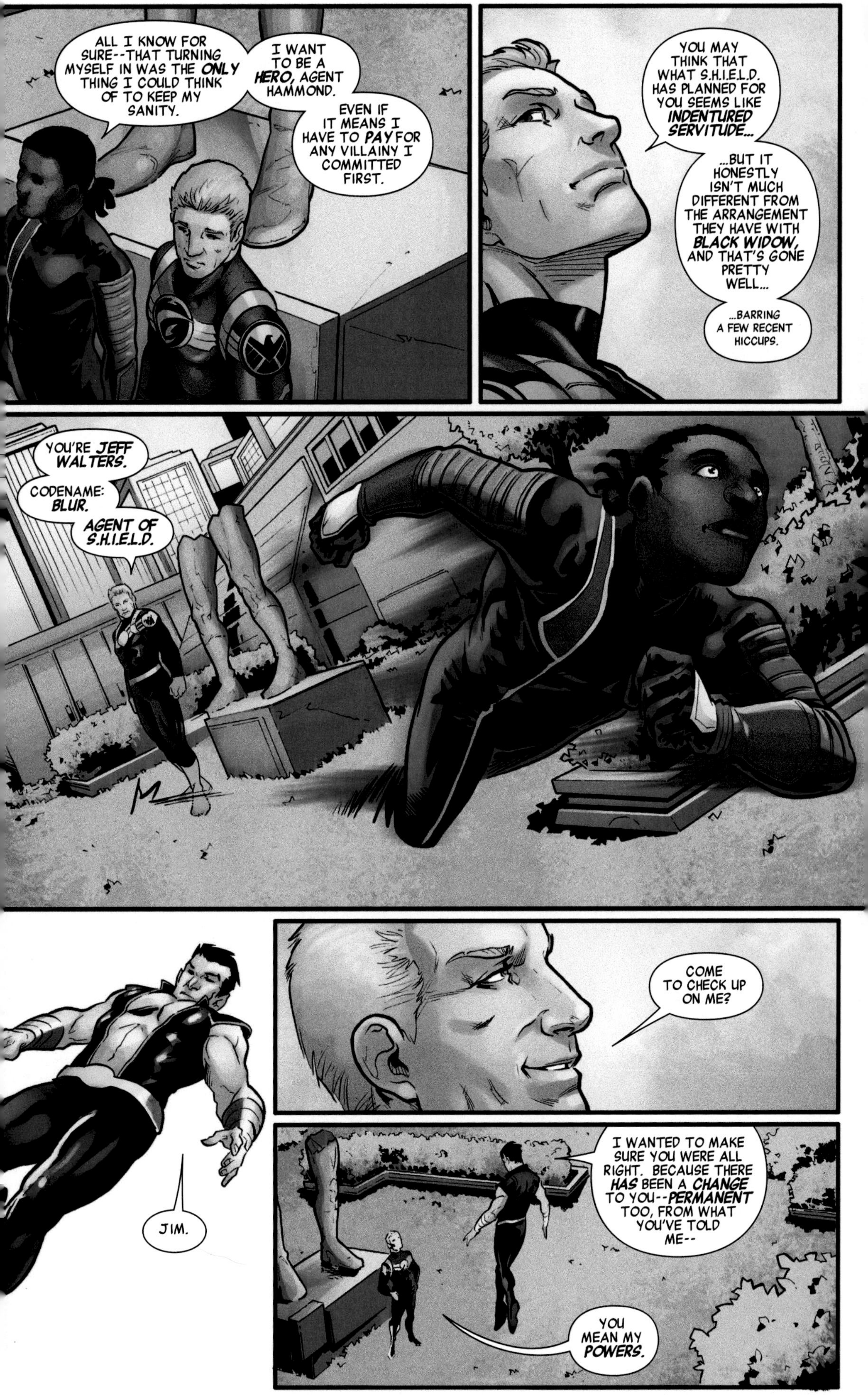
ALL I KNOW FOR SURE--THAT TURNING MYSELF IN WAS THE ONLY THING I COULD THINK OF TO KEEP MY SANITY.
I WANT TO BE A HERO, AGENT HAMMOND.
EVEN IF IT MEANS I HAVE TO PAY FOR ANY VILLAINY I COMMITTED FIRST.
YOU MAY THINK THAT WHAT S.H.I.E.L.D. HAS PLANNED FOR YOU SEEMS LIKE INDENTURED SERVITUDE...
...BUT IT HONESTLY ISN'T MUCH DIFFERENT FROM THE ARRANGEMENT THEY HAVE WITH BLACK WIDOW, AND THAT'S GONE PRETTY WELL...
...BARRING A FEW RECENT HICCUPS.
YOU'RE JEFF WALTERS.
CODENAME: BLUR.
AGENT OF S.H.I.E.L.D.
COME TO CHECK UP ON ME?
JIM.
I WANTED TO MAKE SURE YOU WERE ALL RIGHT. BECAUSE THERE HAS BEEN A CHANGE TO YOU--PERMANENT TOO, FROM WHAT YOU'VE TOLD ME--
YOU MEAN MY POWERS.

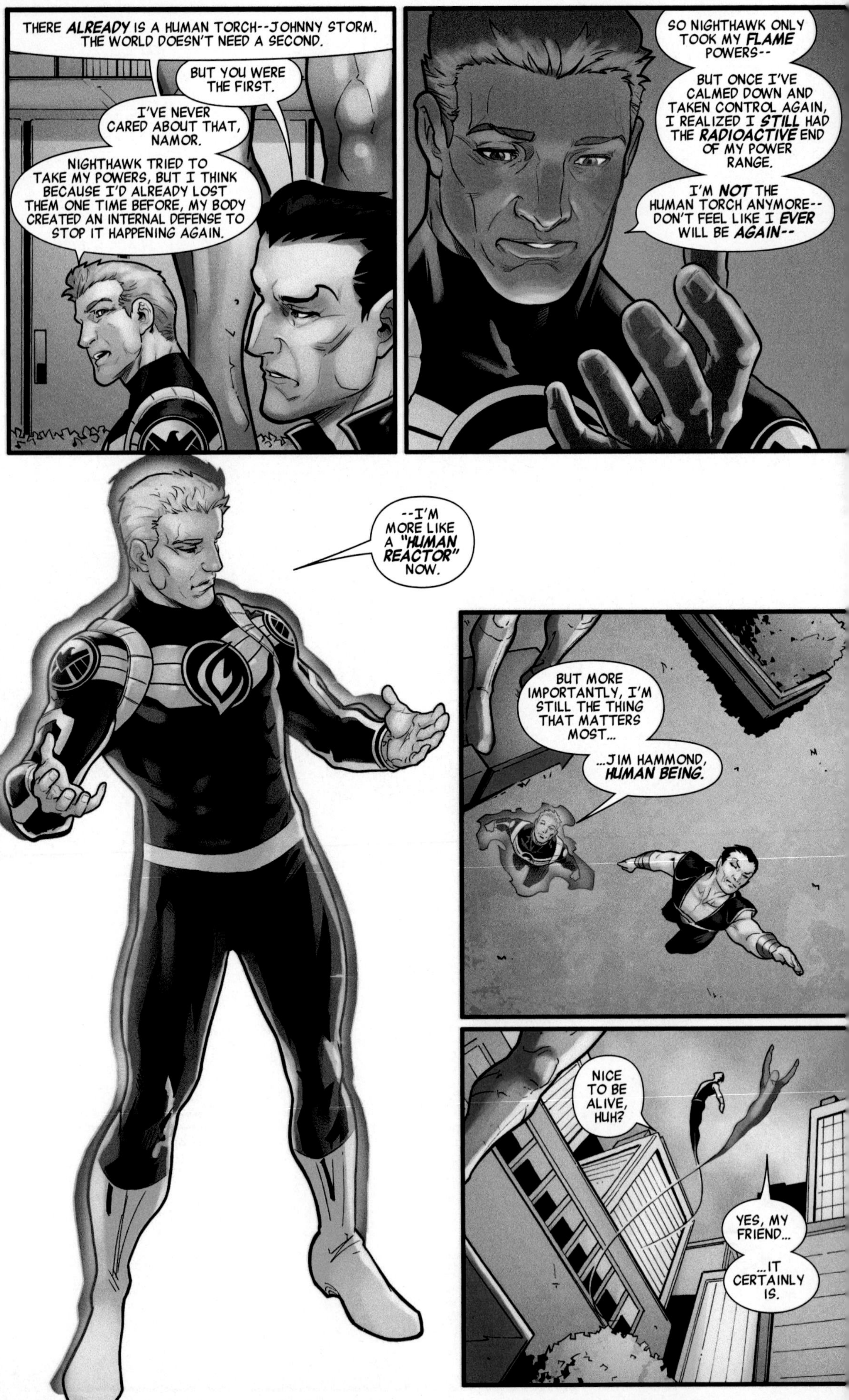
THERE ALREADY IS A HUMAN TORCH--JOHNNY STORM. THE WORLD DOESN'T NEED A SECOND.
BUT YOU WERE THE FIRST.
I'VE NEVER CARED ABOUT THAT, NAMOR.
NIGHTHAWK TRIED TO TAKE MY POWERS, BUT I THINK BECAUSE I'D ALREADY LOST THEM ONE TIME BEFORE, MY BODY CREATED AN INTERNAL DEFENSE TO STOP IT HAPPENING AGAIN.
SO NIGHTHAWK ONLY TOOK MY FLAME POWERS--
BUT ONCE I'VE CALMED DOWN AND TAKEN CONTROL AGAIN, I REALIZED I STILL HAD THE RADIOACTIVE END OF MY POWER RANGE.
I'M NOT THE HUMAN TORCH ANYMORE--DON'T FEEL LIKE I EVER WILL BE AGAIN--
--I'M MORE LIKE A "HUMAN REACTOR" NOW.
BUT MORE IMPORTANTLY, I'M STILL THE THING THAT MATTERS MOST...
...JIM HAMMOND, HUMAN BEING.
NICE TO BE ALIVE, HUH?
YES, MY FRIEND...
...IT CERTAINLY IS.

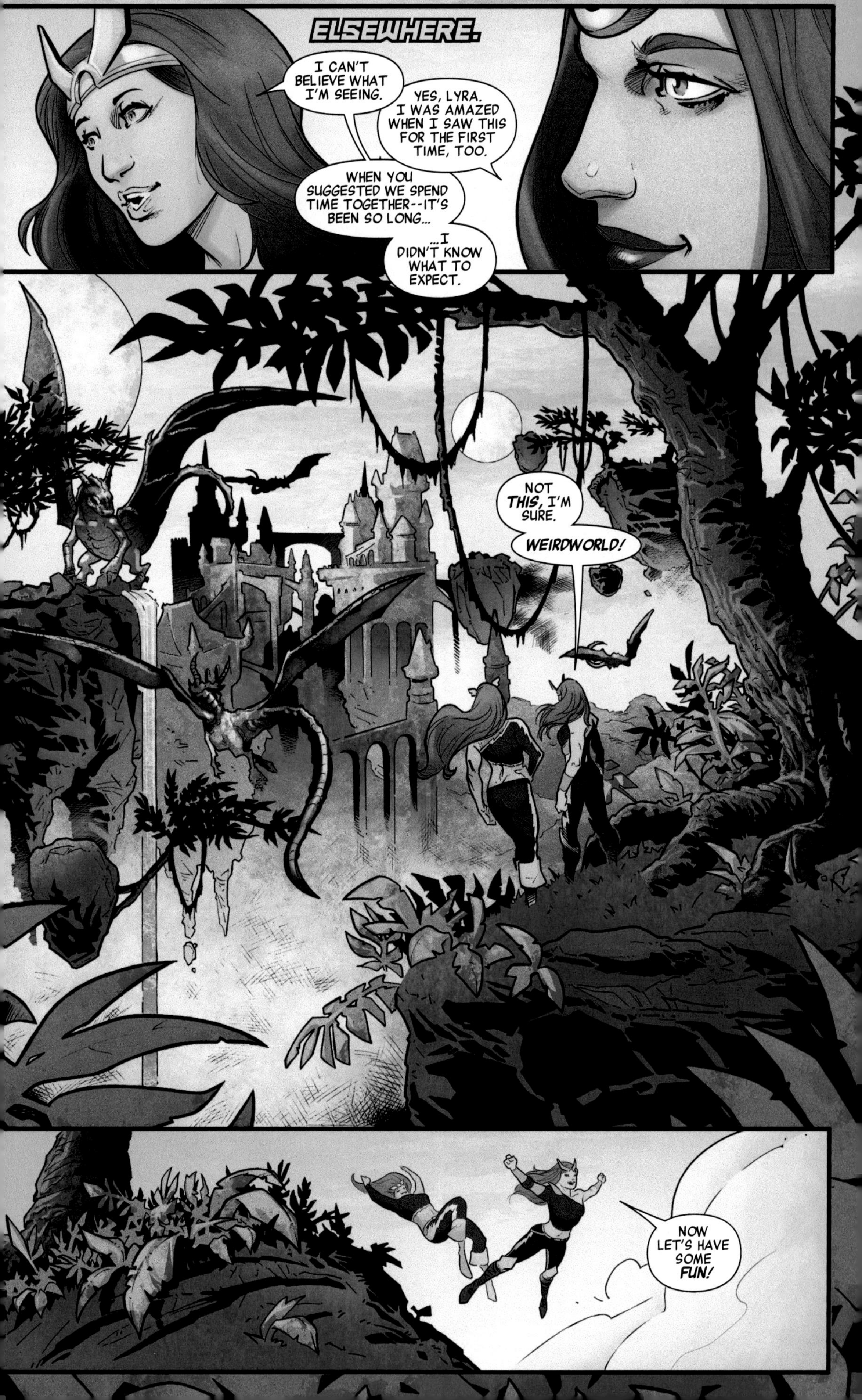
ELSEWHERE.
I CAN'T BELIEVE WHAT I'M SEEING.
YES, LYRA. I WAS AMAZED WHEN I SAW THIS FOR THE FIRST TIME, TOO.
WHEN YOU SUGGESTED WE SPEND TIME TOGETHER--IT'S BEEN SO LONG...
...I DIDN'T KNOW WHAT TO EXPECT.
NOT THIS, I'M SURE.
WEIRDWORLD!
NOW LET'S HAVE SOME FUN!

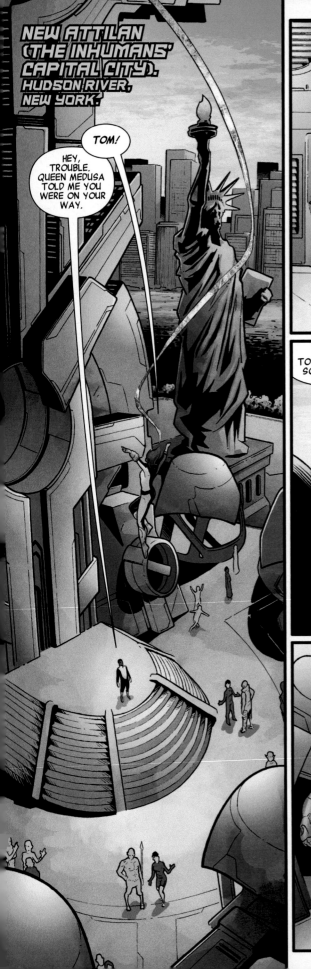

NEW ATTILAN (THE INHUMANS' CAPITAL CITY). HUDSON RIVER, NEW YORK:

TOM!

HEY, TROUBLE. QUEEN MEDUSA TOLD ME YOU WERE ON YOUR WAY.

I NEED A PLACE LIKE THIS WHERE I CAN FEEL SAFE.

YEAH, Y'DO.

YOU NEED TO UNDERSTAND SOMETHING--

--TOOK A WHILE FOR ME TO REALIZE IT, MYSELF.

YES?

THE PAST IS THE PAST. YOURS, MINE, ALL OF IT.

SO WELCOME TO YOUR FUTURE. YOU'RE AMONG THE INHUMANS NOW...

...AND THAT MAKES YOU FAMILY.

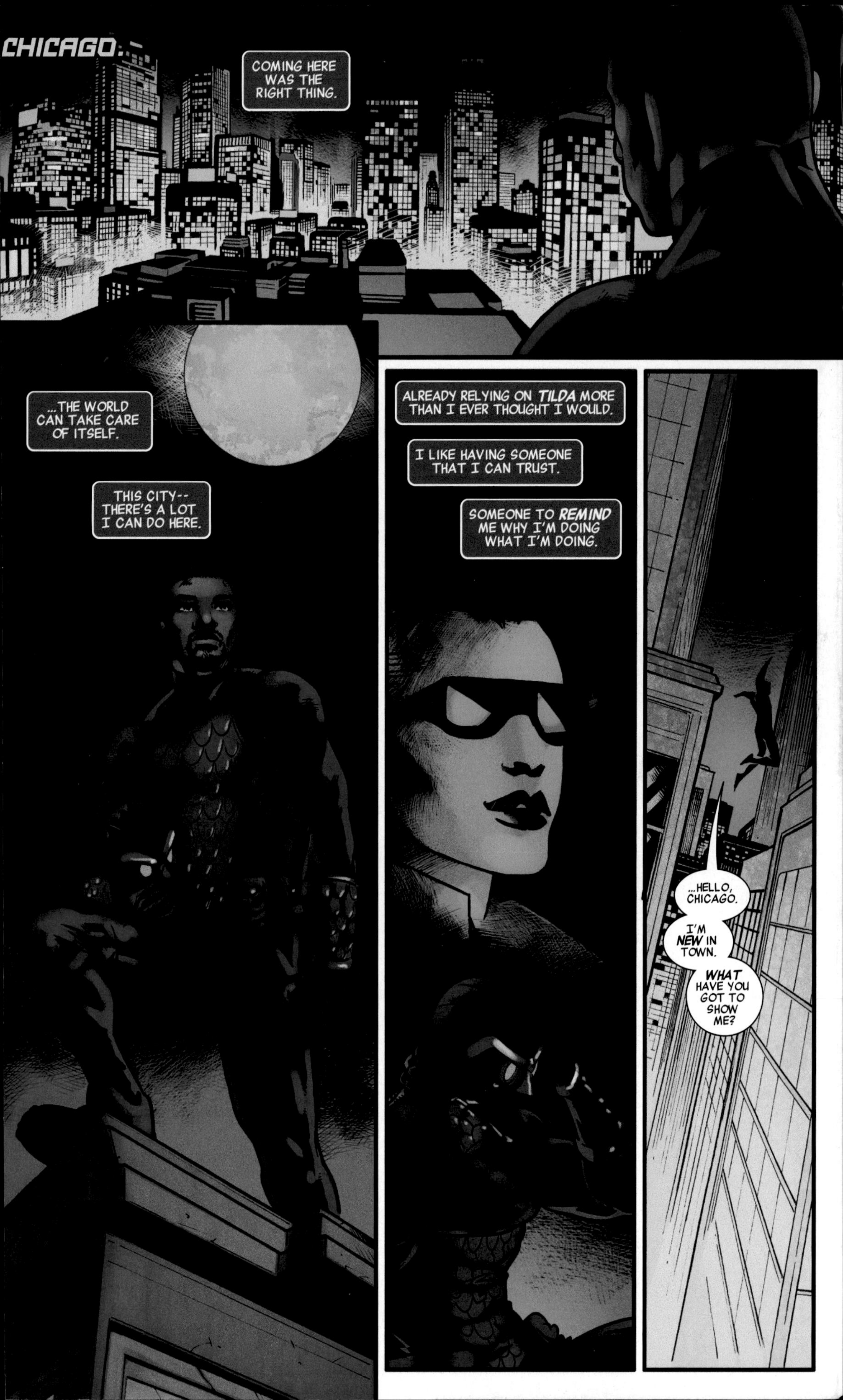
CHICAGO:
COMING HERE WAS THE RIGHT THING.
...THE WORLD CAN TAKE CARE OF ITSELF.
THIS CITY-- THERE'S A LOT I CAN DO HERE.
ALREADY RELYING ON TILDA MORE THAN I EVER THOUGHT I WOULD.
I LIKE HAVING SOMEONE THAT I CAN TRUST.
SOMEONE TO REMIND ME WHY I'M DOING WHAT I'M DOING.
...HELLO, CHICAGO.
I'M NEW IN TOWN.
WHAT HAVE YOU GOT TO SHOW ME?

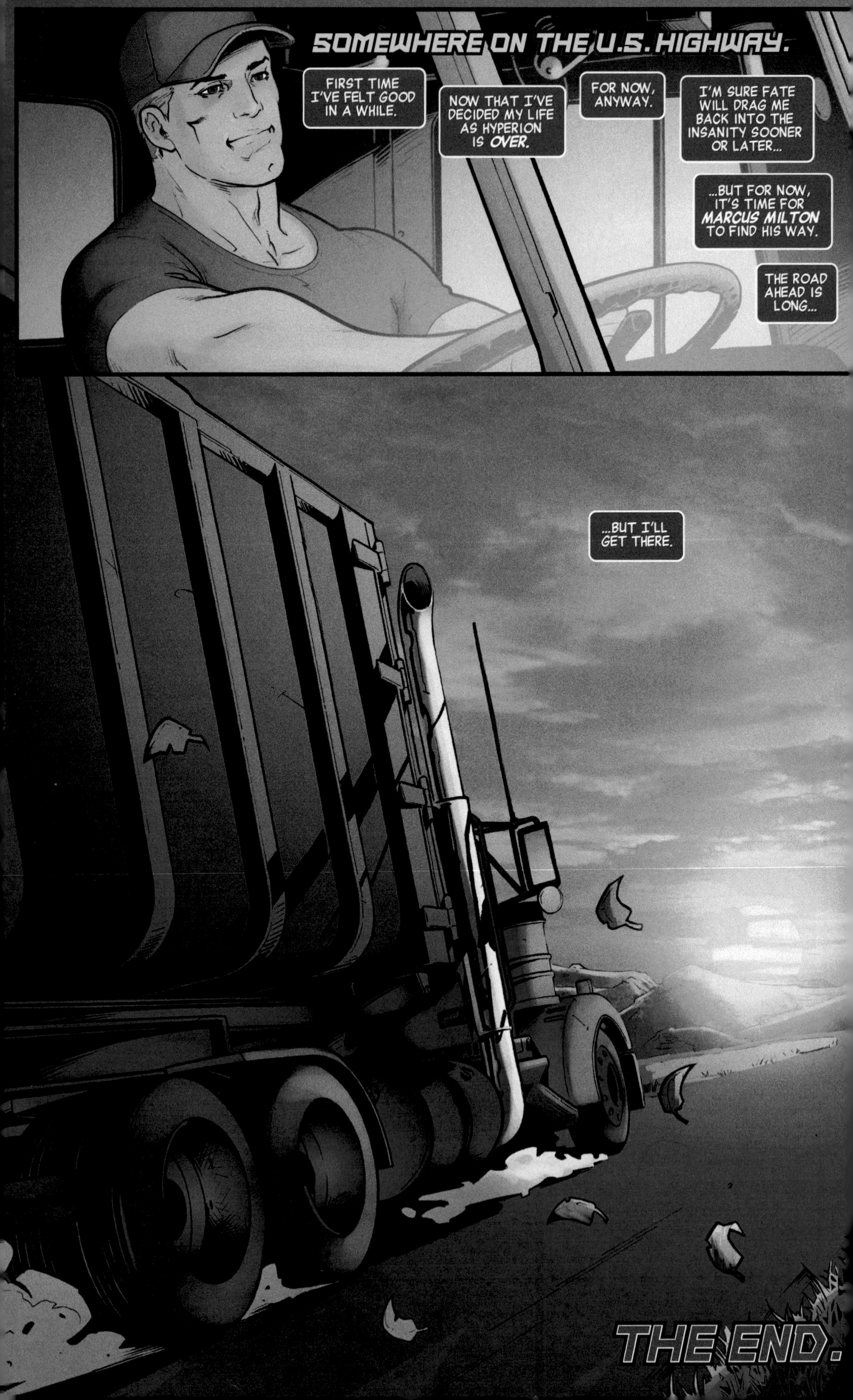
SOMEWHERE ON THE U.S. HIGHWAY.
FIRST TIME I'VE FELT GOOD IN A WHILE.
NOW THAT I'VE DECIDED MY LIFE AS HYPERION IS OVER.
FOR NOW, ANYWAY.
I'M SURE FATE WILL DRAG ME BACK INTO THE INSANITY SOONER OR LATER...
...BUT FOR NOW, IT'S TIME FOR MARCUS MILTON TO FIND HIS WAY.
THE ROAD AHEAD IS LONG...
...BUT I'LL GET THERE.
THE END.

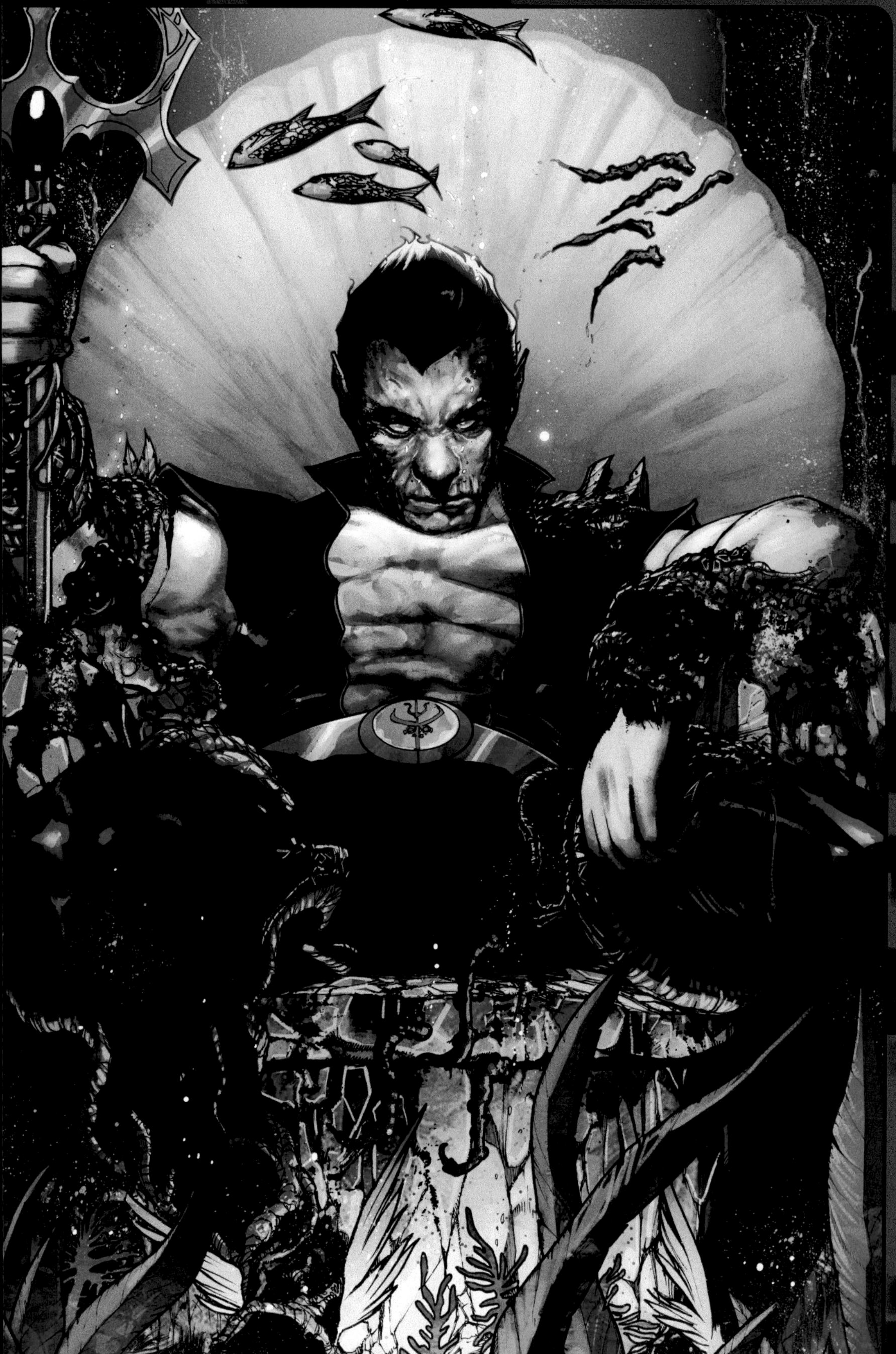

#13 VARIANT BY ALEX SANCHEZ & ROMULO FAJARDO JR.